Saqifa

The Study of the Establishment of Government after the Prophet's Death

Sayyid Murtaza Askari
Dr. Mahdi Dashti

English Translation by
Elham Ebadi

Revision and Editing
Yasir Alexander

Title: Saqifa

Authors: Sayyid Murtaza Askari and Dr. Mahdi Dashti

Translation: Elham Ebadi

Revision and Editing: Yasir Alexander

ISBN: 979-8-9861941-1-0

Year: 2022

Contents

Chapter 6

The Economic War Against Ahl al-Bayt **91**

Chapter 7

Fāṭimah on Bed Rest **107**

Chapter 8

The Situation in Islāmic Lands and Imams' Policies

Chapter 9

Abū Bakr's Will and 'Umar's Caliphate

Chapter 10

The Government Status in 'Umar's Time

Chapter 11

'Uthmān's Caliphate Era

Chapter 12

Translator's Note

It is impossible to express the gratitude I am feeling for the blessing I obtained in translating this book. Since the text was in fact a collection of speeches, there were some inevitabe mistakes and ambiguities that had to be corrected and supplemented in the translation, cautiously and without importing any fundamental change into the context. Most of the errors were in the footnotes, insomuch that the number of books in the bibliography indicates this correction process. Of course, I tried to make the least changes so as not to be involved in the credibility of the text and content of the book. Although it may seem that the main work was done by me, but the truth is that this publication has been created as a result of the effort of many whom are hoped to be rewarded by the Almighty God.

Firstly, I'm extremely grateful to Mrs. Saeedeh Taheri who chose to trust me with the work and also offered all kinds of help. Not only is she a precious researchist of the Islām ic studies, but also a valuable scholar whose work in advertising Islām and Shi'a is heartwarming. May God bless her.

Secondly, I'd like to express my deepest thanks to Mr. Manuchehr Naderi who actually pulled the trigger on starting the work and helped out greatly with the translation of some chapters. May God bless him.

Thirdly, this project would not have been possible without the wonderful friendship of Dr. Zaynab Amiri, our mutual friend, whose role we wouldn't want to ignore. May God bless her.

Finally, my admiration and love goes to my father whose knowledge and understanding is limitless and was a great help in this project. May God bless him.

Last but not least, I would like to pay my special regards to all my Muslim friends who have been an encouragement throughout my life in order to lead me to succeed in translating such a book. May the Prophet (pbuh) himself and his Ahl al-Bayt help us out in this life and the definite life afterwards.

Elham Ebadi

January 2022

Foreword

In the name of God, the Beneficent, the Merciful

Praise to God, the Lord of the worlds, and prayer and peace be upon Muḥammad and his family

This book was originally a collection of speeches given at the Muharram and Ṣafar mourning ceremonies in 1419 AH/ 1998 CE, and after typing down the lectures from the recorded cassette tapes by two Shi'as of the Ahl al-Bayt who did not want to be introduced, Dr. Mahdi Dashti took the trouble to compile and edit and do research of the authenticity, and now it is ready for publication.

Saqīfa, in 'Arabic, means a canopy considered as a guest house in which the tribesmen would gather and discuss all the affairs of the tribe.

The Anṣār of the Holy Prophet (pbuh) were from the two tribes of Aws and Khazraj, both of which were originally from Yemen, and their ancestors had come to Medina to be at the company of the Prophet (pbuh) and help him out in his prophecy.

The famous Saqīfa in history was the meeting place of Banū Khazraj of Anṣār in Medina, and its leader was Sa'd ibn 'Ubadah, for whose allegiance they had gathered after the death of the Prophet (pbuh); while his blessed body laid among his family and they were busy in giving it Ġusl (ablution). When the news of the Saqīfa gathering reached the group of followers of Abū Bakr and 'Umar, they too, quickly joined the gathering of Saqīfa.

Social Impacts of Saqīfa

Due to that gathering under that canopy in Saqīfa, the Shari'a of Islām was completely changed after the Holy Prophet (pbuh)!

Due to Saqīfa, the history of Islām was altered.

Due to Saqīfa, the door of Fāṭimat az-Zahrā's house was set on fire and what should have not, took place.

Due to Saqīfa, Ibn Muljam's sword cut open 'Alī 'Amīr al-Mu'minīn's head.

Due to Saqīfa, Imam Ḥasan (as) was martyred by poison.

Due to Saqīfa, Imam Ḥusayn (as) was martyred and Zaynab (sa) and other ladies from the Prophet's family were taken captive.

Due to Saqīfa, the course of human history was changed.

The effect of Saqīfa continues from that day until now and until the advent of Imam Mahdī (May God hasten his reappearance)!

And today, all the followers and lovers of Imam 'Alī (as) and the other Imams wish that with his advent, Imam Mahdī (May God hasten his reappearance) would reveal the truth about Saqīfa and take revenge of his immaculate ancestors on the organizers and executives of that community. Amen!

Sayyid Murtaza Askari
Ḏū al-Qa'dah 1421 AH/ 2000 CE

Introduction

Saqīfa and its place in the history of Islām have long been discussed in many books, independently or occasionally which, of course, are not of equal value and importance. In most of these books, Saqīfa has been seen in just one day and therefore the events of that day have been merely examined. Although in some cases, the incidents that took place a couple of weeks before and after it are also mentioned.

Among the older books, only few books can be found that have not narrated its occurance. A look at the thirty outstanding works from the sources of the first Islāmic millennium in which the story of Saqīfa is discussed, sometimes briefly and sometimes in detail, reveals the fact that the experts of history, traditions of the Prophet (pbuh) and hadith have not ignored this event.[1]

---

[1] These books are in chronological order: 1. *Sirat ibn Hisham* (Decd. 213 AH/ 828 CE) 2. *Kitāb aṭ-Tabaqāt al-Kabīr*, Ibn Sa'd (Decd. 230 AH/ 845 CE) 3. *Musnad Aḥmad ibn Ḥanbal*, (Decd. 241 AH/ 855 CE) 4. *Sunan al-Darimi* (Decd. 255 AH/ 869 CE) 5. *Ṣaḥīḥ al-Bukhārī* (Decd. 256 AH/ 870 CE) 6. *Al-Akhbār al-Muwaffaqīyāt*, Az-Zubayr ibn Bakkār (Decd. 256 AH/ 870 CE) 7. *Ṣaḥīḥ Muslim* (Decd. 261 AH/ 875 CE) 8. *Al-Imāma wal-Siyāsa*, Ibn Qutayba al-Dīnawarī (Decd. 270 or 276 AH/ 884 or 889 CE) 9. *Sunan ibn Mājah* (Decd. 273 AH/ 886 CE) 10. *Ansāb al-Ashrāf*, al-Balāḏurī (Decd. 279 AH/ 892 CE) 11. *Al-Akhbar al-Tuwal*, Dīnawarī (Decd. 282 AH/ 895 CE) 12. *Tārīkh Ya'qūbī* (Decd. 292 AH/ 905 CE) 13. *Tārīkh al-Ṭabarī*, (Decd. 310 AH/ 922 CE) 14. *Al-'Iqd al-Farīd*, Ibn 'Abd Rabbihi (Decd. 328 AH/ 940 CE) 15. *At-Tanbih wal-'Ishraf*, al-Mas'ūdī (Decd. 346 AH/ 957 CE) 16. *Murūj aḏ-Ḏahab*, al-Mas'ūdī (Decd. 346 AH/ 957 CE) 17. *Kitab al-Aghani*, Abū al-Faraj al-Iṣfahānī (Decd. 356 AH/ 967 CE) 18. *Al-Irshad*, al-Mufīd (Decd. 413 AH/ 1022 CE) 19. *Al-Amalī*, al-Mufīd (Decd. 413 AH/ 1022 CE) 20. *Al-Isti'ab*, Ibn Abd al-Barr al-Andalusi (Decd. 463 AH/ 1071 CE) 21. *Safwat u-Safwah*, Ibn al Jawzi (Decd. 597 AH/ 1201 CE) 22. *Al-Kāmil fit-Tārīkh Ibn al-Athir*, al-Jazari (Decd. 630 AH/ 1233 CE) 23. *Usd al-Ġābah*, Ibn al-Athir (Decd. 630 AH/ 1233 CE) 24. *Sharḥ Nahj al-Balāgha*, Ibn Abī l-Hadīd (Decd. 655 or 656 AH/ 1257 or 1258 CE) 25. *Al-Riaz un-Nazra*, Muḥibb al-Dīn Aḥmad ibn 'Abd Allāh

Contemporary writers have also made efforts in this regard and have presented remarkable works. These include, the late Muḥammad Riḍā Muẓaffar[2], Muḥammad Baqir Behbudi[3], 'Abd al-Fattāḥ 'Abd al-Maqṣūd[4], and Wilferd Madelung.[5]

In his book *al-Saqīfa*, the late Muẓaffar has tried to look at this matter with the method of theology and proved that what happened in Saqīfa firstly, was not based on the authority and consensus of the nation and secondly, was against the religious teachings. Of course, this is not a new view, and before him, many Shi'a scholars had looked at it from this perspective; e.g. the late Shaykh al-Mufīd (Decd. 413 AH/ 1022 CE), in the book *Al-Amalī*, and the late Sayyid Ibn Ṭawūs (Decd. 664 AH/ 1266 CE) in his valuable book *Al-Muhajjal Samaratal Muhajja*.

In his book *Sireye Alawi*, Muḥammad Baqir Behbudi has examined the events after the death of the Holy Prophet (pbuh) until the martyrdom of 'Alī (as), and in the meantime, has mentioned a detailed and useful narration about

---

Ṭabarī Shāfi'ī (Decd. 694 AH/ 1295 CE) 26. *Tārīkh al-Islām al-Kabir*, aḏ-Ḏahabī (Decd. 748 AH/ 1347 CE) 27. *Al-Bidaya wa an-Nihaya*, Ibn Kathir (Decd. 774 AH/ 1373 CE) 28. *Tārīkh al-Khulafā'*, As-Suyūṭī (Decd. 911 AH/ 1505 CE) 29. *Tārīkh al-Khamis*, Husayn ibn Muḥammad Diyar Bakri (Decd. 966 AH/ 1559 CE) 30. *Kanz al-Ummāl*, al-Muttaqi al-Hindi (Decd. 975 AH/ 1568 CE)

[2] The late Muẓaffar (1904-1964) was a scholar of seminary in Najaf. His book *al-Saqīfah* has been translated into Persian by Muḥammad Javad Hujjati Kermani, with the title *Asrār Saqīfah*. Earlier, the late Sayyid Ġulām Riḍā Sa'īdī had translated this book into Persian under the title *Mājarāye Saqīfa*.

[3] Author of the book *Sireye Alawi*, published in 2007.

[4] 'Abd al-Fattāḥ 'Abd al-Maqṣūd is an Egyptian Sunnite author and scholar. His book *Al-Saqīfah wa al-Khilāfah* has been translated into Persian by Sayyid Hasan Iftikharzadeh under the title *Khāstgāh Khilāfat*.

[5] Wilferd Madelung is an originally German Islāmist who was professor of Arabic at the University of Oxford from 1978 to 1998. He has written extensively on the early history of Islam and has taught Islāmic studies at the Oxford University. His book is entitled *The Succession to Muḥammad: A Study of the Early Caliphate* and has also been translated and published in Persian.

Saqīfa. He sees Saqīfa as the result of a pre-planned scheme that pitted Muslims with what was done; however, he does not see the scope of this plan until the time of 'Uthmān and Mu'awiyah, and therefore his narration, despite its accuracy and scientific citation, remains unfinished.

'Abd al-Fattāḥ 'Abd al-Maqṣūd considers Saqīfa to be the site of a pre-planned operation in which there was neither a council, nor a place for the ruling of a council. In his view, Saqīfa could be the beginning of the governorship of those who wanted the government to be passed around amongst them.[6]

Although 'Abd al-Fattāḥ 'Abd al-Maqṣūd also sees clear signs of prior planning in this story,[7] but ultimately, he considers the narrations that specify 'Umar naming people who, if were alive, would be appointed to the caliphate after him to be fake,[8] and contrary to what he presents at the beginning of his book, he considers the collusion of these three friends (Abū Bakr, 'Umar and Abū 'Ubaydah ibn al-Jarāḥ) on the usurpation of the Caliphate and its rotation among themselves, weak and does not accept it.[9]

As for the German-born Orientalist Wilferd Madelung, in his book, he first introduces Lammens' theory of the "Triumvirate of Abū Bakr, 'Umar and Abū 'Ubaydah ibn al-Jarāḥ"[10] and states from L. Caetani that in this triumvirate, the main inspiration came from 'Umar,[11] and concludes that the Holy Prophet (pbuh) did not intend Abū Bakr to be his natural successor at all and was not happy for this appointment.[12] He emphasizes that the privileged position of

---

[6] *Al-Saqīfah wa al-Khilāfah,* p. 241 onwards.

[7] *Ibid.,* p. 241 onwards.

[8] *Ibid.,* p. 437.

[9] *Ibid.,* pp. 438-439.

[10] *The Succession to Muḥammad,* pp. 15-16.

[11] *Ibid.,* p. 18.

[12] *Ibid.,* p. 32.

ruling over the Islāmic community - which Abū Bakr had assigned to the Qurayshites - had no basis in the Qur'ān.[13]

However, Madelung does not believe in the Prophet's statement about the succession of 'Alī (as) either, and regarding the incident of Ghadīr Khumm he opines:

'Apparently, that time was not adequate to appoint 'Alī as his successor. Perhaps, Muḥammad delayed this decision in the hope that his life would be long enough to ascertain one of his grandsons.'[14]

Finally, he concludes that the Prophet (pbuh) died without appointing a successor.[15] In addition, Madelung considers the reports from 'Abdullāh ibn 'Abbās, in which 'Umar's explicit confessions as to why 'Alī (as) was rejected of becoming the caliph have been reported, invalid,[16] without presenting any plausible reason.

In the final part of his book, Madelung goes even further and declares the non-appointment of a successor the Prophet's tradition, and even says that perhaps it was according to this tradition that 'Alī (as), too, did not want to choose a successor during his caliphate; although, he eventually assigned Ḥasan (as) in his will.[17] Of course, Madelung believes that Abū Bakr sought the caliphate and before the death of the Prophet (pbuh), had undoubtedly decided that the caliph should be himself, without being nominated for this position by the Prophet (pbuh). Hence, he decided to make this wish of his come true by destroying his powerful opponents - who were from Ahl al-Bayt (members of the Prophet's household) - and awaited the opportunity. The opportunity was given to him by Anṣār's hasty mistake in choosing a leader from among themselves.[18]

---

[13] *Ibid.*, p. 84.

[14] *Ibid.*, p. 34.

[15] *Ibid.*, p. 35.

[16] *Ibid.*, p. 40.

[17] *Ibid.*, p. 427.

[18] *Ibid.*, pp. 62 & 63.

14

Thus, Madelung also emphasizes the plotting of a pre-planned scheme to secure the caliphate by Abū Bakr, however, he considers the emergence of this decision in Saqīfa as a coincidence and with the help of several other Qurayshite men in this matter, effective in subjugating the majority of Qurayshites and Anṣār to the Caliphate of Abū Bakr. Especially since Abū Bakr had deceived them by saying that the Qurayshites have a tribal right to rule, and they were glad that the government, like prophethood, would not remain in the monopoly of the family of the Prophet (pbuh).

*****

An overview of what has been written about Saqīfa from its beginning until recent time was necessary in order to better understand the value and importance of the work of researcher, Allameh Sayyid Murtaḍā Al-'Askarī, in the book before you.

According to this book, Saqīfa is not limited to one day and designed by one person for the caliphate; rather, Saqīfa is considered to be the beginning of the emergence of a designed plan in which certain individuals from the Quraysh were to take over the government one after the other in order to continuously keep it away from the Ahl al-Bayt who, according to the Prophet's direct speech, were the successors, and be kept among the Umayyads. This plan was executed, but 'Uthmān's assassination which led to the caliphate of 'Alī (as) messed it up and caused it to remain unfinished. This analysis, which is based on the first-rate resources of the caliphate school of thought, is unique in its kind since it regulates, completes and corrects the scattered, incomplete and sometimes inaccurate material of the old and contemporary narrations about Saqīfa, and is very comprehensive and instructive for a better understanding of the history of Islām, from the time of the Prophet's death until now.

Congereh Publication seized the opportunity and obtained permission from the author and researcher, Allameh Sayyid Murtaḍā Al-'Askarī, made the publication of this valuable work a priority and to complete its usefulness, using authentic resources, included some footnotes of the documents of hadithes and historical narrations quoted in this book, and in some cases, explanations of some contents. Hopefully, this effort would be considered acceptable in the eyes of 'Alī (as), the Commander of the Faithful; God willing.

And lastly, we pray that praise be to God, the Lord of the worlds.

Mahdi Dashti

Winter of 1379 SH/ 2000 CE – Tehran

Chapter 1

The Establishment of Saqīfah during Prophet Muḥammad's Life

To study how Saqīfah was established during Prophet Muḥammad's life, we need to review the following verses of Qurʾān:

In the few first verses of Surah al-Taḥrim, God states:

يَا أَيُّهَا النَّبِيُّ لِمَ تُحَرِّمُ مَا أَحَلَّ اللَّهُ لَكَ تَبْتَغِي مَرْضَاتَ أَزْوَاجِكَ وَاللَّهُ غَفُورٌ رَحِيمٌ* قَدْ فَرَضَ اللَّهُ لَكُمْ تَحِلَّةَ أَيْمَانِكُمْ وَاللَّهُ مَوْلَاكُمْ وَهُوَ الْعَلِيمُ الْحَكِيمُ * وَإِذْ أَسَرَّ النَّبِيُّ إِلَى بَعْضِ أَزْوَاجِهِ حَدِيثًا فَلَمَّا نَبَّأَتْ بِهِ وَأَظْهَرَهُ اللَّهُ عَلَيْهِ عَرَّفَ بَعْضَهُ وَأَعْرَضَ عَنْ بَعْضٍ فَلَمَّا نَبَّأَهَا بِهِ قَالَتْ مَنْ أَنْبَأَكَ هَذَا قَالَ نَبَّأَنِيَ الْعَلِيمُ الْخَبِيرُ* إِنْ تَتُوبَا إِلَى اللَّهِ فَقَدْ صَغَتْ قُلُوبُكُمَا وَإِنْ تَظَاهَرَا عَلَيْهِ فَإِنَّ اللَّهَ هُوَ مَوْلَاهُ وَجِبْرِيلُ وَصَالِحُ الْمُؤْمِنِينَ وَالْمَلَائِكَةُ بَعْدَ ذَلِكَ ظَهِيرٌ

O' Prophet, why do you prohibit [yourself from] what Allāh has made lawful for you, seeking the approval of your wives? And Allāh is Forgiving and Merciful. Allāh has already ordained for you [Muslims] the dissolution of your oaths. And Allāh is your protector, and He is the Knowing, the Wise. And [remember] when the Prophet confided to one of his wives a statement; and when she informed [another] of it and Allāh showed it to him, he made known part of it and ignored a part. And when he informed her about it, she said, "Who told you this?" He said, "I was informed by the Knowing, the Aware." If you two repent to Allāh, [it is best], for your hearts have deviated. But if you unite against him, then indeed Allāh is his protector, and Gabriel and the righteous of the believers and the angels, moreover, are [his] supports.[1]

The Reason behind Revelation of these Verses

In these verses, three things are stated:

---

[1] al-Taḥrīm 1-4.

A. Prohibition of the Holy Prophet (pbuh) on himself of what God had made lawful for him to please his wives and that God has declared the way of violating oaths.

B. The Prophet (pbuh) telling a secret to one of his wives and her revealing the secret to his another wife and then God informing the Prophet (pbuh) of the revelation of the secret.

C. God threatening the two wives of the Prophet (pbuh) until the end of the Surah.

In these verses, it has not been stated what the Prophet (pbuh) forbade for himself from for the sake of his wife and what secret was revealed by that wife and what happened afterwards that God expressed such threatening words.

It is worth remembering that God has said,

وَأَنْزَلْنَا إِلَيْكَ الذِّكْرَ لِتُبَيِّنَ لِلنَّاسِ مَا نُزِّلَ إِلَيْهِمْ

Also sent down to you this Holy Qur'ān that you may explain to the people clearly what is sent down to them.[2]

In the Matter of Qur'ān, Two Kinds of Revelations Were Revealed to the Prophet

1. The Qur'ānic revelation, which is the text of the Qur'ān that has been available to everyone since the time of the Prophet (pbuh) until today.

2. The expressive revelation with which the interpretation of the Qur'ān has been stated.

In expressing the first verse, it is narrated that the Prophet (pbuh) went to bed with his maid Maria on the day which was Ḥafṣah's turn and when Ḥafṣah found out about it, Prophet (pbuh) forbade himself from Maria to appease Ḥafṣah.[3]

---

[2] al-Nahl 44.

[3] *Tafsīr al-Ṭabarī*, 28: p. 101 and similar to this narration in *Kitāb aṭ-Ṭabaqāt al-Kabīr, Ibn Sa'd*, 8: p. 135. [Translator: There are other interpretations that are not in conflict with the infallibility of the Prophet (pbuh).]

18

In the second verse, God removes this prohibition.

In the third verse, it is stated that the Prophet (pbuh) shares a secret with his wife, Ḥafṣah, but she reveals it. God informs his prophet (pbuh) of what she has done and he informs Ḥafṣah of revealing that secret. Ḥafṣah asks the Prophet (pbuh), "Who told you this?" The Prophet (pbuh) says, "I was informed by the Knowing, the Aware."[4]

In the fourth verse, the tone changes and He addresses the two women saying, "If you two [wives] repent to Allāh, [it is best], for your hearts have deviated. But if you unite against him [the Prophet (pbuh)], then indeed Allāh is his protector, and Gabriel and the righteous of the believers ['Alī][5] and the angels, moreover, are [his] supports."

What happened that in the following verses God threateningly says:

There is hope that if he divorces you, his Lord will replace you with better wives than you, women who are (Muslims) surrendered, believers, humble, repentant, devout, immigrants, widows and virgins!

O' Believers! Guard yourselves and your families against the Fire fueled by people and stones, over which there are harsh and stern angels who never disobey Allah in that which He orders and follow His orders (completely). O' Unbelievers! Make no excuse for yourselves on this Day since you shall be recompensed only according to your deeds.

O' Believers! Turn to Allah in sincere repentance. Your Lord may acquit you of your sins and admit you to Gardens underneath which rivers flow on a Day when Allah will not degrade the Prophet and those who believe with him. Their light will run before them and on their right hands, and they will say, "Our Lord! Complete our light for us and forgive us. Surely, you have power over all things." O' Prophet! Fight against the unbelievers and the hypocrites and take it hard on them. Hell shall be their refuge, an evil arrival!

Allah has given as an example for the unbelievers, the wife of Noah and the wife of Lot. They were married to two of Our righteous worshipers, but they

---

[4] *Tafsīr al-Ṭabarī*, 28: p. 101.

[5] *al-Durr al-Manthur*, 6: p. 244.

betrayed them and (their relationship with Noah and Lot) did not avail them anything (against the divine punishment) and they were both told, "Enter the Fire with those who shall enter it."[6]

What seditions took place in the Prophet's house and around him? Which of these seditious actions did the Prophet (pbuh) mention and which ones did he not talk about? What were the two mentioned Prophet's wives' and their associates' plans, for whom all those warnings were required through expression of the results of the similar acts of the two prophets' wives (Noah and Lot) by stating explicitly that those two women were hypocritical and betrayed the two prophets and as a result were ordered to be sent to hell? Our findings in this regard in the books about caliphs are as follows:

The Prophet (pbuh) had told Ḥafṣah, 'Umar's daughter, "Your father and Ā'ishah's father (Abū Bakr) would rebel to take power after me." The Prophet (pbuh) had said this as a secret and in confidence, but Ḥafṣah shared it with Ā'ishah and Ā'ishah reported it to her father and Abū Bakr shared it with 'Umar. 'Umar asked Ḥafṣah, "What is going on? Tell us (in order to prepare ourselves)." And she revealed the Prophet's secret to her father.

The Prophet (pbuh) stated only a part of the story, i.e. that the two women had revealed his secret, and refrained from telling the rest. What could the secret be other than the preparedness of their fathers to seize power after the Prophet (pbuh)?

In order to narrate the cause of revelation of the Surah from the mouth of the second caliph, Ibn Abbas smartly told him, "It's been about a year that I have wanted to ask you a question but your awe keeps me back." 'Umar said, "What is it?" He said, "My question is about a verse of the Qur'ān." The caliph said, "Ibn Abbas, you know that I bear some of the knowledge of the Qur'ān and you don't ask me?!" Here, Ibn Abbas asked him, "About whom was Surah al-Taḥrim in the Qur'ān revealed about?" 'Umar said, "About Ā'ishah and Ḥafṣah."[7]

---

[6] at-Taḥrīm 5-10

[7] *Tafsīr al-Ṭabarī*, 28: pp. 104-105; *Ṣaḥīḥ al-Bukhārī*, 3: pp. 137-138 & 4: p.22; *Ṣaḥīḥ Muslim*, book of al-Talaq, hadīth 31, 32, 33 & 34; *Musnad Aḥmad ibn Ḥanbal*, 1: p. 48; *Musnad al-*

In the book *al-Durr al-Manthur* we read:

And when the Prophet secretly communicated a piece of information to one of his wives… Ḥafṣah bint 'Umar, that indeed the caliph after him would be Abū Bakr and after Abū Bakr it would be 'Umar.[8]

Tayalisi, hadīth 23. In the books about caliph, the Prophet's prediction about Abī Bakr and 'Umar becoming caliphs is interpreted as His annunciation to them taking power! Which is not unduly because not only based on the Qur'ān that explicitly indicates reproaches and threats them and also stipulates the betray of two of the Prophet's wives to be like Noah's and Lot's wives, it shows complete contradiction with annunciation. The Prophet (pbuh) has had many predictions of events that refer to disasters, evil deeds and oppressions such as, warning his wives about the bark of dogs in Haw'ab. (*Al-Bidaya wa an-Nihaya,* 6: p. 212; *al-Khasa'is al-Kubra,* 2: p. 136; *al-Mustadrak,* 3: p. 119; *Al-Ijāba,* p. 62; *al-'Iqd al-Farīd,* 3: p. 108; *As-Sirat al-Halabiah,* 3: 320-321). This turned to be true about Ā'ishah in the Jamal battle. (*Tārīkh al-Ṭabarī,* 7: p. 475 and in the European publication 1: p. 3108; *Musnad Aḥmad ibn Ḥanbal,* 6: p. 97; *Al-Bidaya wa an-Nihaya,* 7: p. 230; *al-Mustadrak,* 3: p. 120) when this happened Ā'ishah was devastated and said, "Take me back, Take me back! This is the water which the Prophet (pbuh) warned me about and said: Lest you be the woman whom the dogs of Haw'ab bark on." (*Tārīkh Ya'qubi,* 2: p. 157; *Kanz al-Ummāl,* 6: p. 83-84) But Zubayr rushed to her saying, "Whoever told you this is Haw'ab has lied to you." (*Al-Bidaya wa an-Nihaya,* 7: p. 230; *Tārīkh Abī al-Fada',* p. 173) Ṭalḥa confirmed Zubayr's words and fifty other men arrived and attested that the place was not Haw'ab. (*Murūj aḏ-Ḏahab,* 2: p. 6-7). Also the Prophet's prediction about Imam Husayn's Martyrdom where he said, "Gabriel informed me that he [Husayn] will be killed in Iraq." (*al-Mustadrak,* 4: p. 398; *Al-Mu'jam al-Kabir,* hadīth 55; *Tārīkh Dimashq Ibn 'Asākir,* hadīth 621-629; *Kitāb aṭ-Tabaqāt al-Kabīr,* translation of al-Husayn, hadīth 267; *Tārīkh al-Islām al-kabir aḏ-Ḏahabī,* 3: p. 11; *Ḏakhā'ir al-Uqbā,* pp. 148-149; *Al-Bidaya wa an-Nihaya,* 6: p. 230; *Kanz al-Ummāl,* 16: p. 266) And also said, "God's rage is extremely severe for the murderer of Husayn." (*Tārīkh Dimashq Ibn 'Asākir,* hadīth 623; *Tahzīb Ibn 'Asākir,* 4: p. 325; *Kanz al-Ummāl,* 23: p. 112; *ar-Rawḍ an-Naḍīr,* 1: p. 93) None of these are annunciation and they are all predictions of oppression and evil deeds and the injustice which would take place after the death of the Prophet (pbuh).

[8] *al-Durr al-Manthur,* 6: p. 241.

We can infer from this story that Abū Bakr and 'Umar were plotting to assume power. They had a plan for it when the Prophet (pbuh) was alive[9] and a plan for the period after him. What is relevant to our discussion at the moment is their plan for the period after when the Prophet (pbuh) would pass away, which formed the basis of Saqīfah. That plan was such that Abū Bakr, 'Umar, Abū 'Ubaydah ibn al-Jarāḥ, Sālim Mawlā Abī Ḥudayfah and 'Uthmān swore allegiance to the government after the Prophet (pbuh) and wrote it down as a consent in a letter and entrusted it to Abū 'Ubaydah ibn al-Jarāḥ.[10] This is why 'Umar used to say, "Abū 'Ubaydah is the trustee of this nation."[11] Also, it was because of this agreement that the second caliph would say in many cases, "If Abū 'Ubaydah or Sālim Mawlā Abī Ḥudayfah were alive, I would cede them the caliphate."[12]

In the event of the designation of the second caliph, this trend became more evident where Abū Bakr, at the time of his death, sent after 'Uthmān and said, "Write: In the name of God, the Compassionate the Merciful. This is Abū Bakr 'Abdullāh Ibn Abī Quhāfah's will to the Muslims. Furthermore..."

Here, Abū Bakr passed out. 'Uthmān continued and wrote: Furthermore, I assign 'Umar ibn al-Khaṭṭāb as caliph over you and have not abandoned

---

[9] The plan they had for the Prophet (pbuh) while he was alive could have been when they scared the Prophet's camel on the way back from the Battle of Tabuk to cause him a fall into the valley and be martyred, which in God's will did not come about. According to Ibn Hazm al-Andalusī one of the greatest scholars of the caliph's school of thought in his precious book the *Al-Mohalla*, 11: p. 244 says some of those who had taken part in this plan and scared the Prophet's camel were Abī Bakr, 'Umar and Uthmān. Although, Ibn Hazm al-Andalusī considers this narration to be invalid because it is narrated by Walīd ibn Abdullah ibn Jamī' Zuhrī. But his claim is untrue and unduly for Muslim and Bukhārī have both introduced it to be valid. Bukhārī in his book *Al-Adab al-Mufrad* and Ibn Hajar al-'Asqalānī in his book *Tahdīb al-Tahdīb* mention the translation by Walīd ibn Abdullah ibn Jamī' and indicate that Muslim and Bukhārī have narrated from him and thus his is also accurate.

[10] *Bihar al-Anwar*, 2: p. 596, hadīth 5.

[11] *al-'Iqd al-Farīd*, 4: p. 274.

[12] *Ibid.*, 4: p. 274.

22

goodwill for you. After regaining his consciousness, Abū Bakr said: 'Read.' 'Uthmān read what he had written and Abū Bakr said: "Allāhu Akbar (God is the Greatest). You feared that the nation would fall into (the trap of) disagreement after me; yes, I also wanted to say what you said."[13]

How did 'Uthmān get informed about the person who was going to be appointed as caliph by Abū Bakr? It is quite clear that there was a compromise among them that dictated Abū Bakr, 'Umar, Sālim, Abū 'Ubaydah and 'Uthmān to be caliph one after the other and in this order. This can be inferred from two acts of the second caliph:

1. When 'Umar was hit and injured by Abū Lu'lu'a, because Sālim and Abū 'Ubaydah[14] were dead at that time, 'Umar arranged the caliphate council in a way that 'Uthmān would have the highest vote to be selected as caliph.[15]

2. It can be understood from the following event that the third caliph was selected during 'Umar's life:

Ibn Sa`d (the author of *Kitāb aṭ-Tabaqāt al-Kabīr*) narrates from Sa'īd ibn al-'Ās al-Umawī that he asked the second caliph for a piece of land next to his lodging to expand his house; he did this because 'Umar conferred such boons in some cases. The caliph told him, "After the Morning Prayer return and I will fulfill your request. Sa'īd referred to the caliph after the Morning Prayer and they both went to the desired part of the land. 'Umar drew a line on the ground with the tip of his foot and said, "This patch is yours." Sa'īd ibn al-'Ās says, "I said O' Amīr al-Mu'minīn! I have a big family. Give me more." 'Umar said, "For now, this plot is enough for you, but I will tell you a secret; keep it to yourself. There will emerge a caliph after me who will become your kinsfolk and will fulfill your demand." Sa'īd says I waited during the caliphate period of 'Umar

---

[13] *Tārīkh al-Ṭabarī,* and in the European edition 1: p. 2138 and in the Egyptian edition 3: p. 52.

[14] In the second year of 'Umar's caliphate, Sālim Mawlā Abī Huḍayfah was killed in battle against Musaylimah al-Kaḍḍāb, and in the 18th Hijri year, Abū 'Ubaydah who was the commander in war against Romans in Sham which used to be called the Eastern Roman Empire, died due to the plague disease. (*al-'Iqd al-Farīd*, 4: 274-275)

[15] *Ansab al-Ashraf*, 5: pp. 15- 19; *Kitāb aṭ-Tabaqāt al-Kabīr*, 3: p. 43; *Tārīkh Ya'qubi*, 2: p. 160.

and after his death 'Uthmān took power, and as 'Umar had said, became a relative of mine through marriage and provided me my wish."[16]

It becomes clear from this narrative that the second caliph knew, from the plot he had devised for the period after him, that Sa'īd al-Umawī's relative, i.e. 'Uthmān, would become the caliph.

Moreover, it is evident from the following happenings that the second caliph had planned that after 'Uthmān, 'Abd al-Rahman ibn 'Awf and after him Mu'awiya would seize power. Proof to this is that in "'Ām al-Ra'af" (the year of nosebleeds) 'Uthmān developed a nosebleed and was about to die. Therefore, he secretly nominated 'Abd al-Rahman ibn 'Awf as the substitute for caliphate after himself in a letter. 'Abd al-Rahman got very upset and said, "I overtly made him caliph but he covertly gives me caliphate in a written form."[17]

Thus, a severe enmity between the two arose and the curse of 'Alī (as) came true at this time. He had said, "May God bring about a dispute between you."[18] 'Uthmān recovered from that disease while 'Abd al-Rahman died during the caliphate of 'Uthmān.[19]

On the same day 'Abd al-Rahman ibn 'Awf pledged allegiance to 'Uthmān and backed him to become caliph, 'Alī (as) told him, "I swear to God that you backed 'Uthmān to take the caliphate only because (one day) he will return the caliphate to you."[20]

We will discuss 'Umar's inclination for appointing Mu'awiya as caliph in the section of "**Mu'awiya in 'Umar's Time**" in chapter 10. Here, we will just mention that 'Umar basically wanted to keep caliphate in Quraysh and hinder

---

[16] *Kitāb aṭ-Tabaqāt al-Kabīr*, 5: pp. 20-22.

[17] *Siyar A'lam al-Nubala* and *Tārīkh Dimashq Ibn 'Asākir*, in the biography of Abdur-Rahman ibn 'Awf

[18] *Sharḥ Nahj al-Balāgha* by Ibn Abī l-Hadīd 1: p. 188, sermon 3 and 9: p. 55, sermon 139. This sentence was a proverb in the Age of Ignorance (*Jahiliyyah*).

[19] For more information on the enmity between Uthmān and Abdur-Rahman ibn 'Awf, see *Ansab al-Ashraf*, 1: part 4: pp. 546-547.

[20] *Tārīkh al-Ṭabarī*, 3: p. 297 under the events of the 23rd Hijri year; *Al-Kāmil fit-Tārīkh Ibn al-Athir*, 3: p. 37.

it from being taken by Banī Hāshim. He and his associates, not only in their time but also after their period, did not allow Banī Hāshim to come to power.[21]

---

[21] More detail in this book in the chapter titled Government in 'Umar's Caliphate; The conversation between Ibn Abbas and 'Umar. Also see: *Al-Isti'ab*, 1: p. 253; *al-Iṣābah*, 3: p. 413; *Al-Bidaya wa an-Nihaya*, 8: p. 120; *Murūj aḏ-Ḏahab*, 2: pp. 321-322; *Musnad Aḥmad ibn Ḥanbal*, 1: p. 177; *Tārīkh al-Ṭabarī*, 5: p. 2768 & 2770-2771 & 2787; *Sharḥ Nahj al-Balāgha* by Ibn Abī l-Hadīd 6: p. 12-13.

Chapter 2

How Did the Event of Saqīfah Take Place?

A: The Illness and Death of the Prophet

On the last ten days of the month Ṣafar in the year 11 AH/ 632 CE, the Prophet (pbuh) got sick. Meanwhile, he appointed Usama ibn Zayd, who was a freed slave by the Prophet (pbuh) and eighteen years old at that time,[1] to go to Sham (Syria) and, as the commander of the expeditionary force, fight the Christians of the Eastern Roman Empire. He ordered that Abū Bakr, ʻUmar, Abū ʻUbaydah ibn al-Jarāḥ, Saʻd ibn ʻUbadah, and the other leaders of the Anṣār (Helpers) and the Muhājirūn (Emigrants) to participate,[2] and emphasized that none of the above-mentioned people violate the order to go with that army. The Prophet (pbuh) said, "May God curse anyone who turns away from Usama's army (and does not accompany it)."[3]

After that, the Prophet's condition got severe due to the illness. Usama's army was informed that the Prophet (pbuh) was moribund. Those who wanted to interfere in the Caliphate affair returned to Medina and on Monday morning gathered around the Prophet's bed. The Prophet (pbuh) said, "Bring me a quill

---

[1] *Al-Istiʻab*, 12; *Usd al-Ġābah*, 1: pp.65-66

[2] *Kitāb aṭ-Tabaqāt al-Kabīr*, 2: pp. 190-192, *Uyūn al-Athar*, 2: p. 281; In many resources it has been indicated that Abī Bakr and ʻUmar were members of Usama's army: *Kanz al-Ummāl*, 5: p.312; *Muntakhab Kanz al-Ummāl*, 4: p. 180; *Ansab al-Ashraf*, 1: p. 474; *Kitāb aṭ-Tabaqāt al-Kabīr*, 4: p. 44; *Tahzīb Ibn ʻAsākir*, 2: p.391; *Tarīkh Yaʻqubi*, 2: p.74; *Al-Kāmil fit-Tārīkh Ibn al-Athir*, 2: p.123.

[3] *Sharḥ Nahj al-Balāgha* by Ibn Abī l-Hadīd 6: p. 52.

and a paper. I want to write a letter (a will) for you, which secures you from going astray."[4]

'Umar said, "Illness has overcome the Prophet [an irony to imply that the Prophet (pbuh) is not aware of what he is saying] and you have the Book of God and the Book of God suffices us."[5] But a group of them said, "Do as the Prophet (pbuh) has ordered." And that group who wanted to follow the Prophet's order was dominant.[6]

It is referred in some narrations as mentioned in the *Kitāb aṭ-Tabaqāt al-Kabīr Ibn Sa'd* that one of the attendees said, "Indeed, the Prophet of God (pbuh) has become delirious [may God have mercy on us]."[7]

O' sky! Cry blood. One of the Aṣḥāb (Companions) stated such an undue matter in the face of the Prophet (pbuh) and in front of the other Aṣḥāb. Although the narrator has not been mentioned in this narration, according to what we quoted earlier from *Ṣaḥīḥ al-Bukhārī*, who could dare put to words such an impudent speech other than 'Umar?! Yes, the speaker was the same person who said, "The Book of God is enough for us."[8]

---

[4] For detailed account of this incidence known in history as Raziyat Yawm al Khamis (The Calamity of Thursday) please see: *Black Thursday* by Dr. Muhammad Al-Tijani Al-Samawi. Ansariyan Publications, Qum (2014).

[5] *Ṣaḥīḥ al-Bukhārī*, book of al-Ilm Min Kitāb al-Ilm 1: p.22; *Musnad Aḥmad ibn Ḥanbal*, hadīth 2992; *Kitāb aṭ-Tabaqāt al-Kabīr, Ibn Sa'd,* 2: p. 244.

[6] *Ṣaḥīḥ al-Bukhārī*, book of al-Ilm Min Kitāb al-Ilm 1: p.22; *Musnad Aḥmad ibn Ḥanbal*, hadīths 2676 & 2992; *Kitāb aṭ-Tabaqāt al-Kabīr, Ibn Sa'd,* 2: pp. 223-244.

[7] *Kitāb aṭ-Tabaqāt al-Kabīr*, 2: p. 242; *Ṣaḥīḥ al-Bukhārī*, book of Java'ez al-Vafd Min Kitāb al-Jihad 2: p.120 & part Ikhraj al-Yahud Min Jaziret al-Arab 2: p. 136 says: 'They said the Prophet (pbuh) became delirious.' And in *Ṣaḥīḥ Muslim*, part Man Tarak al-Wasieh 5: p. 76; *Tārīkh al-Ṭabarī*, 3: p. 193 says: 'Indeed the Prophet (pbuh) becomes delirious.'

[8] 'Umar has confessed to this himself. According to Abu al-Faḍl Ahmad ibn Abī Tahir in *History of Baghdad* & Ibn Abī l-Hadīd in *Sharḥ Nahj al-Balāgha*, 3: p. 97 in the memoir of 'Umar: One day through a serious discussion that took place between ibn Abbass and 'Umar, 'Umar said, "During his illness, the Prophet had in mind to mention his name [Alī ibn Abī Ṭālib's] specifically but I did not allow it." Also see: *al-Murāja'āt*, pp. 442-443.

O' God, what calamity can be greater than this!

After this talk and argument, some of those who were present were willing to provide a pen and a paper, but the Prophet (pbuh) said, "After what [do you bring what was asked]?"[9] If they had brought the required material after these comments and the Prophet (pbuh) had written a will in which 'Alī (as) was mentioned, the opponents could bring some people and testify that the Prophet (pbuh) wrote that will in a state of delirium [may God have mercy on us].

Following this profanity, the Prophet (pbuh) said, "Get away from me for it is not appropriate to quarrel in the presence of the Prophet (pbuh)."[10]

What Happened in the Dawn that Led to That Day?

Whenever Bilāl called to prayer, he would come to the Prophet's door and say, "Prayer, Prayer! O' Messenger of God."[11] At the dawn of that Monday when it was time to call to prayer, Bilāl came to Prophet's house and made his usual address. The Prophet (pbuh) was in Ā'ishah's chamber, unconscious with his head in 'Alī's lap. Ā'ishah appeared behind the door and told Bilāl, "Get my father to come and offer the congregational prayer." Abū Bakr showed up and started to hold the Morning Prayer. The Prophet (pbuh) woke up and realized that the congregational prayer was being held in the mosque, while 'Alī (as) was sitting by his side. The Prophet (pbuh), while sick and weak, performed ablution and leaned on the arms of Faḍl ibn Abbas and 'Alī (as). He was brought to the mosque while his legs were pulled on the ground because of the severity of his illness. Abū Bakr was performing the prayer. The Prophet (pbuh) placed himself in front of him and cut his prayer and started his own prayer in a sitting position. The Aṣḥāb followed him and said the Morning Prayer behind the

---

[9] *Kitāb aṭ-Ṭabaqāt al-Kabīr*, 2: p. 242.

[10] *Tārīkh Abī al-Fada'*, 1: p.151; *Ṣaḥīḥ al-Bukhārī*, book of al-Ilm Min Kitāb al-Ilm 1: p.22 we read: "The Prophet (pbuh) said, 'Get away from me for it is not appropriate to quarrel in my presence.'"

[11] The door to the Prophet's house opened into the mosque and so it is probable that Bilāl notified the Prophet (pbuh) of the presence of the worshipers who had come to pray.

Prophet (pbuh).[12] The rest of the events took place on that same Monday and it was on that same day that the Prophet (pbuh) passed away.

B: Ġusl and the Preparing the Prophet for Burial

Those who performed Ġusl (Full-Body Ritual Ablution) on the pure and holy body of the Prophet (pbuh) and participated in his funeral ceremony were: 'Alī ibn Abī Ṭālib, Abbas the Prophet's uncle, Faḍl ibn Abbas, and Ṣāliḥ (the freed slave by Prophet (pbuh)). This is how the Aṣḥāb left the body of the Prophet (pbuh) for the members of the family and only the mentioned took the responsibility to prepare the body of the messenger of God for the burial.[13]

According to another narration, 'Alī (as) along with Faḍl and Qutham (sons of Abbas) and Shuqran (a freed slave by the Prophet (pbuh)) and, according to one quote, Usama ibn Zayd did the whole task of preparing of the Prophet's body for burial[14] and Abū Bakr and 'Umar were not present in the funeral ceremony.[15]

At this point, Prophet's uncle, Abbas, said to 'Alī (as), "O' son of my brother! Let me pledge my allegiance to you, so that after I do so, no one will

---

[12] *Sharḥ Nahj al-Balāgha* by Ibn Abī l-Hadīd 9: p. 197, sermon 156 & *Sharḥ Nahj al-Balāgha* published in Egypt 2: p. 458; *Al-Irshad*, pp. 86-87. For more details see: *Ṣaḥīḥ al-Bukhārī*, 1: p. 92; *Ṣaḥīḥ Muslim*, 2: p.23; *Sunan ibn Mājah*, part Ma Ja'a Fi Ṣalāt Rasul Allah: "So Abī Bakr prayed behind the Prophet and people prayed behind Abī Bakr." And words close to these are seen in *Musnad Aḥmad ibn Ḥanbal*, 6: pp. 210 & 224; *Kitāb aṭ-Tabaqāt al-Kabīr, Ibn Sa'd*, 3: p. 179; *Ansab al-Ashraf*, 1: p. 557.

[13] *Kitāb aṭ-Tabaqāt al-Kabīr, Ibn Sa'd*, 2: part 2: p. 70; *Kanz al-Ummāl*, 4: pp. 54 & 60. In one narration Aws ibn Khawlī has been among these four. See *Abdullah ibn Saba'* by Allamah 'Askari 1: p. 110.

[14] *al-'Iqd al-Farīd*, 3: p. 61; Also aḍ-Ḍahabī in his book *Tārīkh al-Islām al-Kabir*, 1: pp. 321,324 & 326 narrates the same.

[15] Ā'ishah was also not attendant at this ceremony and did not know of the preparation and burial except when, as she herself has said, heard the sound of shovels in the middle of the night on Wednesday. *Sirat ibn Hisham*, 4: p. 344; *Tārīkh al-Ṭabarī*, 2: pp. 452 & 455 and in the European edition 1: pp. 1833-1837; *Al-Bidaya wa an-Nihaya*, 5: p. 2704; *Usd al-Ġābah*, 1: p. 34; *Musnad Aḥmad ibn Ḥanbal*, 6: pp. 62, 242 & 274.

oppose you."[16] 'Alī (as) replied, "Right now, it's on us to prepare the Prophet's body for burial."[17]

At the same time, the Aṣḥāb gathered in Saqīfa Banī Sā'ida (the courtyard of the Sā'ida clan) to determine a leader among themselves.[18] This news was spread quickly to a group of the Muhājirūn consisting of Abū Bakr, 'Umar and Abū 'Ubaydah and their companions. They rapidly joined the Aṣḥāb in Saqīfah.[19]

And thus, there was left nobody except the Prophet's relatives at his holy corpse who were: 'Alī ibn Abī Ṭālib, 'Abbas ibn 'Abd al-Muttalib (Prophet's uncle), Usama ibn Zayd (freed by the Prophet (pbuh)), Ṣāliḥ (freed by the Prophet (pbuh)) and Aws ibn Khawlī (from the Anṣār). It was only these who took the duty of Ġusl and the burial of the Prophet (pbuh).[20]

---

[16] *Murūj aḏ-Ḏahab*, al-Mas'ūdī 2: p. 200; *Tārīkh al-Islām al-Kabir aḏ-Ḏahabī*, 1: p. 329; *Duha al-Islām*, 3: p. 291; In the book *al-Imama Wa al-Siyasa* by ibn Qutayba al-Dīnawarī it is said: "Give me your hand and let me pledge my allegiance to you, so that it would be said that the Prophet's uncle swore allegiance to the Prophet's cousin and then your family members will pledge allegiance to you. After that no one will oppose you." In the book *Kitāb aṭ-Tabaqāt*, 2: part 2: p. 38 this is how Ibn Sa'd narrates the event: Abbas said to Alī (as), "Stretch your hand so I would pledge my allegiance to you and therefore people pledge their allegiance to you."

[17] *Sharḥ Nahj al-Balāgha*, Ibn Abī l-Hadīd 1: p. 131.

[18] *Musnad Aḥmad ibn Ḥanbal*, 1: p. 260; *Ibn Kathīr*, 5: p.260; *Safwat u-Safwah*, 1: p. 85; *Tārīkh al-Khamis*, 1: p. 189; *Tārīkh al-Ṭabarī*, 2: p. 451 & in the European edition 1: p. 1830-1831; *Tārīkh Abī al-Fada'*, 1: p. 152; *Usd al-Ġābah*, 1: p. 34 & 35: p. 188; *al-'Iqd al-Farīd*, 3: p. 61; *Tārīkh al-Islām al-Kabir aḏ-Ḏahabī*, 1: p. 321; *Kitāb aṭ-Tabaqāt al-Kabīr, Ibn Sa'd*, 2: 2: p. 70; *Tārīkh Ya'qubi*, 2: p. 94; *al-Bad' wa a-Tārīkh*, 5: p. 68; *Al-Isti'ab*, 4: p. 65.

[19] *Ṣaḥīḥ al-Bukhārī*, book of al-Hudud 4: p. 120; *Sirat ibn Hisham*, 4: p. 336; *Al-Riaz un-Nazra*, 1: p. 163; *Tārīkh al-Khamis*, 1: p.186; *al-Saqīfa* by Abī Bakr Johari narrates from Ibn Abī l-Hadīd 2: p. 2; *Tārīkh al-Ṭabarī*, European edition 1: p. 1839; *al-Bad' wa a-Tārīkh*, 5: p.65.

[20] *Musnad Aḥmad ibn Ḥanbal*, 1: p. 260; *Ibn Kathīr*, 5: p. 260; *Safwat u-Safwah*, 1: p. 85; *Tārīkh al-Khamis*, 1: p. 189; *Tārīkh al-Ṭabarī*, 2: p. 451 & in European edition 1: pp. 1830-1831; Ibn al-Shihnah in sidelines of *Al-Kāmil fit-Tārīkh Ibn al-Athir*, p. 100; *Tārīkh Abī al-*

Praying on the body of the Prophet (pbuh) was objective obligatory for all Muslims present in Medina, i.e. all Muslims one by one were obliged to pray on the Prophet's corpse,[21] and unlike praying on the body of others, Imam of congregation was not necessary for praying on the body of the Prophet (pbuh). As 'Alī (as) used to mention, "The Prophet (pbuh) is the Imam of All." So, the Muslims came in groups of five and six and 'Alī (as) would say the prayer phrases loudly and they would repeat them. Men said the prayers first, and then women and finally children under the age of puberty. This task started on Monday and ended in the evening of Tuesday.[22] The Prophet's body was buried at the night before Wednesday in the very same room he had passed away in.[23] Except close relatives of the Prophet (pbuh) no other person was present at his funeral and the Banī Ghunm clan were fast asleep in their homes only to be awoken by the sound of shovels in the middle of the night.[24] Ā'ishah says, "We were not aware of the burial of the Prophet's body until the sound of the shovels reached our ears amidst the night before Wednesday."[25]

C: The Prophet's Will to 'Alī

Before stating the Prophet's will to 'Alī (as), it is better to give an introduction to gain a better understanding of the matter. In the Qur'ān we read:

Fada, 1: p. 252; *Usd al-Ġābah,* 1: p. 34; *al-'Iqd al-Farīd,* 3: p. 61; *Tārīkh al-Islām al-kabir aḏ-Ḏahabī,* 1: p. 321; *Kitāb aṭ-Tabaqāt al-Kabīr, Ibn Sa'd,* 2: part 2: p. 70; *Tārīkh Ya'qubi,* 2: p. 94; *al-Bad' wa a-Tārīkh,* 5: p. 68; *At-Tanbih wal-'Ishraf,* p. 244.

[21] This part is the author's own inference (Sayyid Murtada Sharif 'Askari) because in spite of the hatred towards delay in burial, the Prophet's body was not put into the ground for two whole days and nights in order for all the inhabitance of Medina, including men, women and children to pray on the holy body.

[22] *I'lam al-Wara Bi A'lam al-Huda,* p. 144; *Kitāb aṭ-Tabaqāt al-Kabīr, Ibn Sa'd,* 2: pp. 256-257; *Bihar al-Anwar,* 22: pp. 525 & 539.

[23] *Kitāb aṭ-Tabaqāt al-Kabīr, Ibn Sa'd,* 2: pp. 292-294; *Sirat ibn Hisham,* 4: p. 343.

[24] *Kitāb aṭ-Tabaqāt al-Kabīr, Ibn Sa'd,* 2: p.78.

[25] *Sirat ibn Hisham,* 4: p. 344; *Musnad Aḥmad ibn Ḥanbal,* 6: pp. 62 & 242 & 274; *Tārīkh al-Ṭabarī,* 3: p. 313; *Kitāb aṭ-Tabaqāt al-Kabīr,* 2: p. 205.

وَمَا مُحَمَّدٌ إِلَّا رَسُولٌ قَدْ خَلَتْ مِن قَبْلِهِ ٱلرُّسُلُ أَفَإِيْن مَّاتَ أَوْ قُتِلَ ٱنقَلَبْتُمْ عَلَىٰ أَعْقَٰبِكُمْ وَمَن يَنقَلِبْ عَلَىٰ عَقِبَيْهِ فَلَن يَضُرَّ ٱللَّهَ شَيْئًا وَسَيَجْزِي ٱللَّهُ ٱلشَّٰكِرِينَ

"Muḥammad is not but a messenger. [Other] messengers have passed on before him. So if he was to die or be killed, would you turn back on your heels [to unbelief]? And he who turns back on his heels will never harm Allāh at all; but Allāh will reward the grateful."[26]

As mentioned earlier, the Sharia (religion) of Islām was sent in two kinds of revelation to the Prophet (pbuh):

A. The Qur'ānic revelation, which is the same text of the Qur'ān we have nowadays and has been preserved as it was to reach us, consisting of the words which have been sent by God and in which the principles of the Sharia of Islām, i.e. the unity of the creator, the monotheism of the Lord (the legislator), re-resurrection (after death), calculation, reward and punishment, the dispatch of the messengers, the necessity of their obedience from the time of Adam to the Last Prophet, and also the Islāmic manners and rulings such as Ṣalāt (prayer), Hajj, Jihād, fasting, Zakāt, Khums, enjoining what is right and forbidding what is wrong and the prohibition of gossip and detraction and etc. are mentioned.

B. The expressive revelation, which is a revelation that was sent along with the Qur'ānic revelation and was used to explain and interpret it. As an example, on the day of Ghadīr Khumm, at the same time of the revelation of verse saying:

يَٰٓأَيُّهَا ٱلرَّسُولُ بَلِّغْ مَآ أُنزِلَ إِلَيْكَ مِن رَّبِّكَ وَإِن لَّمْ تَفْعَلْ فَمَا بَلَّغْتَ رِسَالَتَهُ

"O' Messenger! Announce that which has been revealed to you from your Lord, and if you do not, then you have not conveyed His message"[27], this revelation was sent: "O' Messenger of God! Announce what has been revealed

---

[26] Āl-'Imrān 144.

[27] al-Mā'ida 67.

to you in 'Alī."[28] So, "in 'Alī" was part of the expressive revelation which the Prophet (pbuh) would present in his Hadith and therefore "in 'Alī" was also God's revelation. The Prophet (pbuh) would not state anything from himself. As God says in this regard:

وَمَا يَنطِقُ عَنِ ٱلْهَوَىٰ إِنْ هُوَ إِلَّا وَحْيٌ يُوحَىٰ

"Nor does he speak from [his own] inclination. It is not but a revelation revealed."[29]

And even stronger He says:

وَلَوْ تَقَوَّلَ عَلَيْنَا بَعْضَ ٱلْأَقَاوِيلِ لَأَخَذْنَا مِنْهُ بِٱلْيَمِينِ ثُمَّ لَقَطَعْنَا مِنْهُ ٱلْوَتِينَ فَمَا مِنكُم مِّنْ أَحَدٍ عَنْهُ حَٰجِزِينَ

"And if he [i.e., Muḥammad] had made up about Us some [false] sayings, We would have seized him by the right hand; Then We would have cut from him the aorta. And there is no one of you who could prevent [Us] from punishing him."[30]

Hence, the Qur'ānic revelation is the same text of the Qur'ān in which all words are from God and no one can bring a Surah like it, even if it is as short as al-Kawthar.[31] So, the Qur'ān is the miracle of the holy Prophet (pbuh) which God Himself has taken the responsibility of protecting:

إِنَّا نَحْنُ نَزَّلْنَا ٱلذِّكْرَ وَإِنَّا لَهُ لَحَٰفِظُونَ

"Indeed, it is We who sent down the message [i.e., the Qur'ān], and indeed, We will be its guardian."[32] But, the expressive revelation gets its meaning from

---

[28] *Bihar al-Anwar*, 37: pp. 155 & 189; *Shawāhid al-Tanzīl*, 1: pp. 187 & 190; *Tārīkh Dimashq Ibn 'Asākir*, hadīth 451; *Asbāb al-Nuzūl*, p. 135; *al-Durr al-Manthur*, 2: p. 298; *Fath al-Qadir*, 2: p. 57; *Tafsīr al-Nīsābūrī*, 6: p. 194.

[29] An-Najm 3-4.

[30] al-Ḥāqqah 44-47.

[31] al-Baqarah 23-24.

[32] al-Hijr 9.

God, although its expression is rendered in the Prophet's expression and there is no condition determined for challenge and miracle, and its purpose is to elaborate on the Qur'ānic verses by the Prophet (pbuh). As God says:

$$\text{وَأَنزَلْنَا إِلَيْكَ ٱلذِّكْرَ لِتُبَيِّنَ لِلنَّاسِ مَا نُزِّلَ إِلَيْهِمْ}$$

"And We revealed to you the message [i.e., the Qur'ān] that you may make clear to the people what was sent down to them."[33]

When the Prophet (pbuh) received a verse of Qur'ān through revelation and publicized it, he also mentioned the expression related to that verse, which was sent by God, and thus completed his proselytism in this way.

'Abdullāh ibn Mas'ud, one of the greatest Aṣḥāb of the Prophet (pbuh), says, "I learned seventy Suras from the Prophet (pbuh) himself." For instance when the verse:

$$\text{وَٱلشَّجَرَةَ ٱلْمَلْعُونَةَ}$$

"the accursed tree"[34] was sent, the Prophet (pbuh) would tell him "the accursed tree" means Banū Umayya.[35]

Quoting the Prophet's Aṣḥāb in *Musnad Aḥmad ibn Ḥanbal*, it is narrated, "The Prophet's Aṣḥāb learned the Qur'ānic verses ten by ten and did not start the new ten verses unless they learned the (related) Islāmic concepts and rules that were in the previous ten verses."[36] For example, if a story was mentioned about the previous prophets, the Prophet (pbuh) would tell it, or if a verse was related to the Day of Judgment, he would explain what the Day of Judgment is like, or if it was about orders such as ablution, prayers and tayammum (the Islāmic act of dry ritual purification using a purified sand or stone or mud

---

[33] Part of al-Nahl 44.

[34] Part of al-Isrā' 60.

[35] *al-Durr al-Manthur*, 4: p. 191.

[36] *Musnad Aḥmad ibn Ḥanbal*, 5: p. 410; *Tafsir al-Qurtubi*, 1: p. 39; *Ma'rifat al-Qurrā'*, p. 48; *Majmau' az-Zawa'id*, 1: p. 165; *Tārīkh al-Ṭabarī*, 1: p. 27; *Kanz al-Ummāl*, hadīths 4213 & 4215.

instead of ablution or Ġusl), he would accurately teach the exact practice of the commandments. So, the Prophet (pbuh) did not publicize any verse unless he indicated its expressive revelation to the people as well. For instance in teaching the verse:

$$إِنَّمَا يُرِيدُ ٱللَّهُ لِيُذْهِبَ عَنكُمُ ٱلرِّجْسَ أَهْلَ ٱلْبَيْتِ وَيُطَهِّرَكُمْ تَطْهِيرًا$$

"O' people of the [Prophet's] household! Allāh intends only to remove from you the impurity [of sin] and to purify you with [extensive] purification."[37] the Prophet (pbuh) would add, "the household of Muḥammad are ʿAlī, Fāṭimah, Ḥasan and Ḥusayn."[38]

Also, when revealing the verse:

$$إِن تَتُوبَا إِلَى ٱللَّهِ فَقَدْ صَغَتْ قُلُوبُكُمَا إِن تَتُوبَا إِلَى ٱللَّهِ فَقَدْ صَغَتْ قُلُوبُكُمَا$$

"If you two [wives] repent to Allāh, [it is best], for your hearts have deviated";[39] he explained that the two wives were Umm al-Mu'minin Ḥafṣah and Umm al-Mu'minin Ā'ishah.[40]

In teaching these types of verses, the Prophet (pbuh) also instructed their practice as he taught their meanings. And this was the case, for example, when this verse was revealed saying:

$$فَٱغْسِلُواْ وُجُوهَكُمْ وَأَيْدِيَكُمْ$$

---

[37] Part of al-Ahzāb 33.

[38] *al-Mustadrak ʿala al-Sahihayn*, 3: p. 147; *Ṣaḥīḥ Muslim*, 7: p. 130; al-*Sunan al-Bayhaqī*, 2: p. 149; *Tafsīr al-Ṭabarī*, and *al-Durr al-Manthur*, under verse 33 of al-Ahzāb; *Al-Kashshāf* and *Tafsir al-Razi* under verse Mubahilah; *Usd al-Ġābah*, 2: p. 20.

[39] Part of At-Taḥrīm 4.

[40] *Ṣaḥīḥ al-Bukhārī*, book of al-Tafsīr 3: pp. 137-138; *Ṣaḥīḥ Muslim*, Talaq book of al-Talaq 2: pp. 1108 &1111.

"Wash your faces and your forearms";[41] the Prophet (pbuh) practically taught how and with what kind of water to perform ablution.

In all these cases, regarding what was taught to the Aṣḥāb by the Prophet (pbuh), each of the Aṣḥāb who could write, wrote the Qur'ānic verses with the interpretations that they had heard from the Prophet (pbuh). Thus, all the writers of the Qur'ān among the Aṣḥāb wrote the verses with the interpretations that they themselves had heard from the Prophet (pbuh). Of course, in the Qur'āns of each Companion, the interpretation of all verses was not written, although this was not true about the Qur'ān that existed in the Prophet's house for that one was a complete text accompanied by the complete interpretation of all the verses. It is necessary to explain that what was sent of the Qur'ān and its interpretation, would cause the Prophet (pbuh) to ask each of the Aṣḥāb who was literate and close to him to come, and order them to write what was revealed including the verses of Qur'ān and their interpretations on whatever they had in reach i.e. a piece of paper, board, bone or parchment of sheep and etc., and then He would keep those writings at his house.

At the time of death, the Prophet (pbuh) made a will to 'Alī (as) saying, "After preparing me for burial, do not wear your cloak and do not leave the house until you collect this Qur'ān."[42]

'Alī (as) pierced and passed thread through the verses of the Qur'ān with their interpretations written on parchment, leather, board, paper and so, and thus collected the verses and interpretations of each Surah. This job started from Wednesday (the day after the burial of the Prophet (pbuh)) and ended on Friday. 'Alī (as) accompanied by his freed slave, Qambar, brought that Qur'ān to the mosque. Muslims had gathered for Friday prayers at the Prophet's mosque. He said to them, "This is the same Qur'ān that was in the Prophet's house and I have brought it to you, the Caliphate system." They said, "We do

---

[41] Part of al-Mā'idah 6.

[42] *Umdat al-Qari*, 20: p. 16; *Fath al-Bārī*, 10: p. 386; *al-Itqan As-Suyūṭī*, 1: p. 59; *Bihar al-Anwar*, 92: pp. 48 & 51-52 quoted from *Tafsir al-Qummi*, p. 745.

not need this Qur'ān. We have a Qur'ān of our own!" And so 'Alī (as) said, "You will not see this Qur'ān again."[43]

That Qur'ān with the interpretation of all verses was given after 'Alī (as) to his sons in his progeny one after the other and is in the hands of Mahdī now, and he will disclose it when he emerges.[44] The Qur'ān that we have now is the same Qur'ān as of the time of the Prophet (pbuh) but without its interpretation, i.e. it is only the Qur'ānic revelation void of expressive revelation.[45]

But why didn't they accept the Qur'ān 'Alī (as) had collected which contained the text of verses as well as their interpretations as revealed to the Prophet (pbuh)?! The reason is that in the expressive revelation, which was revealed to the Prophet (pbuh) and was considered as the Hadith of the Prophet (pbuh) in the expression of Qur'ān through his words, there were ideas that opposed the Caliphate system and was a hindrance to their government.

For example, as mentioned earlier when:

وَٱلشَّجَرَةَ ٱلْمَلْعُونَةَ

---

[43] *Mafatih al-Asrar wa Masabih al-Abrar*, introduction p. 15; *Kitāb Sulaym ibn Qays al-Hilālī*, pp. 18-19 (for authenticity see *Qur'ān al-Karīm wa Riwāyāt al-Madrasatayn*, 2: pp. 396-408.

[44] *Al-Kāfī*, 2: p. 633 hadīth 23. For more information regarding the Imams referring their knowledge to Alī (as) and therefore to the Prophet (pbuh) see *Ma'alim al-Madrasatayn*, 2: pp. 312-320.

[45] More to know is that Abī Bakr ordered for the Qur'ān to be written free of interpretation. This mission started in his time and ended in 'Umar's time. 'Umar kept that Qur'ān with Hafsah. In the time of Uthmān, due to the Aṣḥāb's opposition towards him, and their reciting of the verses that were against Banū Umayyah and were mentioned in the Qur'āns containing the interpretations, Uthmān took the interpretation-free Qur'ān from Hafsah and ordered for seven copies to be written from it. He sent six of them to Mecca, Yemen, Damascus, Ḥimṣ, Kūfah and Baṣrah and kept one in Medina. Then he demanded all the Qur'āns which were kept by the Aṣḥāb and included the interpretations heard from the Prophet (pbuh) to be collected and burnt. This is why he is known as the Qur'ān-burner. In the meantime, it was only Abdullah ibn Mas'ud who did not surrender into giving his book and therefore Banū Umayyah forced the narrators to forge lies and fake tales about him.

was revealed to the Prophet (pbuh) that *"the accursed tree"*[46] were Banū Umayya; and this is recorded in some texts. By this narration, 'Uthmān, Mu'awiya, Yazīd, Walīd and such people could not be Caliph anymore.

Or, it was mentioned in accordance with the statement of the menacing verses of the Surah at-Taḥrīm that the two implied women are Ā'ishah and Hafsah.

Or it was mentioned postscript to the verse:

$$\text{يَـٰٓأَيُّهَا ٱلَّذِينَ ءَامَنُواْ لَا تَرْفَعُوٓاْ أَصْوَٰتَكُمْ فَوْقَ صَوْتِ ٱلنَّبِيِّ}$$

"O' you who have believed! Do not raise your voices above the voice of the Prophet";[47] that it was sent about Abū Bakr and 'Umar.[48]

Also, when the first ten verses of Surah at-Tawbah were sent, the Prophet (pbuh) gave the verses to Abū Bakr and 'Umar to be taken to Mecca and announce them to the polytheists. The non-Qur'ānic revelation was revealed that you yourselves or a person in whom you confide should announce this message. After that, the Prophet (pbuh) sent 'Alī ibn Abī Ṭālib (as) to take those verses from Abū Bakr and 'Umar, and 'Alī (as) himself took them to Mecca and announced them to the polytheists during the Hajj ceremony.[49]

Another example would be the verses that were sent in honor of the Prophet (pbuh) and Ahl al-Bayt, in the al-Taṭ'hīr verse:

$$\text{إِنَّمَا يُرِيدُ ٱللَّهُ لِيُذْهِبَ عَنكُمُ ٱلرِّجْسَ أَهْلَ ٱلْبَيْتِ وَيُطَهِّرَكُمْ تَطْهِيرًا}$$

"O' people of the [Prophet's] household! Allāh intends only to remove from you the impurity [of sin] and to purify you with [extensive] purification";[50]

Or in the al-Mubāhala verse:

---

[46] Part of al-Isrā' 60.

[47] Part of al-Hujurāt 2.

[48] *Ṣaḥīḥ al-Bukhārī*, book of al-Tafsīr, interpretation of al-Hujurāt 3: pp. 190-191.

[49] For more information see *Qur'ān al-Karīm wa Riwāyāt al-Madrasatayn*, 1: pp. 226-227.

[50] Part of al-Ahzāb 33.

فَمَنْ حَاجَّكَ فِيهِ مِنْ بَعْدِ مَا جَاءَكَ مِنَ ٱلْعِلْمِ فَقُلْ تَعَالَوْاْ نَدْعُ أَبْنَاءَنَا وَأَبْنَاءَكُمْ وَنِسَاءَنَا وَنِسَاءَكُمْ وَأَنفُسَنَا وَأَنفُسَكُمْ ثُمَّ نَبْتَهِلْ فَنَجْعَل لَّعْنَتَ ٱللَّهِ عَلَى ٱلْكَاذِبِينَ

"Should anyone argue with you concerning him (Jesus), after the knowledge that has come to you, say: Come, let us call our sons and your sons, our women and your women, ourselves and yourselves, then supplicate earnestly [together] and invoke the curse of Allāh upon the liars [among us]".[51]

Or in the al-Ghadīr verse:

يَـٰٓأَيُّهَا ٱلرَّسُولُ بَلِّغْ مَا أُنزِلَ إِلَيْكَ مِن رَّبِّكَ وَإِن لَّمْ تَفْعَلْ فَمَا بَلَّغْتَ رِسَالَتَهُۥ وَٱللَّهُ يَعْصِمُكَ مِنَ ٱلنَّاسِ إِنَّ ٱللَّهَ لَا يَهْدِي ٱلْقَوْمَ ٱلْكَافِرِينَ

"O' Apostle! Announce that which has been revealed to you from your Lord, and if you do not, then you have not conveyed His message. And Allāh will protect you from the people. Indeed, Allāh does not guide the disbelieving people."[52]

And in the verse of the perfection of religion and the blessings:

ٱلْيَوْمَ أَكْمَلْتُ لَكُمْ دِينَكُمْ وَأَتْمَمْتُ عَلَيْكُمْ نِعْمَتِي وَرَضِيتُ لَكُمُ ٱلْإِسْلَـٰمَ دِينًا

"On this day I have perfected for you your religion and completed My favor upon you and have approved for you Islām as religion."[53]

And in the al-Wilāyah verse:

إِنَّمَا وَلِيُّكُمُ ٱللَّهُ وَرَسُولُهُۥ وَٱلَّذِينَ ءَامَنُواْ ٱلَّذِينَ يُقِيمُونَ ٱلصَّلَوٰةَ وَيُؤْتُونَ ٱلزَّكَوٰةَ وَهُمْ رَٰكِعُونَ

---

[51] Āl-'Imrān, 61

[52] al-Mā'idah, 67

[53] Part of al-Mā'idah, 3.

"Your ally is none but Allāh and [therefore] His Messenger and those who have believed - those who establish prayer and give Zakāt, and they bow [in worship]."[54]

And in the al-Najwā verse:

$$\text{يَـٰٓأَيُّهَا ٱلَّذِينَ ءَامَنُوٓاْ إِذَا نَٰجَيْتُمُ ٱلرَّسُولَ فَقَدِّمُواْ بَيْنَ يَدَيْ نَجْوَىٰكُمْ صَدَقَةً ۚ ذَٰلِكَ خَيْرٌ لَّكُمْ وَأَطْهَرُ ۚ فَإِن لَّمْ تَجِدُواْ فَإِنَّ ٱللَّهَ غَفُورٌ رَّحِيمٌ}$$

"O' you who have believed! When you [wish to] privately consult the Apostle, present before your consultation a charity. That is better for you and purer. But if you find not [the means] - then indeed, Allāh is all-forgiving, all-merciful."[55]

In addition, many other verses.[56] Thus, they not only did not accept the Qur'ān of ʿAlī ibn Abī Ṭālib (as), but tried to write the Qur'ān distinct from the expressive revelation[57] and prevented the Prophet's Hadith to be published and tried to conceal, falsify and distort it.[58]

*****

After this introduction to the previous events, now we will introduce the candidates of Caliphate position on the day of Saqīfah.

D: The Candidates of the Caliphate after the Death of the Prophet on the Day of Saqīfah[59]

---

[54] al-Māʾidah, 55.

[55] al-Mujādalah, 12.

[56] For more information see *Qur'ān al-Karīm wa Riwāyāt al-Madrasatayn*, 1: pp. 218-248.

[57] *Qur'ān al-Karīm wa Riwāyāt al-Madrasatayn*, 1: pp. 264-274 & 2: pp. 413-417.

[58] *Qur'ān al-Karīm wa Riwāyāt al-Madrasatayn*, 2: pp. 417-431 & pp. 510-515 & pp. 572-582; *Maʿalim al-Madrasatayn*, 1: pp. 329-392 & pp. 402-483; *Ahadīth Umm al-Muʾminin Āʾishah* p. 2; *Naqshe Aʾimah Dar Ihyaʾe Din*, pp. 2, 5 & 9.

[59] Caliph means the successor of the Prophet meaning the one who after Prophet takes the role of governing and ruling. This word is neither a lexical word nor an Islāmic expression and was only invented by the caliphate's school of thoughts after the Prophet (pbuh) passed away because the word means some'one's substitute that does

'Alī ibn Abī Ṭālib: He was sent for the leadership of this Ummah (the Islāmic community) by God and the holy Prophet (pbuh) announced this to the Muslims.

---

the work in his absence (*Al-Mufradat* under the word khalaf). According to the Qur'ān, the main duty of the Prophet (pbuh) and all other prophets is the propagation of religion to people and not ruling or governing them (al-Mā'idah 98) & (al-Nahl 35). Thus most of the prophets such as Jesus Christ, John, Zachariah, Noah and etc. did not govern or rule. Also, this word has no religious basis because the Prophet (pbuh) has stated that his successor is the one who narrates his words and behaviors to people (*Ma'ānī l-'Akhbār*, pp. 374-375; *Man lā Yahduruhu al-Faqīh*, 4: p. 420; *al-Fath al-Kabir*, 4: p. 233; *Sharaf As'hab al-Hadīth*, p.30). Also, this word does not mean the representative of God on earth because that would be one whom is selected by God to present God's religion to people through revelation (if he is a prophet) or through the Prophet (if he is the substitute of the Prophet such as an Imam). Although governing is part of this status, but representative of God has no responsibility to go after it unless people ask him to govern and lead them with their assistance, like the Prophet (pbuh) who governed Medina because people swore allegiance to him and aided him through the ruling, unlike Mecca (where people did not want him to rule and offered no help) which he did not take the government and instead stuck to his main duty which was propagating God's religion. Regarding Alī ibn Abī Ṭālib (as) the same applies. His and every other Imam's main duty just like the Prophet (pbuh) was to preserve and propagate God's religion to people and if they asked and assisted him to govern, he would be obligated to take the role, but they didn't except three people (*Tārīkh Ya'qubi*, 2: p. 105; *Sharh Nahj al-Balāgha* by Ibn Abī l-Hadīd, 2: p.4) or four and five people (*Sharh Nahj al-Balāgha* by Ibn Abī l-Hadīd, 2: p. 47) up to where Alī (as) said, "If I had found forty determined men, I would have ruled." But after 25 years and after the murder of Uthmān, because people came to Alī's door and persistently requested him to take the government, he accepted (*Sharh Nahj al-Balāgha* by Ibn Abī l-Hadīd 2: p. 50; *Taḏkirat al-Khawāṣ*, part 6). This was exactly what the Prophet (pbuh) had asked him to do (*Usd al-Ġābah*, 4: p. 31). Now consider that if Alī's name is mentioned in the list of the candidates, it does not mean he desired it and proceeded to take it. This represents the opinion of a few people of Medina who wanted him to be the governor because of his states knowing him as the administer of the Prophet (pbuh) and ruling his right (i.e. Salmān, Abū Ḏarr, Miqdād, Ammār), or due to family prejudice (i.e. Abbas ibn 'Abd al-Muttalib, Prophet's uncle) or clan prejudice (Abū Sufyān) insisted on his ruling.

Sa'd ibn 'Ubadah: He was the candidate of Banū Khazraj, but not all the Anṣār (the Aṣḥāb).

Abū Bakr: He was the candidate of a group of the Muhājirūn (refugees or emigrants of Quraysh), but not all of them.

E: The Mottos of the Congregators in Saqīfah

The mottos of the Anṣār

The Anṣār helped Islām[60]

The Anṣār drew their swords for the ideals of the Prophet (pbuh)[61]

Medina is the city of the Anṣār[62]

The Mottos of the Muhājirūn (Quraysh)[63]

The Prophet (pbuh) is from the Quraysh clan

Arabs do not accept that a person other than a member of their own clan to be their ruler, and so the Prophet's substitute should be a person from Quraysh.

After expressing what happened there, we can have a clear understanding of Saqīfah coup d'état.

F: The Saqīfah Coup D'état and Allegiance to Abū Bakr

After the death of the Prophet (pbuh), the Anṣār gathered at Saqīfa Banī Sā'ida. The members of Banū Khazraj wanted to appoint Sa'd ibn 'Ubadah as the Prophet's substitute.[64] This was not done unintentionally and/or because they didn't know the successor and trustee of the Prophet (pbuh); No, this is not the case. They did it out of tribal prejudice.

---

[60] *Abdullah ibn Saba'* by Allamah 'Askari 1: p. 113.

[61] *Ibid.*, 1: p. 113.

[62] *Ibid.*, 1: p. 115.

[63] *Ibid.*, 1: pp. 115-116.

[64] *Abdullah ibn Saba'* by Allamah 'Askari 1: p. 113.

Meanwhile, a group of the Muhājirūn who had heard about the assembling in Saqīfah joined them.[65] All these people left the corpse of the Prophet (pbuh) to some of his close relatives and came to argue and dispute for his substitution.

The Aus clan did not like Sa'd ibn 'Ubadah to take that position. Among Banū Khazraj, Bashir ibn Sa'ad who was one of the honorable persons in this clan, envied Sa'd and did not see eye to eye with him.[66]

G: Saqīfah in the Words of the Second Caliph

In *Ṣaḥīḥ al-Bukhārī*, the happenings of Saqīfah is mentioned on behalf of 'Umar as such:

"When the Prophet (pbuh) passed away, we were informed that the Anṣār had assembled in Saqifa Banī Sā'ida. I proposed to Abū Bakr to come so that we could join our brothers from the Anṣār. So, we hurried to reach Saqīfah. 'Alī (as) and Zubayr and their Aṣḥāb were not with us. When we arrived at Saqīfah, we understood that the Anṣār clan had brought a man wrapped in blanket with them and claimed that he was Sa'd ibn 'Ubadah and said that he had fever. We sat beside them and their preacher stood up and after reminding the grandeur of Almighty God said: We are the helpers of God and the fighting men and the compact force of Islām; You, the Muhājirūn, are people in limited number and ..."

"I ('Umar) wanted to say something as a response but Abū Bakr pulled my sleeve and demanded me to be calm. Then he himself stood up and began to talk. I swear to God that he didn't abandon any points that I had intended to point out in my speech. He either mentioned the same points or expressed something better. He said, "O' The group of Anṣār! What you mentioned about your goodness and your distinctions in superiority are correct with no doubt and you deserve it. Caliphate and ruling belongs only to the Quraysh clan because they are distinguished in terms of lineage and honor and this clan is

---

[65] Abī Bakr, 'Umar, Abū 'Ubaydah ibn al-Jarāḥ, Mughīra ibn Shu'ba and Abd al-Rahman ibn 'Awf: *Abdullah ibn Saba'* by Allamah 'Askari p. 113-115.

[66] *Sharḥ Nahj al-Balāgha* by Ibn Abī l-Hadīd, 2: p. 2 narrated from *al-Saqīfa* by Abī Bakr Johari.

eminent among the Arab clans. Because of this, I propose two people to be selected as Caliph and you can swear the oath of allegiance to either of them as you like." He said this and took Abū 'Ubaydah's hand and mine and introduced us for this position to them. It was only his last sentence that I disliked. At this time, a person from the Anṣār stood up and said, "I am like a stick with which camels scratch their backs.[67] And a tree that under its branches they take refuge. You, the Muhājirūn, choose governing for yourselves and we will choose ruling for ourselves."

"After this speech, controversy and noise arose from every side and the people were differentiated and divided and differences in ideas appeared strongly. I took the chance and told Abū Bakr, "Give me your hand I will pledge allegiance to you." After I finished allegiance to Abū Bakr, we rushed towards Sa'd ibn 'Ubadah as an attack... If someone pledges allegiance to a man for caliphate without consulting Muslims, do not follow him or the person to whom he has pledged; because both of them are worthy of death."[68]

H: Saqīfah as Narrated by Tārīkh al-Ṭabarī

al-Ṭabarī writes about the story of Saqīfah and the allegiance to Abū Bakr as:

The Anṣār clan left the body of the Prophet (pbuh) to his family to prepare for burial and they themselves assembled in Saqīfa Banī Sā'ida. They said, "We select Sa'd ibn 'Ubadah as our leader after Muḥammad (pbuh). They had brought Sa'd there with them, who was ill.

Sa'd praised God, reminded the previous jobs done by the Anṣār for the religion and mentioned their superiority in Islām. He also refreshed the audience about the helps on their side to the Prophet (pbuh) and the battles that they had with the enemies and emphasized that the Prophet (pbuh) left this world while he was pleased with them, and at last said, "Now, you people of

---

[67] This is an idiom from the Arab language. Obviously idioms do not sound as amusing when translated into other languages. This proverb is for those who have gained experience through conflicts and difficulties.

[68] Ṣaḥīḥ al-Bukhārī, book of al-Hudud, part Rajm al-Hubli 4: pp. 119-120; Sirat ibn Hisham, 2: pp. 336-338; Kanz al-Ummāl, 3: p. 139, hadīth 2326.

the Anṣār! Seize the ropes of ruling in your own hands and do not hand it to another person."

In response to Sa'd, all the Anṣār said loudly, "Your speech is quite right and your words are tried and true, and we will never do anything against you and we elect you for ruling and leadership."

After this final agreement, other things came up and they exchanged ideas until they lastly came to ask, "If the Muhājirūn of Quraysh do not accept our decision and say that they are the Muhājirūn and the first helpers of the Prophet (pbuh) and tell us that we do not have the right to oppose them in the ruling and leadership of the Prophet (pbuh), what should we reply?" A group of them replied, "In that case, we will tell them that we will select a chief for ourselves and you select a head for yourselves." Sa'd ibn 'Ubadah said, "And thereby this would be the first defeat and retreat."[69]

When Abū Bakr and 'Umar heard about this gathering, they rushed to Saqīfah along with Abū 'Ubaydah al-Jarāḥ. Usayd ibn Huḍair[70] and 'Uwaym ibn Sā'ideh[71] and 'Asim ibn 'Adi[72] from Banī 'Ajlan, who out of jealousy, didn't want Sa'd to be the Caliph joined them. Moreover, Mughīra ibn Shu'ba and 'Abd al-Rahman ibn 'Awf awaited them there.

---

[69] *Tārīkh al-Ṭabarī*, events of the year 11 Hijri 1: p. 838.

[70] Usaid ibn Hudair was of the Anṣār who took part the second battle of Aqaba, the battle of Uhud and battles of the Islāmic era. Abī Bakr never considered any of the other Anṣār better than him. He passed away in year 20 or 21 Hijri and 'Umar was one of whom carried his coffin. *Al-Isti'ab*, 1: pp. 31-33; *al-Iṣābah*, 1: p. 64.

[71] He was one of the Anṣār and had taken part in the battle of Aqaba, Badr and other battles in the Islāmic era. He passed away in 'Umar's caliphate time. In the book *Siyar A'lam al-Nubala*, he is introduced as 'Umar's brother. When at his tombstone, 'Umar said, "Nobody can claim that I'm better than the owner of this tomb." *Al-Isti'ab*, 3: p. 17; *al-Iṣābah*, 3: p. 45; *Usd al-Ġābah*, 4: p. 158.

[72] He was a confederate to the Anṣār and the head of clan to Bani 'Ajlan. He also took part in the Battle of Uhud and other battles in the Islāmic era. He passed away in year 45 Hijri. *al-Iṣābah*, 2: p. 237 *Al-Isti'ab*, 3: p. 133; *Usd al-Ġābah*, 3: p. 75.

46

After hindering 'Umar from talking in that assembly, Abū Bakr stood up and expressed praise and gratitude to God and reminded everyone of the record of the Muhājirūn and pointed out that they were pioneers in acknowledging the mission of the Prophet (pbuh) and said, "Muhājirūn were of the first people who worshipped God on earth and believed in his Prophet (pbuh). They are close relatives and friends of the Prophet (pbuh) and for this reason, after His holiness, are more deserving for this position, and so because of this accomplishment nobody will oppose their ruling except the evildoers."

After this speech, Abū Bakr talked about the goodness of the Anṣār and continued, "Of course, besides the Muhājirūn and the forerunners in Islām, nobody will have your rank and status in our eyes. May government and command be ours and the reputation of ministering be yours."

Then Hubab ibn al-Munḏir stood up and addressed the Anṣār, "O' the group of the Anṣār! Take the responsibility of government in your own hands since this group of the Muhājirūn live in your city and under your command and no rebel can dare not be submissive to your orders. So, avoid disagreeing and discord, for conflict will lead you to decay and corruption and you will be defeated and (as a result) you will lose governance and administration. If they do not accept and say nothing other than what we heard from them, in that case, we will choose a ruler among ourselves and they can also select a governor for themselves.

At this point, 'Umar rose and said:

"This will never be done, for two swords cannot be contained in one sheath. I swear to God that Arab will not surrender to your ruling when their prophet is not one of you. But Arab will not oppose the ruling of a person who is from the lineage of prophets and messengers. We have decisive argumentation against those who try to oppose us. Who can seize the government and ruling of Muhammad from us and fight for it and be against us while we are one of his relatives and a member of his dynasty;[73] except a person who has gone astray

---

[73] When Alī (as) heard Muhājirūn's reasoning he said, "They ratiocinate the family tree but have ignored its fruit." Sarcastically meaning that because they are from the Quraysh clan and the Prophet (pbuh) was also from that clan, therefore the caliphate

or been polluted with sin or a person who has been thrown in the whirl of destruction."

Hubab stood up once again and said, "O' the group of Anṣār! Stay hand in hand and do not listen to the words of this man and his Aṣḥāb, otherwise you will lose your rights in governance and administration. If they do not obey your demands, kick them off your lands and have your own way and take control of the affairs, for I swear to God that you deserve leadership and ruling more than they do; needless to say the infidels surrendered to your swords and converted to this religion.

I am like a stick with which camels scratch their back[74] (an irony to imply that at hard times they take refuge to their own ideas) and I am like a corpulent tree that is an asylum for the weak. I swear to God that if you desire, I will restart war and bloodshed."

'Umar said, "In that case, God will kill you."[75]

Hubab replied, "God will kill you."

Considering this situation, Abū 'Ubaydah addressed Anṣār saying, "O' the group of Anṣār! You were from the pioneers who helped the Messenger of God (pbuh). So, do not be the first people who change and modify the religion and the basis of unity of Muslims!"

After the tactful speech of Abū 'Ubaydah, Bashir ibn Sa'ad Khazraji[76] stood up and said, "O' the group of Anṣār! By God we have gained a high status in Jihād with the pagans and in being pioneers to accept Islām and we did not

---

position is their right and not the Anṣār's. Alī (as) states, "According to this reasoning, we who are the fruit of the tree of the Prophet's family, deserve it more than you Muhājirūn, but you forgot us and trampled our rights. *Sharḥ Nahj al-Balāgha* by Ibn Abī l-Hadīd 2: p. 2.

[74] This Arabic proverb applies to those who have gained experience through conflicts and difficulties.

[75] This was a murder threat.

[76] He was Nu'mān ibn Bashīr al-Ansārī's father and one of the distinct people of the Khazraj clan and there was a record of jealousy between him and Sa'd ibn 'Ubadah. *Sharḥ Nahj al-Balāgha* by Ibn Abī l-Hadīd 2: pp. 2-5.

request anything in return but the satisfaction of God and following the Prophet (pbuh) and patience and restoring our souls. So, with all these virtues it is not appropriate to be haughty to people and lay them under obligations and make them a tool to gain our worldly riches and possessions. God is our master. He has laid obligation on us in this regard. O' people! Know that Muḥammad (pbuh) is from Quraysh and the members of his clan are closer to him and more deserving than the others in taking the responsibility and leadership of his government; I ask God not to let me be seen fighting with them in the affair of ruling. So, you also fear God and do not oppose them and, in the case of government, do not have enmity and hostility towards them."

When Bashir finished his speech, Abū Bakr rose and said, "This is 'Umar and that is Abū 'Ubaydah: Select and swear allegiance to whichever you like." 'Umar and Abū 'Ubaydah spoke in one voice saying, "We swear to God that, in your presence, we would never dare forerun you in the affair of ruling, for you are the companion of the cave to the Prophet (pbuh)."

Meanwhile, 'Abd al-Rahman ibn 'Awf stood up and uttered some words, "O' the group of Anṣār! Although you have a high and brilliant status, but nobody can be found among you similar to 'Umar and Abū Bakr." Also, Munḍir ibn Abī'l-Arqam stood and addressed 'Abd al-Rahman saying, "We do not deny the superiority of the people you named, especially that there is a person among them whom if had wanted to come forward to take control of governing, nobody would have opposed. [Munḍir meant 'Alī ibn Abī Ṭālib (as)]."[77]

Then, some of the Anṣār said out loud, "We will only swear allegiance to 'Alī (as)." 'Umar says himself, "There was noise and murmur amongst the attendees everywhere and vague words were heard from every corner, so I feared the dissensions would make our affair dispersed in the core. That's why I turned to Abū Bakr and demanded: "Give me your hand so that I can have allegiance to you."[78]

---

[77] What is in brackets is from *Tārīkh-e Yaq'ubi*, 2: p. 123.

[78] After 'Umar dissuaded the Anṣār from swearing allegiance to Sa'd ibn 'Ubadah, the Anṣār asked for Alī (as) saying, "We will only swear allegiance to Alī." 'Umar feared the tendency towards Alī (as) and thought to himself that if that meeting did not reach

But, before 'Umar could put his hand in the hands of Abū Bakr, Bashir ibn Sa'ad pre-empted and shook hands with Abū Bakr and swore allegiance to him.[79]

Hubab ibn al-Mundir who was watching this event shouted at Bashir, "O' Bashir! O' the one cursed by his family! You separated from your relations and envied your cousin to achieve power?!" Bashir said, "I swear to God this is not true; but I didn't want to reach out for the rights of people whom God has destined this right for."

When the Aus clan considered what Bashir ibn Sa'ad did and what claims Quraysh had on one hand and on the other hand, what Banū Khazraj had intended by causing Sa'd ibn 'Ubadah to take the leadership, some of them addressed the other members of their clan including Usayd ibn Hudair [who was one of their representatives] and said, "We swear to God that if Banū Khazraj seize the power, this will be their eternal merit and they will excel you in glory and will never let your partnership in government come true. So, get up and swear allegiance to Abū Bakr."

Then they all stood together and swore allegiance to Abū Bakr, and therefore Sa'd ibn 'Ubadah and the members of Banū Khazraj's plan of taking control of the government led to useless pursuits. People from every corner rushed to swear allegiance to Abū Bakr so that Sa'd ibn 'Ubadah, who was ill, was about to be trodden upon by them. At this time, one of his relatives shouted, "O' people! Watch out not to tread upon Sa'd." 'Umar said loudly in his response, "Kill him so that God kills him!" Then pushed the people aside and went to his lying place and said, "I wanted to tread you so hard no part of your

---

a conclusion and the Anṣār came to meet the Banū Hāshim family, who now were done with the Prophet's burial, they would take the power out of the hands of Abī Bakr, 'Umar, Abū 'Ubaydah ibn al-Jarāḥ, Sālim Mawlā 'Abī Hudayfah, and Uthmān for good. Therefore he hastily swore allegiance to Abī Bakr.

[79] The caliphs gave a huge amount of money and high positions to three of the Anṣār; one was Bashir ibn Sa'ad Khazraji, the first who swore allegiance to Abī Bakr. The second being Zayd ibn Thabit who was 'Umar's substitute in Medina whenever he was on a journey. And the third was Hasan ibn Thabit, a famous poet who never swore allegiance to Alī (as); *Al-Irshad*, 1: p. 237.

body would stay undamaged!" Qays ibn Sa'd who was standing at his father's bed stood up, took hold of 'Umar's beard in his hand and said, "By God if you so much as harm a hair on my father's head, I will make you pay back." Abū Bakr ordered 'Umar to be calm and said, "In this situation, only calmness and peacefulness work, not violence and agitation." Hearing this from Abū Bakr, 'Umar turned his back to Qays and walked off. But Sa'd addressed 'Umar and said, "I swear to God if I were not ill and had the ability to get up, you would hear me roar so loudly in the passages and alleys of Medina that you and your Aṣḥāb would hide in the thickets and copses out of fear, and I also swear by God, I would send you to the level of those for whom you were subordinate and obedient until yesterday, while you are their lord and superior (now)!" Then he told his Aṣḥāb to help him up and take him home, and so they did.

In his book *Saqīfah*, Abū Bakr al-Johari states:

On the same day of Saqīfa Banī Sā'ida, the day of allegiance to Abū Bakr, 'Umar wrapped something around his waist and ran before Abū Bakr shouting, "Attention! Attention! The people have sworn allegiance to Abū Bakr."[80] And by this, the groups who were present in Saqīfah and accompanied him on that day, would drag anyone they saw and take allegiance.

It is stated in *Tārīkh al-Ṭabarī* that:

On the day of Saqīfah, people from Banū Aslam had all come to Medina for grocery shopping. Their crowd was so big that walking around was made difficult for people in all alleys. 'Umar states this fact as, "I was not sure about the victory until the Banū Aslam arrived and filled and crowded the alleys of Medina."[81]

I: The Role of Banū Aslam in the Allegiance to Abū Bakr

This story is mentioned in the book of *al-Jamal* by Shaykh al-Mufīd as follows:

At that time, the Arab nomads came to cities for grocery shopping in clans, because the Sahara was not safe and if they came in few numbers, they might

---

[80] Narrated from *Sharḥ Nahj al-Balāgha* by Ibn Abī l-Hadīd, 1: p. 133.

[81] *Tārīkh al-Ṭabarī*, 1: p. 1843.

have gotten killed or robbed by bandits. So, the members of the clan came to shop for groceries all together. The men of Banū Aslam had come from the desert to Medina to get provisions. When they entered Medina, the allegiance to Abū Bakr was done. 'Umar and the others said, "Come and help collect allegiance for the caliph of the Prophet (pbuh); and if you do so, you will be given gratis groceries." That promise excited and provoked them and so they themselves rushed and swore allegiance first, and then became Aṣḥāb (companions) of Abū Bakr. After that, they wrapped their Arabic shawls round their waists and filled the alleys of Medina searching everywhere they could which included the bazaar, the alleys and etc. bringing in whomever they saw to swear allegiance to Abū Bakr. In this way, by the help of Banū Aslam, Abū Bakr became the caliph.[82]

J: The Reasons of Selecting Abū Bakr to Caliphate

The companions of Abū Bakr state the reasons for his selection as the caliph as:

1. Because the Prophet (pbuh) is from Quraysh, his substitute should also be from Quraysh[83] (this was the tradition of Arabs).

2. The other reason is that Abū Bakr had been one of the companions of Prophet and a former Muslim.[84]

'Alī (as) has a saying here. He says, "They ratiocinated the family tree of prophet hood (which was from Quraysh) for their argumentation and ignored its fruit (which was his cousin and groom).[85] They reasoned that they are from the lineage of the Prophet (pbuh) while, they ignored the fruit of this tree which is Banī Hāshim. The value of a palm tree or grape shrub is not in its branches or leaves, but the true value is in its fruit.

---

[82] *al-Jamal*, p. 43; *al-Muwafaqiat*, 6: p. 287 published by Dār Ihya' al-Kutub al-Arabi Publications, "Abī Bakr got stronger by Banū Aslam and he had no idea when they had appeared." Also see *al-Ṭabarī*, 1: p. 1843.

[83] *Ṣaḥīḥ al-Bukhārī*, book of al-Hudud 4: p. 120; *Sirat ibn Hisham*, 4: p. 339.

[84] *Abdullah ibn Saba'* by Allamah 'Askari, p. 121, narrated from *Tārīkh al-Ṭabarī*.

[85] *Sharḥ Nahj al-Balāgha* by Ibn Abī l-Hadīd, 2: p. 2.

In regard of saying Abū Bakr is from the Prophet's Companions, 'Alī (as) has also said, "They say that Abū Bakr should be the substitute of the Prophet (pbuh) because he is his Companion. If being the caliph depends on being a Companion, why doesn't it matter where both being a close relative and a Companion come together (that being true about 'Alī ibn Abī Ṭālib who is both a Companion and a close relative of the Prophet (pbuh))." We all know that 'Alī ibn Abī Ṭālib was a little child when the Prophet (pbuh) took him from his father, 'Abī Ṭālib's house and brought him to his own home. 'Alī (as) himself talks about it as, "The Prophet (pbuh) softened the food and put it in my mouth. He made the pleasing aroma of his body reach my nose. I was in Hira cave with the Prophet (pbuh) when the very first verse of Qur'ān was revealed to him."[86] 'Alī (as) was with the Prophet (pbuh) in every condition until the end of the Prophet's life. The Prophet's head was on 'Alī's chest when he passed away.[87] 'Alī (as) was both the Prophet's Companion and His holiness Dawi l-Qurbā (close relative whose friendship is mentioned in Qur'ān) and like a shadow, always followed him everywhere.

K: The General Pledge of Allegiance

After the allegiance to Abū Bakr in Saqīfah, those who had sworn allegiance to him took him happily like a bridegroom who is taken to Hejleh (the bridal chamber) to the mosque of the Prophet (pbuh).[88] When Abū Bakr and his followers entered the mosque, the affair of Caliphate was established. The mosque of the Prophet (pbuh) was the Government House; a place for setting up the flag (of fight), dispatching the military force, performing the Prophet's visits and resolving the quarrels of Muslims. In fact, all the matters of Muslim society in those times would take place and be dealt with in Masjid an-Nabawi (The Prophet's Mosque). The pulpit of the Prophet (pbuh) was like the radio and television today. In every revolution, people who commit coup d'état try to occupy and seize the radio and television center and the Government House. If

---

[86] *Nahj al-Balāgha*, sermon 192, pp. 300-301; *Sharḥ Nahj al-Balāgha* by Abduh 1: p. 182.

[87] *Kitāb aṭ-Ṭabaqāt al-Kabīr*, 2: p. 263; *Kanz al-Ummāl*, 2: pp. 262-263 & 7: pp. 178-179; *Waq'at Ṣiffīn*, p. 244.

[88] *Al-Riaz un-Nazra*, 1: p. 164; *Tārīkh al-Khamis*, 1: p. 188.

they seize these three centers, they will succeed in taking the government in their hands.

On Tuesday, the day after taking allegiance with Abū Bakr in Saqīfa Banī Sā'ida, the men who had staged the coup d'état brought Abū Bakr and placed him on the Prophet's pulpit. Before Abū Bakr could say a word, 'Umar stood up and after mentioning grandeur and praise of God and said that his speech, the previous day, i.e. denying the death of the Prophet (pbuh), was neither based on the book of God nor sent as a command on the side of the Prophet (pbuh), and that he had thought that the Prophet (pbuh) would proceed with and take care of the affairs in person and that His holiness was the last person who would leave this world![89] He added at the end, "God has left his book among you, which was also the means of leading his Prophet (pbuh). If you seize upon it, God will lead you in the same way that he led his Prophet (pbuh). Now, God has made you congruous and well-matched for the leadership of the best of you, who was the companion of the cave for the Prophet (pbuh). So, rise and swear allegiance to him."[90] Hence, after the pledge of some in Saqīfah, the majority of people swore allegiance.

It is stated in *Ṣaḥīḥ al-Bukhārī*:

After a group of people swore allegiance to Abū Bakr in Saqīfa Banī Sā'ida, the general allegiance was performed on the height of the pulpit of the Prophet (pbuh).[91]

Ans ibn Malik says, "On that day, I myself heard 'Umar repeatedly tell Abū Bakr to go up the pulpit and so he finally did and when seated on the pulpit, all the audience swore allegiance to him." That is when Abū Bakr preached his sermon and said, "O' people! Though I am not better than you, I took the control of the government for you. So, if you found my behavior good and appropriate,

---

[89] *Abdullah ibn Saba'* by Allamah 'Askari 1: p. 121 narrated from *al-Ṭabarī* and other documents.

[90] *Ibid.*, 1: p. 121 narrated from *al-Ṭabarī* and other documents.

[91] *Ṣaḥīḥ al-Bukhārī*, book of al-Baiah 4: p. 165.

54

help me and if I deviated and made mistakes, guide me back to the right path…
Now, rise and say your prayers[92] so that your God may have mercy on you."[93]

After that, he started to hold the prayer for them and then they returned
home (from Monday until the evening of Tuesday, the people of Medina were
unaware of the burial of their Prophet (pbuh)!). During this period, they were
busy first with the speeches given in Saqīfa Banī Sā'ida, and then with taking
allegiance in the alleys of Medina and after that with the general allegiance to
Abū Bakr in The Prophet's Mosque, and at last with his sermon and 'Umar's
speech, and finally with Abū Bakr's rise to hold the congregational prayer for
them.

------

[92] It seems that he meant the Noon Prayer.

[93] *Sharḥ Nahj al-Balāgha* by Ibn Abī l-Hadīd 1: p. 134; *Safwat u-Safwah*, 1: p. 98.

Chapter 3

The Prophet's Companions's Opinion and Judgment about Allegiance to Abū Bakr

1. Faḍl ibn Abbas

Banī Hāshim family was preparing the Prophet's body for burial when they heard about the allegiance to Abū Bakr. Faḍl ibn Abbas rushed out and announced: O' people of Quraysh! You will not take over the caliphate position by luring people and hiding the truth. It is us who deserve caliphate, not you; our lord 'Alī (as) or any of us are more worthy of becoming the caliph than any of you.

2. 'Utbah ibn Abū Lahab

When hearing about the allegiance to Abū Bakr, he also composed the following in the form of a poem:

I never thought that the caliphate would be taken away from the Banī Hāshim clan, especially from 'Alī (as), because 'Alī (as) is the one who exercised faith prior to anyone else and nobody doubts his superior record in Islām. Compared to anyone else he is more knowledgeable in Qur'ānic sciences and the Prophetic traditions. And he is the only person who attended to offer service to the very last moments of the Prophet's life, with the assistance of Gabriel, performing Ġusl for the Prophet (pbuh) and wrapping his body in the white shroud preparing him for burial. He alone possesses the good traits and spiritual virtues of others, but others are void of his spiritual perfection and ethical excellence.[1]

3. Salmān

Abū Bakr al-Johari has narrated:

Salmān and Zubayr as well as the Anṣār tended to pledge allegiance to 'Alī. Therefore, when allegiance was sworn to Abū Bakr, Salmān al-Fārisī said, "You gained little virtuousness seizing the caliphate, for you lost the mine and source of virtuousness. You selected an old man and abandoned the clan of your Prophet. Had you left the caliphate in the Prophet's clan, no two people would have ever gotten into a disagreement and you could have benefitted from the fruit of this tree more and with a higher pleasure."[2]

Salmān's other statement was "you did but you didn't", i.e. it would have been better if you hadn't, and what you did do was not right. Had the Muslims pledged allegiance to 'Alī (as), God's mercy and divine blessings would have come to them in every way and they would have reached the all-encompassing bliss and glory.[3]

4. Abū Ḍarr

When the Prophet (pbuh) passed away, Abū Ḍarr was not present in Medina. By the time he was back Abū Bakr had already seized control of power.

---

[1] *Tārīkh Ya'qubi*, 2: p. 103; *Sharḥ Nahj al-Balāgha* by Ibn Abī l-Hadīd 1: p. 287; *al-Muwafaqiat*, pp. 580-607. It is said that at this point Alī (as) send someone to Faḍl Ibn Abbas and forbid him from reciting the rest of the poem and said, "The well-being of religion matters more to us than anything else." *Sharḥ Nahj al-Balāgha* by Ibn Abī l-Hadīd 2: p. 8. In *al-Iṣābah*, by Ibn Hajar al-'Asqalānī 2: p. 263 and also in *Tārīkh Abī al-Fada'*, 1: p. 164 these poems have been attributes to Faḍl Ibn Abbas ibn Utbah ibn Abū Lahab Hāshimī which we do not consider correct.

[2] *Sharḥ Nahj al-Balāgha* by Ibn Abī l-Hadīd 2: pp. 131-132 & 6: p. 17 narrated from *al-Saqīfa* by Abī Bakr Johari.

[3] *Ansab al-Ashraf*, 1: p. 591 & Jāḥiẓ in *'Uthmāniyah*.

In this regard Abū Ḍarr said, "You gained little and remained satisfied with what you achieved and instead you lost the clan of the Prophet (pbuh). Had you surrendered the affair to the clan of the Prophet (pbuh), no two people would have ever turned against you or disagreed on anything to your detriment."[4]

5. Miqdād ibn 'Amr

The narrator says:

One day I dropped by the Prophet's mosque where I saw a man sitting on his knees sighing in such pain and desperation as if he used to own the world and now he had it taken away from him. Wallowing in despair he was uttering, "How astonishing is what Quraysh did taking away the affair from the members of their Prophet's household (Ahl al-Bayt), when the first who took faith was among these people."[5]

6. Nu'man ibn 'Ajlan

Nu'man ibn 'Ajlan, in response to what 'Amr ibn al-'Āṣ composed in the event of Saqīfah, composed an ode of which some verses are as following:[6]

"You said that appointing Sa'd ibn 'Ubadah as the caliph is Haram (forbidden) and appointing Abū Bakr is correct and Halal (permissible). We wanted 'Alī (as). 'Alī (as) deserved this task. For, he was the executor of Prophet's will and his cousin. It was him who had killed the warriors of diversion and disbelief. So, if there was no fear of God, you would never attain this position. However, patience suits this virtue (=Islām) better."

7. Umm Mistah ibn al-Uthātha

She recited these poems at the Prophet's grave:

---

[4] *Sharḥ Nahj al-Balāgha* by Ibn Abī l-Hadīd 6: p. 5 narrated from *al-Saqīfa* by Abī Bakr Johari.

[5] *Tārīkh Ya'qubi*, 2: p. 114.

[6] *Sharḥ Nahj al-Balāgha* by Ibn Abī l-Hadīd 6: p. 31 narrated from *al-Muwafaqiat*.

"O' Prophet! After you there were important discussions and events. Had you been alive, none of these plights and disasters would have occurred. Just like a land that is barren and receives no rain and thus loses its vitality and life, you left us alone and people went corrupt. O' Prophet! Watch and witness them."[7]

8. A Woman from Banī Najjar

When the allegiance to Abū Bakr was established, he sent a quota from Bayt al-mal (House of Wealth) to the women of the Anṣar and the Muhājirūn. He entrusted the quota for a woman from Banū 'Adi ibn al-Najjar to Zayd ibn Thabit to deliver. Zayd went to her and offered her the money. The woman asked, "What is this?" And Zayd said, "This is a quota Abū Bakr has assigned for women." She said, "Do you want to deceive me out of my religion through bribery? I swear to God I will not accept anything from him." And thus she sent that quota back to Abū Bakr.[8]

9. Abū Sufyān

The Prophet had sent Abū Sufyān out of town to run an errand therefore at the time of the Prophet's death, he was not in Medina. On his way back he came across a person returning from Medina. He asked, "Did Muḥammad die?"[9] The man answered, "Yes." Then he asked, "Who replaced him?" The man replied, "Abū Bakr." Abū Sufyān continued, "How did those two oppressed poor men, 'Alī (as) and Abbas, react?" The man responded, "They are forsaken at home." Abū Sufyān then said, "I swear to God, if I get a chance to live for them, I will raise them high. I foresee a cloud of dust that will only quench by bloodshed."

---

[7] *Sharḥ Nahj al-Balāgha* by Ibn Abī l-Hadīd 2: pp. 131-132 & 6: p. 17.

[8] *Sharḥ Nahj al-Balāgha* by Ibn Abī l-Hadīd 2: p. 133 narrated from *al-Saqīfa* by Abī Bakr Johari; *Kitāb aṭ-Tabaqāt al-Kabīr*, 2: p. 129.

[9] By this statement we figure that he did not believe in the Prophet being the messenger of God, otherwise he would have used the term "God's messenger".

When he finally arrived in Medina, he wandered in its alleys reciting these poems:

"O Banī Hāshim! Cut the greed of ruling, especially on Taym and Adi clans (clans of 'Umar and Abū Bakr). This government is yours, has been yours, and should be given back to you. Nobody deserves ruling except Father of Ḥasan, 'Alī (as).[10]

Ya'qubi narrates the following as well:

O' Father of Ḥasan, 'Alī! Take hold of the government in your resourceful, powerful hands for, you are strong and capable enough for what is hoped for. And of course, you are the man whom Quṣayy[11] supports. And your right cannot be trodden upon and only (the surrogates of) Quṣayy are from the overcoming, victorious generations.[12]

As narrated by al-Ṭabarī,[13] Abū Sufyān came forward saying, "O' children of Abd Manāf, what does Abū Bakr have to do with you?! Where are 'Alī (as) and Abbas, those two oppressed, offended men?"[14] Then he went to 'Alī (as) and said, "O Father of Ḥasan, 'Alī give me your hand so that I swear allegiance to you." 'Alī (as) refrained and did not accept and said, "If there were forty decisive and determined men [i.e. who have faith in his mastery] I would confront them, but I am left with no helpmate."[15]

---

[10] al-'Iqd al-Farīd, 3: p. 62; Sharḥ Nahj al-Balāgha by Ibn Abī l-Hadīd 3: p. 120 narrated from al-Saqīfa by Abī Bakr Johari.

[11] Banī Hāshim and Banī Umayyah were the descendants Abd Manāf who was Quṣayy's son. In this poem Abū Sufyān tells Alī (as) that the Quṣayy clan will support him.

[12] Tārīkh Ya'qubi, 2: p. 105. In the al-Muwafaqiat narration the story is mentioned in more detail. See: Sharḥ Nahj al-Balāgha by Ibn Abī l-Hadīd 6: p. 7.

[13] Tārīkh al-Ṭabarī, 2: p. 449 & 1: pp. 1827-1828 in the European edition.

[14] Abū Sufyān did not believe in the Prophet being the messenger of God and only due to tribal prejudice would say, "Ruling must belong to our clan."

[15] Tārīkh al-Ṭabarī, 1: p. 1827 in the European edition; Lisan al-Mizan, 4: p. 384; There are more details in Abdullah ibn Saba' by Allamah 'Askari 1: pp. 146-151.

It may be asked why Alī (as) didn't agree to Abū Sufyān's suggestion. A thorough answer is presented in *Abdullah ibn Saba'* by Allamah 'Askari 1: pp. 146-151 but here is the brief version:

After the death of the Prophet (pbuh), family and tribal prejudices were revived. The Anṣār gathering in Saqīfa and their attempt to pledge allegiance to Sa'd ibn 'Ubadah was only based on these prejudices, because in fact they already knew that among the *Muhājirūn*, Alī (as) deserved to replace the Prophet (pbuh). Also, Aws's allegiance to Abī Bakr had no basis other than tribal prejudice. They wanted to prevent the leadership from falling into the hands of the Khazraj clan. In addition, 'Umar's speech in Saqīfa (*Ṣaḥīḥ al-Bukhārī*, 4: p. 120) clearly implies that his people were also influenced by tribal prejudices in their allegiance to Abī Bakr.

Abū Sufyān, like others, had tribal prejudice and only, in order for the leadership to remain in the members of his tribe, Banī Abd Manāf, demanded allegiance to the Alī (as). Meanwhile, it was only Alī (as) whose anticipation and depth of thoughts was higher and expander than taking control by the force of prejudice. If Ali (as) demanded the right of sovereignty for himself, it was because he wanted to establish a government based only on Qur'an and religion. He needed companions like Salmān, Abū Darr, Miqdād and Ammār to support him, men for whom there is no factor or stimulus to help but the source of divine belief; not like Abū Sufyān, who had no other motive than materialistic expectations and family prejudice. Therefore, if Ali (as) had accepted Abū Sufyān's offer of allegiance, all the efforts he and the Prophet (pbuh) had put into restoring the divine nature of the society and destroying ignorant prejudices in the last 23 years would have practically gone to waste. It is worth mentioning that when Ali (as) disappointed Abū Sufyān, he accepted bribery from of the rulers in exchange for allegiance to Abī Bakr, and thus fully revealed his material and worldly motives. Based on 'Umar's suggestion, Abī Bakr surrendered whatever za'kat from the Bayt al-mal Abū Sufyān had hold of back to him. (*al-'Iqd al-Farīd*, 3: p. 62) He also appointed Abū Sufyān's son, Yazīd as the commander of the army that was sent to Shām. (*Tārīkh al-Ṭabarī*, 1: p. 1827 in the European edition.)

10. Khālid ibn Sa'īd

Khālid ibn Sa'īd ibn al-'As (from Banū Umayya) was one of the people who foreran in the acceptance of Islām.[16] He was one of the people who immigrated to Abyssinia (Ethiopia). After Islām was reinforced, the Prophet (pbuh) appointed him and his two brothers (Abān and 'Amr) to collect Zakāt from the Maḏ'hij tribe. Afterwards, they became his representative in Ṣan'ā in Yemen. They were not in Medina at the time of the Prophet's death. On their return to Medina, they said to Abū Bakr, "We, the children of Uḥayḥa, will not be the agent of anybody after the Prophet (pbuh)."[17] And Khālid visited 'Alī (as) and said, "O' 'Alī! Give me your hand so that I can pledge allegiance to you, for I swear to God that there is nobody more honorable than you compared to the Prophet (pbuh)."[18] When Banī Hāshim swore allegiance to Abū Bakr, Khālid swore allegiance, too.[19]

11. 'Umar ibn al-Khaṭṭāb

In the last year of his life when in Hajj, 'Umar heard that 'Ammār had said, "Allegiance to Abū Bakr was a fault that appeared at last. If 'Umar dies, we will swear allegiance to 'Alī (as)."[20] This statement made 'Umar distraught and he said, "When I reach Medina…" And when he did reach Medina, on the very first Friday he climbed the pulpit in the Prophet's mosque and announced, "Allegiance to Abū Bakr was a mistake that took place and should be passed

---

[16] In his book *Kitāb al-Ma'ārif*, p.128, Ibn Qutaybah says that he had accepted Islām prior to Abī-Bakr.

[17] *Al-Isti'ab*, 1: pp. 398-400; *al-Iṣābah*, 1: p. 406; *Usd al-Ġābah,* 2: p. 82; *Sharḥ Nahj al-Balāgha* by Ibn Abī l-Hadīd 6: pp.13 & 16.

[18] *Tārīkh Ya'qubi,* 2: p. 105.

[19] *Usd al-Ġābah,* 2: p. 82; *Sharḥ Nahj al-Balāgha* by Ibn Abī l-Hadīd 1: p. 135 narrated from *al-Saqīfa* by Abī Bakr Johari.

[20] *Sharḥ Nahj al-Balāgha* by Ibn Abī l-Hadīd 2: p. 123.

over. Yes, that was the case but God protected everyone from the evils of that blunder."[21]

12. Mu'awiya

In a letter to Mohammad ibn Abū Bakr, Mu'awiya wrote: We, including your father (Abū Bakr), knew the superiority and virtue of Abī Ṭālib's son and considered his right an obligation on ourselves. But when God selected to run His will on His Prophet (pbuh), and fulfilled His promise and revealed His call and enlightened His reasoning and took his soul, your father and his distinguisher 'Umar, were of the first who arrogated 'Alī's right and opposed him. They united first and then asked 'Alī (as) for allegiance. When 'Alī (as) refrained and kept away, they made inadmissible decisions (and wanted to murder 'Alī (as)) and had dangerous plans for him until 'Alī (as) finally surrendered and pledged allegiance to them.[22]

13. Sa'd ibn 'Ubadah

Sa'd was left unnoticed for a few days after the gathering in Saqīfah took place, and then (they) sent after him to show up and pledge allegiance reasoning that all his relatives had pledged allegiance to Abū Bakr. Sa'd responded saying, "By God I will not pledge allegiance to you unless I throw all my arrows towards you and color my spear bloody red with your blood. What have you thought (of me)? As far as I take hold of the hilt of my sword, I will stab it on your heads, and with the help of my family and my followers, I will fight you to the last breath of my life and will not pledge allegiance to you. I swear to God

---

[21] *Sharḥ Nahj al-Balāgha* by Ibn Abī l-Hadīd 2: pp. 22-23 & 6: p. 47 & 11: p. 13 & 12: p. 147; *Tārīkh Ya'qubi,* 2: p. 160; *Ansab al-Ashraf,* 5:p. 15; *Sirat ibn Hisham,* 4: pp. 336-338; *Ṣaḥīḥ al-Bukhārī,* book of al-Hudud 4: p. 119-120; *Kanz al-Ummāl,* 3: p. 139, hadīth 2326. It should be said that Abī-Bakr, himself has said the same thing about his own caliphate. *Sharḥ Nahj al-Balāgha* by Ibn Abī l-Hadīd 6: pp. 47 & 50.

[22] *Murūj aḏ-Ḏahab,* 2: p. 60; *Waq'at Ṣiffin,* p. 135; *Sharḥ Nahj al-Balāgha* by Ibn Abī l-Hadīd 1: p. 284 & 2: p. 65.

64

that if all Jinns and human beings unite in your government and ruling, I will not bow to you and will not consider you to be righteous and valid and I will never swear allegiance to you until the day my deeds are measured in the divine court of justice."

When Abū Bakr heard about Sa'd's speech, 'Umar told him, "Don't ignore Sa'd unless he pledges allegiance to you." But Bashir ibn Sa'ad said, "He is being obstinate and will not swear allegiance to you, even if he loses his life over this. Killing him is not that simple for he can be killed only when his family, children, and relatives are all killed with him. Leave him alone,[23] since ignoring him will not harm you because he is only one person who isn't pledging allegiance to you."

They accepted Bashir's advice and abandoned Sa'd. Sa'd did not participate in any of their gatherings and did not attend their Congregational or Friday prayers and was not seen with them in the religious performance of Hajj! This went up to when Abū Bakr's governing was over and it was time for 'Umar's to become caliphate.[24]

---

[23] *Tārīkh al-Ṭabarī*, 3: p. 459; *Al-Bidaya wa an-Nihaya*, 2: p. 126. These two resources have narrated the story up to this point. But in *Kanz al-Ummāl*, 3: p. 134, hadīth 2296; *al-Imama Wa al-Siyasa*, 1: p. 10; *As-Sirat al-Halabiah*, 4: p. 397 & *Tārīkh al-Ṭabarī*, 1: p. 1844 in the European edition we also read: Sa'd would never greet any of them if he came across them.

[24] *Tārīkh al-Ṭabarī*, 3: p. 459 & 1: p. 1844 in the European edition; *Al-Bidaya wa an-Nihaya*, 2: p. 126; *Kanz al-Ummāl*, 3: p. 134, hadīth 2296; *al-Imama Wa al-Siyasa*, 1: p. 10; *As-Sirat al-Halabiah*, 4: p. 397; *Al-Riaz un-Nazra*, 1: p. 168.

Chapter 4

Caliphate's Way of Dealing with the Opponents out of Medina

The Murder of Malik ibn Nuwayrah

Malik ibn Nuwayrah was one of the Prophet's Companions and his agent and collector of the alms[1]. He was a brave man, a poet and the head of part of Banī Tamīm.

After the death of the Prophet (pbuh), Malik did not send the alms he had collected to Medina and instead, returned them back to their owners and recited these verses:

"I said take your property back without fear and worry of the future events; if a person stands up for religion, we shall follow him and say: Religion is the religion of Muḥammad (pbuh).[2]

All historians including al-Ṭabarī, Ibn Kathīr and Ya'qūbī have referred to this story that says:

Abū Bakr sent Khālid ibn al-Walīd with an army to the tribes that had not sworn allegiance to him after the death of the Prophet (pbuh) or did not give Zakāt to his collectors, in order to enforce them to pay their Zakāt. 'Umar said to Abū Bakr, "Wait a while before you attend to this matter." Abū Bakr responded, "No. I swear to God if they do not give me so much as a camel harness they used to give to the Prophet (pbuh), I will start war." And so he sent Khālid ibn al-Walīd with an army to fight them. The land in which Malik ibn Nuwayrah inhabited was called Butāh. Abū Qatāda, one of the Companions narrates that:

---

[1] Nowadays it is called za'kat whereas "alms" is the correct term.

[2] *al-Iṣābah*, 3: p. 336.

They raided that land at night (whereas the Prophet (pbuh) would never agree to night-attacks); because the troops surrounded them at night, Malik's tribe was terrified. They wore their armors and rose to confront the enemy. Abū Qatāda says: We told them that we are Muslims. They responded, "We are Muslims, too." The head of the division said to them, "Then, why are you armed?" They answered, "Why have you, yourselves taken hold of weapons?" Abū Qatāda says: We said to them, "If you are telling the truth, then put your weapons down." And they did. Then we performed our prayers and they joined us.[3]

In another narration, it is mentioned that the moment they put their weapons down, their hands were tied up like slaves and they were taken to Khālid.[4]

Malik's wife accompanied him. There, Abū Qatāda and 'Abdullāh ibn 'Umar witnessed in front of Khālid that, "These people are Muslims and we saw them saying their prayers." All historians have mentioned that Malik's wife, who was with them, was very beautiful. Khālid turned to Ḍiraar ibn al-Azwar and said, "Behead Malik!" Malik pointed to his wife and said, "This woman is the cause of my death." And Khālid replied, "God is the one killing you because you forsook Islām." Malik said, "I am a Muslim and I abide by Islām." Khālid turned to Ḍiraar saying, "Decapitate him." And so he beheaded Malik.[5] They also killed the other Muslims and on that very same night, Khālid slept with Malik's wife.[6]

Abū Qatāda went back to Medina and reported what had happened to Abū Bakr and swore not to go to Jihad under the banner of Khālid ever again, because he had killed Malik who was a Muslim.[7] 'Umar told Abū Bakr that

---

[3] All historians of the caliphate school of thoughts agree on this.

[4] *Abdullah ibn Saba'* by Allamah 'Askari 1: p. 181 narrated from *Sharḥ Nahj al-Balāgha* by Ibn Abī l-Hadīd.

[5] *Tārīkh Abī al-Fada'*, p. 1514; *Wafayat al-Ayan*, 5: p. 66; *Tārīkh Ibn al-Shihnah*, p. 114 written in the margins of *Al-Kāmil fit-Tārīkh Ibn al-Athir*, 11; *Fawat al-Wafayat*, 2: p. 627.

[6] *Tārīkh Ya'qūbī*, 2: p. 110; *Kanz al-Ummāl*, 3: p. 132.

[7] Translation of *Tārīkh Ya'qūbī*, 2: p. 10.

Khālid should be stoned because he committed adultery. Abū Bakr said, "I will not stone him because he has made an Ijtihad, though he made a wrong decision through his Ijtihad."[8] 'Umar said, "He is a murderer and has killed a Muslim and you should dictate Qiṣāṣ (Retribution)." Abū Bakr responded, "I will never kill him; he has just gone wrong in his Ijtihad." 'Umar said, "At least discharge him from his position as the leader of the army." Abū Bakr said, "I will never put the sword that has been drawn by God back in sheath."[9] And this is where the title "Sword of God" was coined for Khālid. On Khālid's return to Medina, 'Umar was hard on him again in the mosque of Medina. Khālid went to Abū Bakr and asked for forgiveness and his apology was accepted. So Khālid went back and showed aggression towards 'Umar.[10]

This was one example of the way those surrounding the caliphate dealt with people who were out of Medina and disapproved of the allegiance.

Another Example

Abū Bakr's agent in Yemen, Ziyād ibn Labīd, had collected the alms and at that time they used to receive camels from camel breeders. Among these charity items, there was a calf. The owner of the calf, who was a teenager, said to Abū Bakr's agent, "I care for this calf. Don't take it from me. I will give you a camel instead." Abū Bakr's agent refused saying, "No way. This has been considered as Sadaqāt and it is not possible to return it back." The teenager complained to Ḥaritha ibn Suraqah, the head of the tribe. Haritha told Abū Bakr's agent, "This

---

[8] In the caliphate system, whoever did something against religious rules, as a justification it would be said, "He made an Ijtihad and if a Mujtahid does right in his Ijtihad he gains two rewards and if he does wrong he gains only one." See the topic of Ijtihad in the 2nd volume of *Two Schools of Thought in Islām*, p. 89 onwards.

[9] Narrated from *Tārīkh Abī al-Fada'*, & *Kanz al-Ummāl*, 3: p. 132, hadīth 228 & under "Wathimah" in *Wafayat al-Ayan* & *Fawat al-Wafayat*.

[10] *Abdullah ibn Saba'* by Allamah 'Askari 1: pp. 184-185 narrated from *al-Ṭabarī*.

teenager is passionate about his calf. Take a camel instead." But he refused again and the argument intensified and led to a clash.[11]

When the residents of "Daba"[12] heard about this event, they kicked Abū Bakr's agent out of the city. Ziyād ibn Labīd besieged the Daba city with the help of other nomads. They, along with the other first opponent, fought with Ziyād ibn Labīd's army, but both sides were defeated. The inhabitants of Daba had fortified structures and bars and hid there, taking refuge in their enclosures, but were defeated once again. At last, they said to Abū Bakr's agent, "We will pay Zakāt and surrender. The agent said, "I will only forgive you if you admit that we are right and you are wrong, and our killed forces will go to heaven and yours to hell, and accept any verdict issued against you." They agreed but only out of compulsion. Then, he ordered them to leave their city without any arms or weapons and so they did.

Then the troops entered the city and beheaded their seniors one by one and held their children and women captive and took their properties as booty and sent them to Abū Bakr in Medina. After that, they attacked the Kinda tribe. They beheaded the aristocrats of the tribe and sent the rest to Medina. Abū Bakr wanted to decapitate the men and take the women as slaves but 'Umar prohibited him. These captives were kept under arrest till 'Umar's caliphate era. In his time, 'Umar set them free and sent them back to their tribe.[13]

The caliphate system made no distinction between Muslims and the infidels in the matter of opposition and treated them all equally, i.e. the same way the

---

[11] *Kitāb al-Futūḥ*, 1: p. 48-49. Haritha ibn Suraqah, the head of the tribe has a conversation with the teenager which is interesting. He tells him, "Take your calf and if anyone complained to you, cut his nose off with a sword. We only obeyed the Prophet (pbuh) and nobody but him, when he was alive and if anyone of his household had rose to govern, we would definitely have followed his demands as well. But I swear to God that we have no duty to obey or take allegiance with the son of Abī Quhāfah (Abī Bakr). Then he composed these verses: We obeyed God's messenger as long as he lived, and what a wonder are those who obey Abī Bakr.

[12] See translation of "Daba" in *Mu'jam al-Buldān*.

[13] *Kitāb al-Futūḥ*, 1: pp. 60-61.

Arabs did at the Age of Ignorance. At the Age of Ignorance, when they fought and were victorious, they took the men as slaves and the women as maids and plundered their properties. Indeed, the government named all these people infidels and in historical books they are still referred to as infidels.[14]

---

[14] For more detail see *Abdullah ibn Saba'* by Allamah 'Askari 1: pp. 165-192 & 2: pp. 21-99.

Chapter 5

Caliphate's Encounter with the Opponents out of Medina

A. Killing Sa'd ibn 'Ubadah

After becoming caliphate, once 'Umar came across Sa'd ibn 'Ubadah in an alley in Medina. Upon that encounter he said, "O' you Sa'd!" And Sa'd immediately responded, "O' you 'Umar!" The caliph asked, "Was it not you who said those words [against me]?" Sa'd said, "Yes. It was me. And now you have taken the seat of the Caliphate. I swear to God that I liked your friend more. God knows how I hate being in your vicinity." 'Umar said, "A person who dislikes his neighbor moves." Sa'd replied, "I have considered that. I will take up a neighborhood of which people better than you live in."

It did not take long, during the early years of 'Umar's caliphate, before Sa'd emigrated to Sham (Syria) where the Yamanis tribes lived.[1]

In his book, *Ansāb al-Ashrāf* (Genealogies of the Nobles), Balādurī writes:

Sa'd ibn 'Ubadah did not swear allegiance to Abū Bakr and went to Sham. 'Umar sent someone after Sa'd telling him, "Get Sa'd to swear allegiance and use any deceit or trick you can to make him do it. But if you didn't succeed in convincing him and he refused to accept allegiance, then with the help of God kill him!"

---

[1] *Kitāb aṭ-Tabaqāt al-Kabīr*, Ibn Sa'd part 3, 2: p. 145; *Tārīkh Dimashq Ibn 'Asākir*, 6: p. 90; *Kanz al-Ummāl*, 3: p. 134, hadīth 2296; *As-sirat al-Halabiah* 3: p. 397.

The Anṣār were originally from the Yamani tribes and were called Saba'iyya. They lived in Yemen and after the destruction of the Ma'rib Dam, they were distributed to the borders of Iraq, Sham (Syria) and Medina.

That man went to Sham and visited Sa'd at Huwwarin[2] and proposed the matter of allegiance immediately and asked him to swear allegiance. In response to 'Umar's envoy Sa'd said, "I will not swear allegiance to any man from Quraysh." The envoy threatened him to death and said, "If you do not pledge allegiance, I will kill you." Sa'd answered, "Even so [I will not swear allegiance]!" When the envoy saw his resistance, he said, "Are you not in congruence with the Ummah?" Sa'd replied, "In the matter of allegiance, yes." Once the envoy heard this decisive answer, he shot an arrow to Sa'd's heart causing a tear in the main vein and his died right away.[3]

In the book *Tabsarat al-Awām* we read:

They appointed Muḥammad ibn Maslamah al-Anṣārī to this task. He went to Sham and put an end to Sa'd ibn 'Ubadah's life.

It is also said that Khālid ibn al-Walīd was in Sham at that time and helped Muḥammad ibn Maslamah in killing Sa'd.[4]

In his book, *Murūj aḏ-Ḏahab* (The Meadows of Gold), Mas'ūdī says:

Sa'd ibn 'Ubadah did not swear allegiance, left Medina and headed towards Sham, and was killed there in the year 15 of Hijri Calendar.[5]

Also, Ibn 'Abd Rabbih says, "Sa'd ibn 'Ubadah was found passed away, with an arrow in his heart. Rumors were spread saying because Sa'd urinated standing, Jinns shot two arrows to his heart and recited this poem:

We killed the master of Khazraj, Sa'd ibn 'Ubadah, and hit him with two arrows that were placed exactly in his heart.

In response to this prattle, one of the Anṣar composed the following verses:

---

[2] A famous village in Halab (Syria).

[3] *Ansāb al-Ashrāf,* 1: p. 589; *al-'Iqd al-Farīd,* 3: p. 64-65 with a bit of difference compared to Balāḏurī's narration.

[4] *Tabsarat al-Awām,* : p. 32.

[5] *Murūj aḏ-Ḏahab,* 1: p. 414, 2: p. 194.

74

It is said that the Jinns tore Sa'd's abdomen. Beware that you may have done your job with trickery. Sa'd's sin was not that he urinated standing; his guilt was that he did not swear allegiance to Abū Bakr. [6]

In such manner, Sa'd's life came to an end. But, since the murder of such a bold and hardheaded opponent on the part of the rulers and the government was questionable and was one of the events that historians did not like to talk or write about, some of them disregarded such an important occurrence and ignored it.[7] And some, as mentioned earlier, mixed the matter of his murder with superstitious affairs and attributed it to Jinns.[8] But in spite of proposing such superstitious affairs, these historians have not mentioned what motivated the Jinns' severe hostility and enmity towards Sa'd; and among all those Companions, including the Anṣar and the Muhājirūn, why did their arrows only target Sa'd's heart!

B. Enticing 'Abbās, the Prophet's Uncle

Abū Bakr formed a council including 'Umar ibn al-Khaṭṭāb, Abū 'Ubaydah al-Jarāḥ and Mughīra ibn Shu'ba to decide and determine what to do with those who had not pledged allegiance. The council announced that, 'The best way is to visit 'Abbās and give him and his children a share from the government; in this way, 'Alī will be defeated[9] and 'Abbās's tendency towards you will be a sign of success against 'Alī [and a sign of your righteousness]."[10]

---

[6] *Mu'jam rijāl*, al-ḥadīth 8: p. 73.

[7] Including al-Ṭabarī, Ibn Athir and Ibn Kathīr in their history books.

[8] Including Muḥibb al-Dīn al-Ṭabarī in *Al-Riaz un-Nazra*, and Ibn Abd al-Barr in *Al-Isti'ab*.

[9] 'Umar would heed Ibn 'Abbās ('Abbās's son) to defeat Alī. It was a policy to have Ibn 'Abbās narrate hadīth and interpret but every once in a while he would announce something against the government's policies. (For instance see *Abdullah ibn Saba'* by Allamah 'Askari 1: p. 140-142, the conversation between Ibn 'Abbās and 'Umar, narrated by *Tārīkh al-Ṭabarī*, 2: p. 289, in 'Umar's ways.)

[10] According to the narration of Ibn Abī l-Hadīd 1: p. 225, narrated from *al-Saqīfa* by Johari, this was suggested by Mughīra ibn Shu'ba which is more accurate.

Abū Bakr, along with the members of the afore-mentioned council, went to 'Abbās's house at night[11]. Abū Bakr started praising God and then said, "God sent the Prophet (pbuh), who was the messenger and master of the faithful, and he lived among them until God preferred the other world for him; and he did not determine any successor for after his death[12] and left the issue to the people themselves. And they chose me. And I do not fear anyone but God and so I do not have laxity in my duties. Those who have not pledged allegiance to me are opposing the majority of Muslims and seek refuge in you. Either go along with the majority and swear allegiance, or if you don't, stop them from fighting us."

[This statement from Abū Bakr is good evidence to prove not all the Prophet's Companions had sworn allegiance].

"We want to give you a share from the government that can even be preserved for your descendants, because you are the Prophet's uncle. Although people did consider your position as the Prophet's uncle and also 'Alī's position, but they took the issue (of caliphate) away from you (and did not select you). However, we will give you a share. Banī Hāshim! Be calm, for the Prophet (pbuh) is one of us and one of you. [We are from Quraysh and the messenger of God is also from Quraysh].

Then, 'Umar said in a threatening voice, "We are not here because we need you; we are here because we do not appreciate you opposing in an affair which Muslims have commonly decided upon, as the harmful consequences will both affect you and them. Hence, beware how you behave."

Afterwards, 'Abbās began a prayer of praise to God and said, "As you mentioned, God appointed Muḥammad to be the messenger and a help and support to Muslims. And due to the blessings of his existence, God favored the Ummah up until He called him to His vicinity and chose for him what He had at hand and left the affair of the Muslims to themselves so that they find the true

---

[11] According to the narration of Ibn Abī l-Hadīd in *al-Saqīfa* by Johari, this meeting took place the second night after the Prophet's death.

[12] All prophets appointed successors for after their death. The Prophet (pbuh) had also a successor. To learn more about the subject of Wisayat (successorship) see: *Ma'alim al-Madrasatayn*, 1: pp. 289-345, *Aqā'id al-Islām min al-Qur'ān al-Karīm*, 2: pp. 264-285.

right [the path to God] and select it for themselves, not separate from it and change direction due to the misleading of their inner worldly demands.[13]

If you have taken the affair (of government) in the name of the Prophet (pbuh), you have in fact seized our right because we are the Prophet's relatives and in comparison prior to you. But if you have taken it because you are one of the faithful believers of the Prophet (pbuh), so are we. However, we did not step into the affair that you started first and did not interfere with it, but we constantly disapprove of you. If because of the allegiance of the believers, ruling has become an obligation to you and you have deserved it [and consider yourself so], bear in mind that since we are also of the believers and have not announced consent to your ruling and in fact, dislike it, this right is not proven legitimate and obligatory for you.

What a contradictory that on the one hand, you say people have opposed you and conveyed contempt in the issue of your government, and on the other hand, you say that people have chosen you for ruling. And how far is the name that you have given yourself, the caliph of the messenger of God, [i.e. the person whom the Prophet (pbuh) has announced as his successor] from the concept that you say the Prophet (pbuh) has left the affair of the Muslims to their own choice and they chose you. [This means you are people's caliph and not the Prophet's caliph; and so you are selected by the people and not by the Prophet (pbuh)].

Regarding the idea that you expressed (if I swear allegiance to you) you grant me a share, if what you are offering belongs to the believers, then you have no right in the matter, because you are not allowed to give away others' properties on your own behalf.[14] And if it is our right and belongs to us, you

---

[13] In the position of convincing, sometimes the reasoning is offered only because it is accepted by the presentee, although not believed by the presenter. Apparently, what 'Abbās is presenting here is of the same kind.

[14] In *Sharḥ Nahj al-Balāgha* by Ibn Abī l-Ḥadīd narrated from *al-Saqīfa* by Johari and in *al-Imama Wa al-Siyasa* by Ibn Qutayba al-Dīnawarī which has this extra sentence: "And if it is yours, we want nothing from it."

must hand it fully; we do not want just a share of our right [based on your choice] so that you would give a part and keep the other part.

But regarding your statement saying the Prophet (pbuh) is one of us and one of you, the truth is that the Prophet (pbuh) is from a tree that we are its branches and you are its neighbor.[15]

And you 'Umar! You said you fear the opposition of people to us; this opposing first appeared from your side."

After this speech, they rose and left 'Abbās's house.[16]

C. Caliphate's Encounter with Fāṭimah

1. The Assembly in Fāṭimah's House

'Umar ibn al-Khaṭṭāb says:

After the Prophet (pbuh) passed away, one of the reports we received was that 'Alī and Zubayr and their Companions had gathered in Fāṭimah's house in opposition to us.[17]

Historians name the following people as those who refused to pledge allegiance to Abū Bakr, and together with 'Alī and Zubayr assembled in Fāṭimah's house:

'Abbās ibn 'Abd al-Muṭṭalib, 'Utbah ibn Abū Lahab, Salmān al-Fārisī, Abū Ḍarr al-Ghifārī, 'Ammār ibn Yāsir, Miqdād ibn al-Aswad, Bara' ibn 'Azib,

---

[15] This sentence is sarcastically saying you are strangers and have no relations with the Prophet (pbuh).

[16] *Tārīkh Ya'qūbī*, 2: p. 103; *Sharḥ Nahj al-Balāgha* by Ibn Abī l-Hadīd 2: pp. 13 & 74, narrated from *al-Saqīfa* by Johari 1: pp. 220-221, with a close narration to Ibn Abī l-Hadīd in *al-Imama Wa al-Siyasa*, 1: p. 14.

[17] *Musnad Aḥmad ibn Ḥanbal*, 1: p. 55; *Tārīkh al-Ṭabarī*, 2: p. 466 and in the European edition 1: p. 1822; *Al-Kāmil fit-Tārīkh Ibn al-Athir*, 2: p. 124; *Al-Bidaya wa an-Nihaya*, 5: p. 246; *Safwat u-Safwah* 1: p. 97; *Sharḥ Nahj al-Balāgha* by Ibn Abī l-Hadīd 1: p. 123; *Tārīkh al-Khulafā'*, p. 45; *Sirat ibn Hisham*, 4: p. 338; *Taysīr al-Wusūl*, 2: p. 41.

Ubayy ibn Ka'b, Sa'd ibn Abī Waqqās, Ṭalḥa ibn 'Ubaydullāh and a group of Banī Hāshim, the Muhājirūn and the Anṣār.[18]

The story of 'Alī and his Companions' refraining the allegiance to Abū Bakr and their assembly in Fāṭimah's house, is mentioned at the level of successive hearsay in the books of the Prophet's tradition, history, sihah and masānīd, literature, kalām, the biography of Rijal and Ma'arif, and there is no doubt in its accuracy. However, because the writers of these books did not tend to uncover all the happenings that took place between the group of people who had assembled and the victorious party, they scarcely reported much except parts which were unconsciously spread out through their pens.

Here, we will report Balāḏurī's narration of this important historical event:

When 'Alī did not go under the burden of swearing allegiance to Abū Bakr, Abū Bakr ordered 'Umar ibn al-Khaṭṭāb to bring him ('Alī) to his presence; if necessary by force! 'Umar did as was ordered and as a result formed a conversation to where 'Alī said, "Milk the camel of caliphate the best way you can, for half of it will be your share! I swear to God, the tumult you are making over Abū Bakr's ruling is only to precede others so he would leave the Caliphate to you."[19]

2. The Attack to Fāṭimat az-Zahrā's House

Historians have named the people who attacked Fāṭimat az-Zahrā's House following Abū Bakr's orders as:

'Umar ibn al-Khaṭṭāb, Khālid ibn al-Walīd, 'Abd al-Rahman ibn 'Awf, Thabit ibn Qais ibn Shammās, Ziyād ibn Labīd, Muḥammad ibn Maslamah,

---

[18] Other than the sources mentioned before, there are other sources that clarify these few people did not swear allegiance to Abī Bakr and assembled in Fāṭimah's house. Some of these sources that name those who had assembled in her house to pledge allegiance to Alī are: *Al-Riaz un-Nazra*, 1: p. 167; *Tārīkh al-Khamis*, 1: p. 188; *al-'Iqd al-Farīd*, 3: p. 64; *Tārīkh Abī al-Fada'*, 1: p. 156; *Tārīkh Ibn al-Shihnah*, 11: p. 112; Johari narrated by Ibn Abī l-Hadīd 2: pp. 130-134; *As-Sirat al-Halabiah*, 3: pp. 394-397.

[19] *Ansāb al-Ashrāf*, 1: p. 587.

Zayd ibn Thabit, Salamah ibn Salāma ibn al-Waqash, Salamah ibn Aslam, Usayd ibn Huḍair and etc.[20]

The conditions of the attack and how these people entered Fāṭimah' house and the way they dealt with the people who has assembled there has been reported as follows:

A group of the Muhājirūn including 'Alī ibn Abī Ṭālib and Zubayr who had refused swearing allegiance to Abū Bakr, were in Fāṭimah's house, armed and angry.[21] Abū Bakr and 'Umar receive a report dictating that a group of the Anṣār and the Muhājirūn have gathered around 'Alī ibn Abī Ṭālib in the Prophet's daughter, Fāṭimah's house,[22] and intend to pledge allegiance to him for caliphate.[23] Abū Bakr demanded that 'Umar go to Fāṭimah's house, oust them from there, disperse their gathering and fight them if they showed resistance.

'Umar headed towards Fāṭimah's house to enforce Abū Bakr's demand, holding a torch of fire in his hand and with the intention of setting the house on fire. When they arrived, Fāṭimah stood behind the door and said to 'Umar, "O' son of Khaṭṭāb! Have you come to set our house on fire?" 'Umar answered, "Yes, unless you accompany the Ummah[24] [and swear allegiance to Abū Bakr]."

Regarding this matter, Balāḏurī writes:

To obtain 'Alī's allegiance, Abū Bakr sent after him, but he did not swear allegiance. Then, 'Umar headed towards his house with a torch of fire. At the entrance of the house, Fāṭimah confronted him and said, "O' son of Khaṭṭāb! Have you come to set the door of my house on fire?" 'Umar answered, "Yes… this will strengthen the religion that your father has brought."[25]

---

[20] *Tārīkh al-Ṭabarī*, 2: pp. 443-444; Johari narrated by Ibn Abī l-Hadīd 2: pp. 130-134 & 2: p. 19 & 17 in response to Judge Saani.

[21] *Al-Riaz un-Nazra*, 1: p. 218; Johari narrated by Ibn Abī l-Hadīd 1: pp. 132 & 6: p. 293; *Tārīkh al-Khamis*, 2: p. 169.

[22] *Tārīkh Ya'qūbī*, 2: p. 105.

[23] *Tārīkh Ibn al-Shihnah*, 11: p. 113; *Sharḥ Nahj al-Balāgha* by Ibn Abī l-Hadīd 2: p. 134.

[24] *al-'Iqd al-Farīd*, 3: p. 64; *Tārīkh Abī al-Fada'*, 1: p. 156.

[25] *Ansāb al-Ashrāf*, 1: p. 568.

In *Kanz al-Ummāl* (the treasure of workers) we read:

'Umar said to Fāṭimah, "Nobody was loved more than you by your father, but this will not hinder me from giving the order of setting the house on fire with you in it, if this group gathers in your house."[26]

In the book *Al-Imāma wal-Siyāsa* (Imamat and Politics), it is written that:

'Umar came and addressed 'Alī and the other people who were at his house to come out, but they refused to do so. 'Umar said, "I swear to God who has my life in his hands, either you come out or I will set the house on fire with everyone in it." People told 'Umar that Fāṭimah was in the house. And he said, "Even so, I will set the house on fire."[27]

Ḥāfiẓ Ibrāhīm, the Egyptian poet, has composed so regarding these events:

'Umar made a remark towards 'Alī, both of which are honorable and deserve praise. 'Umar said, "If you do not swear allegiance, I will set the house on fire while you are in it and though Muṣṭafā's daughter is in there, I will not let anybody remain alive."

This remark could not have been said by anyone other than 'Umar, to the leader of fighters 'Adnān (i.e. the great hero of Quraysh) and the best of them, i.e. 'Alī ibn Abī Ṭālib.[28]

In his history book, Ya'qūbi states:

---

[26] *Kanz al-Ummāl*, 3: p. 140.

[27] *Al-Imāma wal-Siyāsa*, 1: p. 12.

[28] *Dīwān Ḥāfiẓ Ibrāhīm*, p. 82. It is worth mentioning that these verses are among an ode that is composed to praise 'Umar ibn al-Khaṭṭāb. See *Al-Ghadīr*, 8: p. 86.

They attacked 'Alī's house accompanied by a group. In the meantime, 'Alī's sword broke[29] and therefore the attackers dared to enter his house and they did so.[30]

In addition, al-Ṭabarī states in his history book that:

'Umar headed towards 'Alī's house, while Ṭalḥa and Zubayr and a group of the Muhājirūn had assembled there. Zubayr ('Alī's cousin) drew his sword to confront 'Umar but slipped and dropped the sword. Then, the invaders rushed and arrested him.[31]

So, the doubt proposed today that the Prophet's houses had no doors so how could 'Umar have set the door to Fāṭimah's house on fire, is not right. According to what has been mentioned in the books of the school of Caliphs and what the Caliphs themselves, including 'Umar and Abū Bakr, have admitted and confessed, they set the door to Fāṭimah's house on fire and entered the house by force. We will discuss this matter for two reasons:

1. Abū Bakr on His Deathbed

When Abū Bakr lay on his deathbed, he said, "I am not upset about anything and do not regret anything in my life except three things that I wish I

---

[29] There are two reasons to why this cannot be true: 1. Before passing away, the Prophet (pbuh) had asked Alī to stay patient. (*Bihar al-Anwar*, 22: pp. 527-528; *Manāqib*, 3: p. 336) And drawing his sword was against the Prophet's will. 2. His bravery in battles is in conflict with him drawing his sword without anyone being killed. It was Zubayr who drew sword.

[30] *Tārīkh Ya'qūbī*, 2: p. 105.

[31] *Tārīkh al-Ṭabarī*, 2: pp. 443-444 & 446, and in the European edition 1 pp. 1819-1820; *Al-Riaz un-Nazra*, 1: p. 167; *Tārīkh al-Khamis*, 1: p. 188; *Sharḥ Nahj al-Balāgha* by Ibn Abī l-Hadīd 1: pp. 58 & 122 & 132 & 134 & 6: p. 2; *Kanz al-Ummāl*, 3: p. 128.

had not done… I wish I had not opened Fāṭimah's house, although they had closed its knob[32] on me for the purpose of quarrel and struggle."[33]

Ya'qūbī has quoted this speech of Abū Bakr in his history book as:

I wish I had not opened [the door to] Fāṭimah's house, the daughter of the Prophet (pbuh) and had not sent the men into her house, although the door to that house was closed on me for the purpose of quarrel.[34]

2. 'Umar ibn al-Khaṭṭāb's Speech to 'Alī 'Amīr al-Mu'minīn

We read in *Kanz al-Ummāl* (the treasure of workers):

"…I would order them to set the door to your house on fire."

This phrase is enough to prove the claim.

The story of burning the door to Fāṭimah's house was so famous that after the passage of many years, when 'Abdullāh ibn Zubayr started talking to Banī Hāshim in Mecca to accept his ruling, because they did not agree to do so and did not pledge allegiance to him, he ordered his troops to imprison them in the valley of a mountain and place a huge pile of firewood in front of the valley to set them all on fire and burn them.

In order to justify his brother's actions, Urwa, 'Abdullāh ibn Zubayr's brother, referred to 'Umar setting fire to the door of Fāṭimah's house in the event of allegiance to Abū Bakr and said, "My brother did this only to prevent division among Muslims and to hinder the destruction of unity in their word. He wanted them all to unify in word by obeying him; as 'Umar ibn al-Khaṭṭāb did so with

---

[32] In Arabic this word represents a small wooden piece that closes the two parts of a door. Due to this word, at that time the houses had doors and according to Abī Bakr's confession, they broke the door and sent armed men into the house.

[33] *Tārīkh al-Ṭabarī*, 4: p. 52, and in the European edition 1: p. 2140; *Murūj aḏ-Ḏahab*, 1: p. 414; *al-'Iqd al-Farīd*, 3: p. 69; *Kanz al-Ummāl*, 3: p. 135; *Al-Imāma wal-Siyāsa*, 1: p. 18; *Al-Mubarrad*, 2: pp. 130-131; *Sharḥ Nahj al-Balāgha* by Ibn Abī l-Ḥadīd 9: p. 130; *Lisan al-Mizan*, 4: p. 189; *Mir'āt al-Zamān* & *Tārīkh Dimashq Ibn 'Asākir*, under the translation of Abī Bakr & *Tārīkh al-Islām al-kabir aḏ-Ḏahabī*, 1: p. 388.

[34] *Tārīkh Ya'qūbī*, 2: p. 115.

Banī Hāshim. When they refused swearing allegiance to Abū Bakr, he provided firewood to set them on fire in the house."[35]

3. The Encounter with ʿAlī

Abū Bakr Johari has quoted that when taken to the mosque without his will to pledge allegiance to Abū Bakr,[36] ʿAlī said, "I am the servant of God and a brother to the Prophet (pbuh) of God."

At last, he was taken to Abū Bakr and proposed to swear allegiance to him but he responded, "I deserve ruling more than you do, so I will not swear allegiance to you. It is you who should pledge allegiance to me. You took the control of this government from the Anṣār on the basis of your kinship to the Prophet (pbuh) and they handed over the control of affairs to you for the same reason. I offer you the same reason you proposed to the Anṣār. So, if you do not follow your inner worldly whims and fear God, treat us, Ahl al-Bayt, fairly and approve of our right of ruling and governing as the Anṣār approved of you, and officially recognize us for the job; otherwise, one day you will have to shoulder the burden of this oppression you deliberately inflicted on us."

ʿUmar said, "You will not be freed unless you pledge allegiance." And ʿAlī answered, "O' ʿUmar. You are milking it for its worth because half of it will end up being yours. Strengthen the basis of his [Abū Bakr's] government, for tomorrow he will leave it to you. I swear to God, I will neither agree to your demand nor obey him."

Abū Bakr added, "If you do not swear allegiance to me, I will not oblige you to do so." And Abū ʿUbaydah Jarāḥ continued, "O' Abū al-Ḥasan, you are young and these are the elderly relatives from Quraysh! You have neither their experience nor their command over the affairs. I see Abū Bakr more capable, more tolerant and more skillful than you to undertake this position. So, agree with him and leave the affair of government to him, for if you stay and live long, you will be more appropriate than anybody else for this position because you

---

[35] *Murūj aḏ-Ḏahab,* 3: p. 86; *Sharḥ Nahj al-Balāgha* by Ibn Abī l-Hadīd 20: 481.

[36] *Sharḥ Nahj al-Balāgha* by Ibn Abī l-Hadīd 6: 285 narrated from *al-Saqīfa* by Johari; *al-ʿIqd al-Farīd,* 4: p. 247; *Ṣubḥ al-Aʿshā,* 1: p. 128.

are more suitable regarding your kinship with the Messenger of God and for your state of being the first to accept Islām and also for your efforts in establishing this religion."

'Alī expressed, "O' members of the Muhājirūn! Take God into consideration and do not take ruling and government from the house of Muḥammad into your own houses and tribes and do not hinder his family from the position and honor that they have among people and do not trod upon their right. O' members of the Muhājirūn! I swear to God, that we, Ahl al-Bayt deserve taking over the affairs of this nation in our hands more than you do, as long as there exists among us a reciter of Qur'ān and a person knowledgeable in religious matters and familiar with the Prophet's traditions and well-informed about the affairs of the vassals. By God we possess all these signs. So, do not follow your sensual desires, for this will depart you from the path of God, step by step."

Hearing Imam's speech, Bashir ibn Sa'ad, turned to him and said, "If the Anṣār had heard these words from you before they swore allegiance to Abū Bakr, not even two of them would have had any difference in opinion in accepting your government and ruling, but what can be done now that it is too late and they have already sworn allegiance to Abū Bakr?!"

Indeed, 'Alī did not pledge allegiance at that time and returned to his house.[37]

Abū Bakr Johari has also narrated that:

When Fāṭimah saw what they did to 'Alī and Zubayr, she stood at the door to her house[38] and turned to Abū Bakr saying, "O' Abū Bakr! How fast did you start deceiving the Prophet's family! By God I will not speak to 'Umar as long as I live."[39]

In another narration, it is stated that:

---

[37] *Sharḥ Nahj al-Balāgha* by Ibn Abī l-Hadīd 6: 285 narrated from *al-Saqīfa* by Johari.

[38] The door to her house opened to the mosque.

[39] *Sharḥ Nahj al-Balāgha* by Ibn Abī l-Hadīd 2: pp. 134 & 286.

While crying hard, Fāṭimah stepped out of the house and started pushing people aside and scattering them off the house.[40]

Ya'qūbī also writes in his history book:

Fāṭimah stepped out and addressed the attackers who had occupied her house and said, "Will you leave my house or I swear to God I will bare my head and complain to God." Hearing this threat, the invaders and others who were in the house, left the place.[41]

Mas'ūdī also writes in his history book, *Murūj aḏ-Ḏahab*:

When the affair of allegiance to Abū Bakr was over in Saqīfah, and on Tuesday, allegiance was renewed in the mosque, 'Alī came out of his house and turned to Abū Bakr and said, "You spoiled Muslim's affairs and did not consult us and ignored our right." Abū Bakr replied, "Yes, that's correct, but I feared sedition and chaos."[42]

D. Ahl al-Bayt's Reaction after Saqīfah

Ya'qūbī says:

A group encircled 'Alī and wanted to swear allegiance to him. 'Alī told them, "Tomorrow morning, be here while you have shaved your heads." But, the next morning, only three of them showed up.[43]

After that, at nights, 'Alī would sit Fāṭimah on a mule and take her door to door to the Anṣār's houses and ask them to help him take his right back. Fāṭimah would also encourage them to help 'Alī, but the Anṣār would reply, "O' daughter of the Prophet! We have pledged allegiance to Abū Bakr and it is all over now. If your cousin had forerun Abū Bakr in taking the rope of the Caliphate in hand, we definitely would not have accepted Abū Bakr.

In response to them 'Alī would say, "Did you expect me to leave the Prophet's corpse unattended in his house, without the ritual ablution and

---

[40] *Ibid.*

[41] *Tārīkh Ya'qūbī*, 2: p. 105.

[42] *Murūj aḏ-Ḏahab*, 1: p. 414; *Al-Imāma wal-Siyāsa*, 1: p. 12-14, slightly different.

[43] *Tārīkh Ya'qūbī*, 2: p. 126; *Sharḥ Nahj al-Balāgha* by Ibn Abī l-Hadīd 2: p. 4.

shroud, and engage in conflict with people to seize the Caliphate position and his substitution?!" And Fāṭimah would add, "Abū al-Ḥasan has done what was appropriate to do, but people have taken measures that they will be accountable for in years and they will need to answer back on it to God."[44]

In a letter that Mu'awiya sent to 'Alī, he referred to this matter where he writes:

I remember days that have passed when, in the dark of the night, you sat your wife (Fāṭimat az-Zahrā) who veiled from the eyes of men on a mule and held Ḥasan and Ḥusayn's hands in your hands, at the time when allegiance was pledged to the truthful Abū Bakr. And you missed no one from the people present at Badr and the pioneers of Islām, from asking them to help you. You would go to their doors accompanied by your spouse and you would present your two children as your evidence and reason, and request their aid against the Companion of the Prophet (Abū Bakr). But eventually only four or five of them accepted your plea. For, I swear on my life, if the right was on your side, they would have undoubtedly followed and supported you; but you had an improper and inaccurate claim and said things that no one believed in and you were determined to do the impossible. Though I may be forgetful, but I recall your speech to Abū Sufyān, who provoked you to an uprising, as you said, "If I could find forty unyielding and determined men, I would rise up against them."[45]

---

[44] *Sharḥ Nahj al-Balāgha* by Ibn Abī l-Hadīd 6: 28 narrated from *al-Saqīfa* by Johari. *Al-Imāma wal-Siyāsa*, 1: p. 12.

[45] *Sharḥ Nahj al-Balāgha* by Ibn Abī l-Hadīd 2: p. 47 & 1: p. 131. In response to this statement from Mu'awiya, Ali said, "I swear to God you meant to condemn. You praise but you tend to scandalize. You yourself got scandalized [for what you said revealed my being oppressed because you confessed that I pledged allegiance unwillingly and with hatred and obligated by cruelty. Therefore you have condemned the Caliphs and scandalized yourself.] And it is totally acceptable for a Muslim to be oppressed if he has no doubts in his religion and no skepticism in his beliefs. (The Translation of *Nahj al-Balāgha* by Feyz al-Islām, letter 28: p. 899-900). In addition to this, in a letter Mu'awiya himself wrote to Abī Bakr, he clearly confesses to Abī Bakr and 'Umar seizing Alī's right

E. The Prophet's Enlightenment

The Prophet (pbuh) had managed the best delicate and programmed plan possible for the Muslims. One item of this plan is the story of the Verse of Purification, about which Umm Salamah has narrated:

One day the Prophet (pbuh) was at our house when he received the Divine Mercy Message. He said, "Send after Ahl al-Bayt." I asked, "Who are your Ahl al-Bayt?" He stated, "'Alī, Fāṭimah, Ḥasan and Ḥusayn."

When they arrived, the Prophet (pbuh) sat Ḥasan and Ḥusayn on his lap and 'Alī and Fāṭimah in front and behind him. Then he took the Yemeni cloak from the bed and spread it on his own head and their heads and said, "O' Lord, these are my Ahl al-Bayt." This is when the Purification verse of the Qur'ān was revealed saying:

$$\text{إِنَّمَا يُرِيدُ ٱللَّهُ لِيُذْهِبَ عَنكُمُ ٱلرِّجْسَ أَهْلَ ٱلْبَيْتِ وَيُطَهِّرَكُمْ تَطْهِيرًا}$$

"Allāh intends only to remove from you the impurity [of sin], O' Ahl al-Bayt, and to purify you with [extensive] purification."[46]

I said, "O' messenger of God, am I not one of the Ahl al-Bayt?" And he said, "You are a good lady, but you are not one of my Ahl al-Bayt; you are one of the Prophet's wives."[47]

After the revelation of this verse, the Prophet (pbuh) would go to the entrance of 'Alī and Fāṭimah's house, which opened to the mosque, five times a day at prayer time, and put his hand on the door and say, "Peace be upon you Ahl al-Bayt", and then he would recite the mentioned verse and afterwards call them to the congregational prayer and announce, "Time for prayer, time for

---

with a schemed plan. (*Murūj aḏ-Ḏahab*, 2: p. 604; *Waq'at Ṣiffīn*, p.135; *Sharḥ Nahj al-Balāgha* by Ibn Abī l-Hadīd 2: p. 65 & 1: p. 284).

[46] Part of Al-Ahzāb 33.

[47] *Tafsīr al-Ṭabarī*, 22: p. 6; *al-Durr al-Manthur*, 5: pp. 198-199, with a different narration in *Jami' at-Tirmiḏi* 13: p. 248; *Musnad Aḥmad ibn Ḥanbal*, 6: p. 306; *Usd al-Ġābah*, 4: p. 29 & 2: p. 297; *Tahḏīb al-Tahḏīb*, 2: p. 297 & in a narration in *al-Mustadrak*, 2: p. 416 & 3: p. 147; *Sahih al-Bayhaqi*, 2: p. 150; *Usd al-Ġābah*, 5: pp. 521 & 589; *Ta'rīkh Baghdād*, 9: p. 126.

prayer."[48] Because the door of Fāṭimah's house opened to the mosque, five times a day all the Companions saw how the Prophet (pbuh) dealt with the house and its residents. This act of the Prophet (pbuh) brought about enlightenment, but we saw the ugliness of some Companions' behavior towards this house and its people.[49]

---

[48] *al-Durr al-Manthur,* 5: p. 199; *Al-Isti'ab,* 2: p. 598; *Usd al-Ġābah,* 5: p. 174; *Majmau' az-Zawa'id,* 9: p. 168 & according to the narration of Anas ibn Malik in *al-Mustadrak,* 2: p. 158. Hakim has considered it an accurate hadīth due to definite conditions. *Usd al-Ġābah,* 5: p. 521; *Musnad Aḥmad ibn Ḥanbal,* 3: p. 258; *Tafsīr al-Ṭabarī,* 22: p. 5 under the verse of purification; *Tafsir Ibn Kathīr,* 3: p. 483; *al-Durr al-Manthur,* 5: p. 199; *Musnad al-Tayalisi,* 8: p. 274; *Jami' at-Tirmiḏi,* 12: p. 85; *Kanz al-Ummāl,* 7: p. 103; *Jami' al-Usul,* 10: p. 101, hadīth 6691; *Taysīr al-Wusūl,* 3: p. 297. For more information on this topic see: *Hadīth al-Kisā fi Kutub Madrasat al-Khulafa was Madrasat Ahl al-Bayt.*

[49] To learn more about the ugliness of this incident, which has also been mentioned in various books from the school of thought of the Caliphs, see: *Abdullah ibn Saba'* by Allamah 'Askarī 1: pp. 128-139; *Ihraq bayt Fāṭimah.*

Chapter 6

The Economic War Against Ahl al-Bayt

The caliphate needed military campaigns to gain allegiance from tribes out of Medina and also carry out other tasks. In addition, those who were in Medina and supporting 'Alī (as) were considered a danger to the caliphate. Therefore, in order to disperse them, Ahl al-Bayt's properties, consisting of Fadak and the share of Khums belonging to the heir of the Holy Prophet (pbuh) was taken away from them, so that the Prophet's family would go poor and people would scatter and leave them.

Confiscation of the Prophet's Property and its Ownership

These two verses verify the financial sources of the Prophet (pbuh) and his Ahl al-Bayt:

First of the Properties:

مَّآ أَفَآءَ ٱللَّهُ عَلَىٰ رَسُولِهِ مِنْ أَهْلِ ٱلْقُرَىٰ فَلِلَّهِ وَلِلرَّسُولِ وَلِذِي ٱلْقُرْبَىٰ وَٱلْيَتَـٰمَىٰ وَٱلْمَسَـٰكِينِ وَٱبْنِ ٱلسَّبِيلِ

"And what Allāh restored to His Messenger from the people of the towns belongs to Allāh and the Messenger and [his] near relatives and orphans and the in-need and the [stranded] traveler [from Banī Hāshim]."[1]

The name of these properties in the Islāmic terminology is "fi'a"[2].

---

[1] Part of al-Hashr 7

[2] Fi'a are the properties that once belonged to the infidels and with no cause of battle or fight fell into the hands of the Muslims; such as Fadak (Although it wasn't only Fadak). *Lisan al-'Arab*, under the word "Fi'a". For more detail on "Fadak" see *Ma'alim al-Madrasatayn*.

Another example of "fi'a" is lands that belonged to the Banī Naḍīr tribe. To clarify we need to explain that there were three Jewish tribes which were settled in Medina and areas around it named Banī Naḍīr, Banī Qaynuqa and Banī Qurayza. According to the promising news they had received in their divine religion about the Last Prophet (pbuh), they were awaiting him and had come to Medina to aid him during his mission. But when the Prophet (pbuh) revealed his mission and immigrated to Medina, the Jews revolted against his prophecy in denial.

Although he was well known to be the Last Prophet (pbuh), but they broke the covenant and resorted to deception, throwing a stone from the roof of a house where next to its wall, he had a gathering with ten of his Companions, in order to wear him down. God informed his Prophet (pbuh) of this deception through revelation. The Prophet (pbuh) hurried to Medina and demanded to the Jews to leave that town due to their perfidy and betrayal. Banī Naḍīr did not give in and encamped in their fort. Though, they finally surrendered after fifteen days, leaving their fort and immigrating to Khaybar and other places.

God earmarked what they left behind including weapons, lands and groves to his Prophet (pbuh). 'Umar turned to the Prophet (pbuh) and said, "Will you not take one fifth of these spoils and distribute the rest among the Muslims?" The Prophet (pbuh) answered, "I do not share what (according to seventh verse of Surah al-Hashr) God has wanted only for me and has not considered a part of it for other Muslims."

al-Waqidi and others have written that:

The Prophet (pbuh) would dedicate from the property that he obtained from Banī Naḍīr and was specifically his, to his family and to whomever he desired and he would not give anything to those he did not want to, and he appointed the administration of the Banī Naḍīr properties to Abū Rāfi', a freed slave of his.[3]

---

[3] *Kitab al-Tārīkh wa al-Maghazi*, 1: pp. 178 & 378; *Imta` al-asma`*, pp. 178-182; *Tafsīr al-Ṭabarī*, surah al-Hashr; *Kitāb aṭ-Tabaqāt al-Kabīr*, Ibn Sa'd, 2: p. 58; *Sunan Abī Dāwūd*, 3: p. 48; *Sunan an-Nasa'i*, part "Fi'a" 2: p. 178; *Sharḥ Nahj al-Balāgha* by Ibn Abī l-Hadīd 4: p. 78; *al-Durr al-Manthur*, 6: p. 192.

In the fourth year of the Prophet's immigration, he voluntarily gifted part of the lands of Banī Naḍīr to Abū Bakr, 'Umar ibn al-Khaṭṭāb, 'Abdur-Rahman ibn 'Awf, Zubayr ibn al-Awam, Abū Dujana Simak ibn Kharasha Sā'idī, Sahl ibn Ḥanīf and others.[4]

These properties were rightful belongings of the Prophet (pbuh) and he gifted from them to his relatives as well as to the orphans and the poor and the Ibnu al-Sabīl, i.e. a stranded traveler from Banī Hāshim. (Ibnu al-Sabīl is the term used for one who is of wealth in his own city, but for some reason, such as being robbed, has become in-need on his trip.) To travelers of this category who are not relatives of the Prophet (pbuh), help is donated from the alms also known as Zakāt.

Second of the Properties:

وَٱعْلَمُوٓاْ أَنَّمَا غَنِمْتُم مِّن شَىْءٍ فَأَنَّ لِلَّهِ خُمُسَهُۥ وَلِلرَّسُولِ وَلِذِي ٱلْقُرْبَىٰ وَٱلْيَتَٰمَىٰ وَٱلْمَسَٰكِينِ وَٱبْنِ ٱلسَّبِيلِ إِن كُنتُمْ ءَامَنتُم بِٱللَّهِ

"And know that anything you obtain of war booty, then indeed, one fifth of it belongs to Allāh and the Messenger and [his] near relatives and the orphans, the in-need, and the [stranded] traveler [related to the Prophet and from Banī Hāshim], if you have belief in Allāh…"[5]

Thus, the Shi'as pay one-fifth of whatever they benefit as Khums.

Third, Forth & Fifth of the Properties:

Three castles from the Khaybar castles. Khaybar consisted of seven or eight castles, three of which belonged to the Prophet (pbuh).

In the books of *Al-Ahkam al-Sultania*, al-Qāḍī al-Māwardī and al-Qāḍī Abū Ya'lā have stated that:

The Prophet (pbuh) obtained three forts from the eight castles of Khaybar which were called "al-Katbiyyah", "al-Watih" and "al-Sulalim" in such a way that he took "al-Katbiyyah" as the Khums of the booty and "al-Watih" and "al-

---

[4] *Kitāb aṭ-Ṭabaqāt al-Kabīr*, Ibn Sa'd 2: p. 58; *Kitāb Futūḥ al-Buldān*, 1: pp. 18-22.

[5] Part of al-Anfāl 41.

Sulalim" were considered divine gifts to the Prophet (pbuh) for he had conquered them in peace and compromise. These three castles, which were to be God's bounty and the Khums of the booty of the battle dedicated to the Prophet (pbuh), were considered to be purely his.[6]

In *Wafā' al-Wafā* we read:

The people of "al-Watih" and "al-Sulalim" acceded to the Prophet (pbuh) in peace. That is why these two were to be his pure belongings and "al-Katbiyyah" was considered part of his Khums. And this was because parts of the Khaybar forts were obtained through battle and conquest, and other parts through negotiation and peace.[7]

Sixth of the Properties:

Fadak was one of the castles of Khaybar. After the Prophet (pbuh) conquered Khaybar and completed the work there, the people of Fadak sent an envoy to the Prophet (pbuh) and offered him half of Fadak and in return suggested peace and compromise. Therefore this was a pure belonging of the Prophet (pbuh) for the Muslims had not galloped their horses on its grounds, nor had they fought for it. Hence, the Prophet (pbuh) would consume its products and outcomes as he wished.[8] And so when the verse:

$$\text{وَءَاتِ ذَا ٱلْقُرْبَىٰ حَقَّهُ}$$

"And give the relative his right"[9] was revealed, the Prophet (pbuh) summoned his daughter Fāṭimah (sa) and gave her Fadak.[10]

---

[6] *Al-Ahkam al-Sultania,* by al-Qāḍī al-Māwardī p. 270; *Al-Ahkam al-Sultania,* by al-Qāḍī Abū Yaʿlā pp. 184-185; *Kitab al-Amwal,* p. 56.

[7] *Wafā' al-Wafā,* p. 1210. Also see: *Sirat ibn Hisham,* 2: p. 404; *Kitab al-Tārīkh wa al-Maghazi,* pp. 683-692; *Ma'alim al-Madrasatayn.*

[8] *Kitāb Futūḥ al-Buldān,* 1: p. 41.

[9] Part of al-Isrā' 26

[10] *Shawāhid al-Tanzīl,* 1: pp. 338-341; *al-Durr al-Manthur,* 4: p. 177; *Mizan al-I'tidal,* 2: p. 228; *Kanz al-Ummāl,* 2: p. 158; *Majmau' az-Zawa'id,* 7: p. 49; *Al-Kashshāf,* 2: p. 446; *Tafsīr al-Qur'ān al-Azim* by Ibn Kathīr 3: p. 36.

Yāqūt al-Ḥamawī writes:

Fadak is a village in Ḥijāz, two or three days away from Medina, full of flowing springs and countless groves.[11]

Seventh of the Properties:

Wadi al-Qura: The villages between Medina and Shām were called Wadi al-Qura. There were seventy villages in that area and all their inhabitants were Jews. They had rebelled, and when the Prophet (pbuh) emerged, they surrendered and closed a deal with him, that indicated one-third of their products would remain to themselves and two-third of it would be given to the Prophet (pbuh) or whomever he assigned.[12]

Eighth of the Properties:

Anṣār gifted the Prophet (pbuh)[13] with lands that were arid and so these properties all belonged to the him.[14]

---

[11] *Kitāb Mu'jam al-Buldān*, under the work "Fadak".

[12] *Kitāb al-Futūḥ al-Buldān*, 1: pp. 39-40; *Kitab al-Tārīkh wa al-Maghazi*, pp. 710-711; Imtaʿ al-asmaʿ, p. 332; *Al-Ahkam al-Sultania*, by al-Qāḍī al-Māwardī p. 170; *Al-Ahkam al-Sultania*, by al-Qāḍī Abū Yaʿlā p. 185.

[13] *Kitab al-Amwal*, p. 282 part al-Iqta.

[14] Of course, there was more to what the Prophet owned. For instance, one of them was "Mahzur" which was a huge land in "Alieh" in which the Jews of Banī Qurayza had built houses and after the expansion of Medina, had turned into a market. He had also inherited the house he was born in from his mother, Aminah bint Wahb, which was located in "Bani Ali" valley in Mecca. In addition he had inherited the house she lived in from his wife Khadija, which was located between "Aṣ-Ṣafā" and "al-Marwah", behind the herb market in Mecca. Although, after the Prophet immigrated to Medina, this house was sold by ʿAqīl ibn Abī Ṭālib (*Ma'alim al-Madrasatayn*, 2: p. 146). When Abī Bakr was selected as caliph, he came up with a story which was only narrated by himself and claimed that the Prophet had said, "We prophets do not receive heritage and so what we leave are alms." (*Ṣaḥīḥ al-Bukhārī*, 2: p. 200, part Manaqib Qarabe Rasulullah; *Sunan an-Nasa'i*, 2: p. 179, part al-Fi'a; *Musnad Aḥmad ibn Ḥanbal*, 1: p. 6 & 9; *Kitāb aṭ-Tabaqāt al-Kabīr*, Ibn Sa'd 2: p. 315 & 8: p. 28). He took all these assets and called them alms and ever since, whatever the Prophet left behind of properties are called

The Cause of Revelation of the Verse "And Give the Relative His Right"

The Prophet (pbuh) had given some of the lands he had to Abū Bakr, 'Umar, 'Uthmān, Ā'ishah and Ḥafṣah,[15] and to others. He had even said to one of his Companions[16] in Wadi al-Qura, "Stand here and shoot your arrow; from this point to wherever it lands is yours."[17]

But the Prophet (pbuh) had not given anything to Fāṭimah (sa) and so in this regard, the verse "And Give the Relative His Right" was revealed. Yes, Fāṭimah's mother, Khadija, had dedicated whatever asset she had in this world to Islām. Therefore, God commanded the Prophet (pbuh) to give Fāṭimah (sa) her right in return for that sacrifice and dedication. And thus the Prophet (pbuh) gifted Fāṭimah (sa) Fadak.[18]

The Caliphs' Behavior Regarding Fadak

As already mentioned, the Prophet (pbuh) had handed over part of the properties he owned to the Muslims and those properties were in their possession. According to the Islāmic ruling, that who possesses an asset is legally its owner and possessor. This ruling is called the "the rule of Zulyad".

Fadak was given to Fāṭimah (sa) by the Prophet (pbuh) and she had occupied it, so it was Zulyad.[19] In spite of all this, Abū Bakr took Fadak away from her. Fāṭimah (sa) said, "Return Fadak to me, because the Prophet (pbuh)

---

alms and only his personal belongings, such as his sword, camel, and shoes were given to Alī and he was told, "Other than these, everything else are alms due to what Abī Bakr said." And only he himself related this hadīth to the Prophet (*Ahkam al-Sultania* by *al-Qāḍī al-Māwardī* p. 171; *Al-Ahkam al-Sultania* by al-Qāḍī Abū Ya'lā p. 186).

[15] *Kitāb aṭ-Tabaqāt al-Kabīr*, Ibn Sa'd 2: p. 58; *Kitāb al-Futūḥ al-Buldān*, 1: pp. 18-22.

[16] Hamzah ibn Nu'mān Udrī

[17] *Kitāb al-Futūḥ al-Buldān*, 1: p. 40.

[18] Also there is a letter left from the Prophet in which he confirms Fāṭimah's ownership of Fadak. *Bihar al-Anwar*, 16: p. 109, hadīth 41, part 6 & 17: p. 378.

[19] When Abī Bakr ordered the usurpation of Fadak, gardeners and workers who were working in it were kicked out. (*Sharḥ Nahj al-Balāgha* by Ibn Abī l-Hadīd 11: p. 211).

has gifted me with it." She was told, "Bring in a witness from the others (i.e. they wouldn't accept those to whom the Prophet (pbuh) had given any property during his lifetime!) Fāṭimah (sa) called Umm Ayman to testify.[20]

In this regard, al-Mas'ūdī writes:

In addition to 'Alī (as) and Umm Ayman, Fāṭimah (sa) also brought Ḥasan and Ḥusayn as her witnesses and they testified and said that the Prophet (pbuh) had gifted Fāṭimah (sa) with Fadak during his lifetime.[21] Abū Bakr said, "This is unacceptable! In testifying there must be two men or one man and two women."[22]

Also, al-Balāḏurī writes:

One slave from the Prophet's slaves named Rabāḥ also testified to the truth that was Fāṭimah (sa).[23]

According to another narration, after the witnesses' testimony, the caliph decided to return Fadak to Fāṭimah (sa). Thus, on a piece of leather, he signed Fāṭimah's name on the property deed of Fadak to document her ownership, but 'Umar showed up, stopped him and tore the deed.[24]

The Usurpation of the Prophet's Heritage

The Prophet's heritage was also taken away from Ahl al-Bayt.[25] Fāṭimah (sa) said to Abū Bakr, "Give me back the Prophet's heritage." Abū Bakr said,

---

[20] Acccording to *Murūj aḏ-Ḏahab*, 2: p. 200.

[21] *Murūj aḏ-Ḏahab*, 2: p. 200; *Wafā' al-Wafā*, 2: p. 160.

[22] *As-Sirat al-Halabiah*, 2: p. 400; *Kitāb al-Futūḥ al-Buldān*, p. 43; *Kitāb Mu'jam al-Buldān*, 4, translation of Fadak.

[23] *Kitāb al-Futūḥ al-Buldān*, p. 43.

[24] *As-Sirat al-Halabiah*, 3: p. 400; *Sharḥ Nahj al-Balāgha* by Ibn Abī l-Hadīd 16: p. 274.

[25] 'Umar said, "When the Prophet passed away, Abī Bakr and I visited Alī and said to him: What do you have to say about the Prophet's heritage? Alī said: We deserve to inherit the Prophet's heritage more than anyone else. I said: Even what belongs to Khaybar? He said: Even those. I said: Even what belongs to Fadak? He said: Even those. I said: I swear to God even if you behead us, there is no way we would give you these stuff." (*Majmau' az-Zawa'id*, 9: p. 39)

"Do you want the furniture of the house or the Prophet's farms and gardens?" Fāṭimah (sa) said, "Both. It is me who inherits these from the Prophet (pbuh), just as your daughters will inherit your heritage after you die." Abū Bakr said, "God knows the Prophet (pbuh) was better than me as you are better than my daughters. But what can I do when the Prophet (pbuh) has said: We prophets do not receive heritage and so what we leave are alms."[26]

Fāṭimah's Sermon in the Mosque

Ten days after the Prophet's death[27] when Fāṭimah (sa) presented all her witnesses and reasons to claim her right and after Abū Bakr's refusal not returning anything from the Prophet's heritage and his dedications to her, she decided to raise the issue before all Muslims and seek the help of her father's Companions and friends. Therefore, according to narrators and historians, she headed for the Prophet's mosque. This matter has been pointed out in the book *al-Saqīfa* by Abū Bakr Johari, according to Ibn Abī l-Ḥadīd Mu'tazili's narration and Ibn Abī Tahir Tayfur's narration in *Balāghāt al-nisā'*.[28] We will quote Abū Bakr Johari who has said:

---

[26] *Sharḥ Nahj al-Balāgha* by Ibn Abī l-Hadīd 4: p. 82; we read there: It is well-known that the story of denying the Prophet's heritage has only been narrated by Abī Bakr and no one but him. Also on p. 85 it says: Most narrations indicate that this hadīth has not been narrated by anyone but Abī Bakr himself. In *Tārīkh al-Khulafā'*, p. 89, where Abī Bakr's story is narrated, As-Suyūṭī writes: hadīth 29 is "We do not receive heritage and so what we leave are alms." Although later on, other hadīths were created and related to people other than Abī Bakr to prove this hadīth has been heard from the Prophet by others as well. (See: *Sharḥ Nahj al-Balāgha* by Ibn Abī l-Hadīd 4: p. 85). *Kitāb aṭ-Tabaqāt al-Kabīr*, Ibn Sa'd 2: p. 36. Also see: *Ma'alim al-Madrasatayn*.

[27] *Sharḥ Nahj al-Balāgha* by Ibn Abī l-Hadīd 4: p. 97.

[28] *Balāghāt al-Nisā'*, pp. 12-14; also in the old version of *Bihar al-Anwar*, 8: p. 108; *Al-Iḥtijāj*, 1: p. 253.

When Fāṭimah (sa) realized that Abū Bakr had decided not to return Fadak to her, she put on her headscarf[29] and wrapped herself in a veil[30], and surrounded by a group of women from her relatives, walking just in the same style as the Prophet (pbuh) himself, while her feet were covered by her dress, entered the mosque. She walked on Abū Bakr, who was sitting among a crowded group of the Muhājirūn, the Anṣār and other Companions. So, a curtain was drawn to separate them from each other. Then (Fāṭimah (sa)) sighed deeply which broke some hearts and brought tears to people's eyes and hence the assembly turned tense. Therefore, she paused for a moment until their tumult subsided and their moans and groans calmed down.

Then, she started by praising the Almighty God and the Prophet (pbuh) and afterwards said, "This is Fāṭimah, Muhammad's daughter... There has certainly come to you a Messenger from among yourselves; what you suffer is grievous to him; [he is] concerned over you [i.e., your guidance] and he is kind and merciful to the believers.[31] If you take a look at him and his lineage and his descendants, you will find him to be my father, not yours, and he is my cousin's brother, not your men's...". (She went on until she said,) "...and you now contemplate that we do not inherit the Prophet (pbuh). "Is it the judgment of Ignorance [era] that you desire? Who is better than Allāh in judgment for people who are certain [in faith]?"[32]

O' son of Abī Quhāfah, how is it that you inherit from your father, but I do not inherit from my father? What a surprising, horrible claim! Now, let Fadak be yours until the Doomsday and consider it like a restrained, saddled camel. God is the righteous judge and the Prophet (pbuh) a competent demandant, and the judgment is on the Doomsday. And on that day the criminals will be the losers."

---

[29] This was a large covering of not only the head and hair, but also the neck and chest which women used and is larger than the usual scarf that just covers the head. In the holy Qur'an we read about this garment in surah an-Noor 31.

[30] This means a cloak-resembling piece or a long dress that covers the whole body.

[31] at-Tawbah 128.

[32] al-Mā'idah 50.

Then she turned to her father's grave and recited these two verses:

"O' Prophet, indeed, after you, much news and hardships and troubles occurred whereas none of these arguments and calamities would have taken place had you been among us. We lost you as if the earth lost its rich allies. Your people became corrupt and deviated from the right path. So witness this all."[33]

[The narrator says that up to that day, he had never seen those people, both men and women, crying and moaning that greatly.] Fāṭimah (sa) then faced the Anṣār and said, "O' those who have been elicited! Strength of the nation and guardians of Islām! What is this weakness you are showing of yourselves in aiding me? You ignore my right and neglect my plea? Did the Prophet not say that a man's rights are protected in regard to his children and that respecting one's child means respecting the father? Isn't it too soon for you to change the religion of God and aren't you being too urgent to start deviations? Now that the Prophet (pbuh) has passed away, have you also destroyed his religion?! I swear on my life that his (the Prophet's) death is a great tragedy and a very deep rift that is constantly widening and will never be sealed. Hopes were dashed after him, and the earth became gloomy and the mountains shattered. After him, the boundaries were lifted and sanctity was scarred and safety and immunity were lost. And all this was announced by the Qur'ān before the death of the Prophet (pbuh) and you were informed about it where it says:

وَمَا مُحَمَّدٌ إِلَّا رَسُولٌ قَدْ خَلَتْ مِن قَبْلِهِ الرُّسُلُ أَفَإِيْن مَّاتَ أَوْ قُتِلَ انقَلَبْتُمْ عَلَىٰ أَعْقَابِكُمْ وَمَن يَنقَلِبْ عَلَىٰ عَقِبَيْهِ فَلَن يَضُرَّ اللَّهَ شَيْئاً وَسَيَجْزِي اللَّهُ الشَّاكِرِينَ

"*Muḥammad is not but a messenger. [Other] messengers have passed on before him. So if he was to die or to be killed, would you turn back on your heels [to unbelief]? And he who turns back on his heels will never harm Allāh at all; but Allāh will reward the grateful.*"[34]

---

[33] *Balāghāt al-Nisā'*, p. 14; *Sharḥ Nahj al-Balāgha* by Ibn Abī l-Ḥadīd 16: p. 251; *Bihar al-Anwar*, 43: p. 195; *Al-Iḥtijāj*, 1: p. 106. Narrated from Two Schools of Thought in Islām, 2: p. 229.

[34] Āl-'Imrān 144.

O' you! They usurp my father's inheritance right before your eyes and you hear my cry for justice, but you take no action! While you have strength and human sources, and you have respect and honor. You are elites that God has chosen and saints that he has selected. You got in battle with the Arabs and accepted the hardships and struggled with problems and overcame them up until Islām was stabled by you and victories were achieved and the fire of war subsided and the fervor of polytheism and idolatry calmed down and chaos broke out and the religious system strengthened. Now, after all this vanguard, have you retreated, and after all your steadfastness, have you failed, and after all that courage have you feared a bunch of retrogressive people, who have abandoned their faith after the covenant they made with their allegiance, and who mock your religion and traditions? "Combat the leaders of disbelief, for indeed, there are no oaths [sacred] to them; [fight them that] they might cease."[35]

I see that you have leaned towards humiliation and leisure, and you have turned to joy and indolence, and you have denied your beliefs, and you have suddenly lost what you easily gained. But know that even if you and all the people on earth disbelieve, God is surely needless.

I shared with you what was to be said; although I was aware of your humiliation, retrogression and indolence. Let this be your way; stay calm, obedient, and fruitful as you receive what is inextricably linked with the divine fire that will flare from the hearts with all its shame and disgrace. God oversees your actions "and soon those who have wronged are going to know to what [kind of] place they will be returned."[36]

The narrator says:

Muḥammad ibn Zakariyyā (from Muḥammad ibn Zahhāk), from Hisham ibn Muḥammad, from 'Awāna ibn al-Ḥakam narrates that when Fāṭimah (sa) shared what she intended with Abū Bakr, Abū Bakr praised God and the Prophet (pbuh) and then said, "O' best of the women and daughter of the best fathers! I swear to God that I haven't done anything against the Prophet's opinion and I haven't disobeyed his command.

---

[35] Part of at-Tawbah 12.
[36] Part of ash-Shu'arā' 227.

A scout does not lie to his caravan mates. You said what you had in mind and conveyed the message and spoke in rage and then turned away. May God have mercy on both you and us. Bear in mind that I handed over the Prophet's weapons, horse and shoes to 'Alī! But regarding stuff other than these, I myself heard the Prophet say: We prophets do not leave gold, silver, lands, properties, assets and houses as our heritages. In fact, our heritage is faith, wisdom, knowledge and tradition!

I have just done what he commanded, and in this path I succeed only when God desires; I trust him and I ask for his help when I am in need!"

According to the narration in the book *Balāghāt al-Nisā'*[37], after hearing Abū Bakr's words, Fāṭimah (sa) said, "O' people! I am Fāṭimah and my father is Muḥammad. As I already said:

$$لَقَدْ جَآءَكُمْ رَسُولٌ مِّنْ أَنفُسِكُمْ$$

"There has certainly come to you a Messenger from among yourselves..."[38] You have deliberately left behind the Book of God and ignored its commands whereas God says:

$$وَوَرِثَ سُلَيْمَٰنُ دَاوُۥدَ$$

"And Solomon inherited David."[39] The Prophet Sulaimān inherited his father, the prophet Dāwūd. Also, in the story of Yaḥyā ibn Zakarīyā, we hear Zakarīyā say:

$$فَهَبْ لِي مِن لَّدُنكَ وَلِيًّا * يَرِثُنِي وَيَرِثُ مِنْ ءَالِ يَعْقُوبَ$$

"So give me from Yourself an heir. Who will inherit me and inherit from the family of Jacob."[40] In addition, God says:

---

[37] *Balāghāt al-Nisā'*, pp. 12-14; *Sharḥ Nahj al-Balāgha* by Ibn Abī l-Hadīd 4: pp. 78-79 & 93.

[38] Part of at-Tawbah 128

[39] Part of an-Naml 16.

[40] Part of Maryam 5&6.

102

وَأُوْلُواْ ٱلْأَرْحَامِ بَعْضُهُمْ أَوْلَىٰ بِبَعْضٍ فِي كِتَٰبِ ٱللَّهِ

"But those of [blood] relationship are more entitled [to inheritance] in the decree of Allāh."[41]

And he says:

يُوصِيكُمُ ٱللَّهُ فِيٓ أَوْلَٰدِكُمْ لِلذَّكَرِ مِثْلُ حَظِّ ٱلْأُنثَيَيْنِ

"Allāh instructs you concerning your children [i.e., their portions of inheritance]: for the male, what is equal to the share of two females."[42]

And:

إِن تَرَكَ خَيْرًا ٱلْوَصِيَّةُ لِلْوَٰلِدَيْنِ وَٱلْأَقْرَبِينَ بِٱلْمَعْرُوفِ حَقًّا عَلَى ٱلْمُتَّقِينَ

"If he leaves wealth [is that he should make] a bequest for the parents and near relatives according to what is acceptable - a duty upon the righteous."[43]

Considering all this, you claim that I have no right from my father and there is no connection and bond between us?!

Has God privileged you with a special verse and excluded His Prophet from it? Or do you claim that we come from two nations [religions] and so we do not inherit from each other?! Aren't my father and I from the same nation? Perhaps you know more about the verses of Qur'ān and its details and general concepts? Are you seeking to revive the laws of the Ignorance era?

...I said what I had to say. And I am aware how weak you are and how you are not willing to help; that's because your spears have weakened and your beliefs have diminished. Fadak can be yours, [but remember] this camel you are riding has a wounded leg [and will not take you to your destination]. This disgrace will remain with you, until it joins God's hell on the Day of Judgment, and God sees your deeds:

---

[41] Part of al-Anfāl 75.

[42] Part of an-Nisā 11.

[43] Part of al-Baqarah 180.

وَسَيَعْلَمُ ٱلَّذِينَ ظَلَمُوٓاْ أَيَّ مُنقَلَبٍ يَنقَلِبُونَ

"And those who have wronged are going to know to what [kind of] place they will be returned."[44]

Ibn Abī l-Ḥadīd writes:

The story of Fadak and Fāṭimah (sa) meeting up with Abū Bakr took place ten days after the Prophet's death; and it is true to say that none of the people, men or women, have said a single word about Fāṭimah's heritage and legacy after she returned from that assembly.[45]

Fāṭimah's Conversation with 'Alī

Within her return from the mosque, Fāṭimah (sa) addressed 'Alī (as) saying, "O' son of Abī Ṭālib![46] You have surrounded yourself just as in a fetal bag in the womb of a mother; you have concealed yourself (from people) and hid in a room as if you are a defendant. You used to break horns of a ram (like 'Amr ibn Abd al-Wud) and now the feather of a featherless bird (an allusion to the ruler of the time) has betrayed you. You humiliated yourself as soon as you dropped your sword. You used to hunt wolves and tear them apart and now you have fallen to the ground. This is the son of Abī Quḥāfah (Abū Bakr) who forcibly took away what my father had gifted me, which was going to be a source of contentment for my two sons.[47] He attempted enmity with me and I found him to be an enemy of words in conversation much so that the Anṣār resisted helping me and the Muhājirūn (who must have mercy due to our kinship)

---

[44] Part of ash-Shu'arā' 227.

[45] *Sharḥ Nahj al-Balāgha* by Ibn Abī l-Ḥadīd 4: p. 97. Narrator says this was because Anṣār (Helpers) did not aid Fāṭimah; a story which will be told in a few pages.

[46] It is Alī's honor to be recognized as Abī Ṭālib's son.

[47] In this part Fāṭimah is not talking about Khums because Alī gets a share of Khums, she isn't talking about heritage either; she is talking about Fadak which the Prophet had gifted her with and she had wanted it to end up belonging to her sons, Hasan and Husayn.

refused their kindness. Woe to me day and night. My supporter and protector (the Prophet (pbuh)) is gone and my strength has diminished. The Muslim community ignored me. (Now) there is no one left to defend me and safeguard me (from my enemies). (I left the house) in rage and returned reluctant. I wish I had died before I was embarrassed. O' you fierce lion! Instead of your help and support, may God help and support me. I will take my complaint to my Lord and I will express my dolor to my father. O' God, you are stronger (than the usurpers of Fadak and the Caliphate)."

Amīr al-Mu'minīn, 'Alī (as) replied to Fāṭimah (sa), "There is no woe to you. The woe is to your enemies. Control this grief, O' daughter of the Prophet (pbuh) and remnant of prophecy. I have not given up on my religion and I have not made mistakes or shown nonchalance in doing what I could. If you need to earn a slight living, your income is guaranteed and God is your guarantor. What God has prepared for you is much better than what they have cut you off from. So consider what they put you through remained with God."

Hence, Fāṭimah (sa) said, "God is sufficient for me and he is the best guarantor."[48]

---

[48] *Bihar al-Anwar*, 43: p. 148, hadīth 4; *Al-Iḥtijāj*, 1: pp. 107-108.

Chapter 7

Fāṭimah on Bed Rest

Fāṭimah (sa) got ill

The first person who gave her a visit was Umm Salamah who said, "O' daughter of the Prophet (pbuh)! How did you spend the night?" Fāṭimah (sa) replied, "Grief and sorrow has filled my heart, because of the death of the Prophet (pbuh) and the oppression of the Prophet's guardian. They violated 'Alī's hijab [an allusion to offending Fāṭimah (sa)]; the man whose position they usurped in contrary to what God has revealed in Qur'ān and what the Prophet (pbuh) had stated. The reason to all of this was the grudges they had held against 'Alī (as) from the Battle of Badr and the revenge and vengeance the sought for the blood he shed in the Battle of Uhud.[1] These hypocrites held on to enmity against 'Alī's, and when they took the caliphate and reached their goal, suddenly, the villains poured rains of tragedy and sorrow upon us. The string of faith was cut in their hearts and they persecuted us as much as they desired, due to their prides. This was all because 'Alī (as) had killed their fathers in challenging battles and martyrdom opportunities."[2]

Fāṭimah's Eagerness to Hearing Bilāl's Aḏān

After the Prophet (pbuh) passed away, Bilāl fell silent and did not recite Aḏān (the call to prayer). One day, Fāṭimah (sa) was eager to hear the Aḏān from her father's Muezzin. When this news reached Bilāl, he recited the Aḏān. Fāṭimah (sa), hearing the sound of Bilāl's Aḏān, recalled her father and his

---

[1] Thirty five people of the seventy elites who were killed in the Battle of Badr had been put to death by Alī (sa). The term in Arabic means seeking revenge for bloodshed. In the Battle of Uhud, at the very beginning, Alī (sa) killed eleven heroes of Quraysh.

[2] *Bihar al-Anwar*, 43: p. 156, hadīth 5 quoted from *Manāqib*,.

lifetime. So she let out a high groan and fell to the ground fainting. People said, "Bilāl! Stop for the Prophet's daughter has passed away." They thought Fāṭimah (sa) had surrendered to death. Bilāl cut the Aḏān short. When Fāṭimah (sa) regained consciousness, she asked him to complete the Aḏān. He resisted and said, "I am afraid of what you would do to yourself when you hear my Aḏān." And so she exempted Bilāl from reciting the Aḏān.[3]

The Women of the Muhājirūn and the Anṣār Visiting Fāṭimah

When Fāṭimah (sa) fell into bed rest with an illness that led to her death, the women of the Muhājirūn and the Anṣār gave her a visit and said to her, "O' Daughter of the Prophet (pbuh)! How are you doing?" Fāṭimah (sa) praised God and sent blessings to her father, then said, "I am fed up with your world; I hate your men and I have thrown them away, after I tested them. Their sluggishness and cowardliness, the cracks on their swords, the weakness of their spears, and the decay of their opinions are hideous. I have leashed them with their own guilt and I have cast the stigma of their acts upon themselves.

Eternal curse on these cunning, oppressive unjust people! Woe to them! They took the Prophet's successor away from his position and distanced him from the base of the mission; from the high, stable mountains of the Prophet's dynasty, from the position of the Prophet (pbuh) and from the spot of revelation, from those who are mystics in the matter of the world and religion. Indeed, this is an obvious loss. What did they find wrong with Abū al-Ḥasan?! Yes, they did not like the sharpness of 'Alī's sword, his kicking them hard, his punishing them severely for their deeds, and his being strict in God's path. These are the causes of their enmity towards 'Alī (as). Had they not avoided the mission the Prophet (pbuh) had entrusted him with, he would have treated them kindly [i.e., he would have had a gentle ruling], so that the government's camel would not have been injured and its rider would not have shaken so hard [i.e., they would have been in comfort at all times], and he would have brought them to a salubrious well filled with pure water pouring from all sides, and the gates of blessings of heaven and earth would have opened on them. [But now

---

[3] *Man lā Yaḥḍuruhu al-Faqīh*, 1: pp. 297-298, hadīth 907; *Bihar al-Anwar*, 43: p. 157.

that none of these have happened] God will punish and interrogate them for what they have done.

So come closer and listen. If you survive, life will show you strange things. If you are one to be surprised, be astonished by what has occurred. On whom, have they relied?! [On Abū Bakr?!] What rope are they holding on to?! Instead of the animal's head, they have clung to its tail [This is an Arabic idiom]. Humiliation be upon those who think they have done a good deed.

أَلَآ إِنَّهُمْ هُمُ ٱلْمُفْسِدُونَ وَلَٰكِن لَّا يَشْعُرُونَ

"Unquestionably, it is they who are the corrupters, but they perceive [it] *not."*[4]

أَفَمَن يَهْدِيٓ إِلَى ٱلْحَقِّ أَحَقُّ أَن يُتَّبَعَ أَمَّن لَّا يَهِدِّيٓ إِلَّآ أَن يُهْدَىٰ فَمَا لَكُمْ كَيْفَ تَحْكُمُونَ

"So is He who guides to the truth more worthy to be followed or he who guides not unless he is guided? Then what is [wrong] with you - how do you judge?"[5]

I swear to God, what you are doing bears sedition and corruption; wait a while until you see its consequences. You will suck blood instead of milk and that is when the descendants will understand what the ancestors did in the past. Be prepared for seditions. Congratulations on the drawn swords and the chaos that will pervade everyone and the tyranny of the oppressors that will rob you of everything. What you sow, the future generations will reap. [Fāṭimah (sa) refers to what happens to the Anṣār after that.]

So, grief and sorrow be upon you. Which way are you headed?! You have lost God's path of truth and mercy. Should we force God's mercy on you even

---

[4] Al-Baqarah 12.
[5] Part of Yūnus 35.

though you dislike it?"[6] And what Fāṭimah (sa) has predicted here actually took place in the Battle of Ḥarrah during Yazīd's reign.[7]

The Women of the Muhājirūn and the Anṣar reported to their husbands what they had heard from Fāṭimah (sa). So, a group of the seniors of the Muhājirūn and the Anṣar visited her to apologize and said, "O' Prior to All Women! Had Abū al-Ḥasan mentioned this matter to us before we established our allegiance and pact with Abū Bakr, we would never have abandoned him and gone in a different direction."

Fāṭimah (sa) declared, "Get away from me, for there is no excuse left after all the dishonest apologies, and there is nothing left to do after your fault [and sin]."[8]

(That is, after being negligent and forcing 'Alī (as) to stay home, after offending the Ahl al-Bayt, after Abū Bakr's envoy raised fire to burn the Prophet's daughter's house based on your allegiance... it is too late now and no excuse is acceptable. The era of oppression and destruction has begun.)

Abū Bakr and 'Umar Visiting Fāṭimah

When Fāṭimah's condition worsened and her illness intensified, Abū Bakr and 'Umar wanted to set a good record for themselves and claim that they visited Fāṭimah and eventually made peace with her and she forgave them. Therefore, they asked 'Alī (as) to seek permission from Fāṭimah (sa) so they can give her a visit and ask about her wellbeing.

Fāṭimah (sa) did not feel like it but 'Alī (as) insisted and so she said, "This house is your house and the lady (of the house) is your lady." Abū Bakr and 'Umar arrived. Fāṭimah (sa) turned her back to them and faced the wall. They

---

[6] *Bihar al-Anwar*, 43: pp. 158-159, narrated from *Ma'ānī l-'Akhbār*; *Al-Iḥtijāj*, 1: pp. 108-109; *Kashf al-Ghumma*, p. 147; *I'lam al-Nisa*, 4: p. 123; *Sharḥ Nahj al-Balāgha* by Ibn Abī l-Hadīd narrated from *al-Saqīfa* by Johari 16: pp. 233-234; *Balāghāt al-Nisā'*, p. 32 which has narrated Fāṭimah's words from *al-Saqīfa* by Johari. Of course, there are slight differences in various books.

[7] The Battle of Harrah will be hopefully discussed in detail at the end of this book.

[8] *Al-Iḥtijāj* 1:p. 109.

110

said, "We have come to ask for your forgiveness." She responded, "I have nothing to say to you unless you promise that you will testify to what I am going to say, if it is true." They agreed. Fāṭimah (sa) then stated, "Do you remember the Prophet (pbuh) saying: Fāṭimah's pleasure is God's pleasure and God gets angry when Fāṭimah gets angry?" They replied, "Yes." Fāṭimah (sa) continued, "God! Be aware that I am angry with these two! And I'm disappointed in both of them."[9]

Abū Bakr pretended to cry, like always and 'Umar rebuked him. Then they got up and left. This was the last thing the two of them did.[10]

Fāṭimah's Will and Her Overnight Burial

Fāṭimah (sa) said, "My wish for after I die is that Abū Bakr and 'Umar do not attend my funeral and pray over me and for my body to be buried during the night."[11]

'Alī (as) made sure Fāṭimah's wish came true[12] and thus buried her in their own house.[13] Afterwards, he created several graves in Baqī' Cemetery and sprinkled water on them to make them look like fresh graves.[14]

The late al-Kulaynī writes:

When Fāṭimah (sa) passed away, 'Alī (as) buried her secretly and destroyed the evidence of where her grave was. Then he turned to the Prophet's tombstone and said, "O' Prophet of God, peace be upon you from me and your daughter,

---

[9] al-Bukhārī writes in *Ṣaḥīḥ*: After the Prophet's daughter asked the caliph for her heritage and he claimed that he had heard the Prophet (pbuh) say: we don't leave heritage, she never spoke to him again as long as she lived. (*Ṣaḥīḥ al-Bukhārī*, 5: p. 177.)

[10] *Bihar al-Anwar*, 42: pp. 170-171; quoted from *Dalā'il al-Imām*, also see: *'Ilal al-Sharāyi'*, 1: pp. 178; *Al-Imāma wal-Siyāsa*, 1: p. 14; *I'lam al-Nisa*, 3: p. 1214; *Sharḥ Nahj al-Balāgha* by Ibn Abī l-Hadīd 16: p. 273.

[11] *Bihar al-Anwar*, 43: pp. 159&182-183; Also see: *Manāqib*, 1: p. 504.

[12] *Kitāb aṭ-Tabaqāt al-Kabīr*, Ibn Sa'd 8: pp. 18-19; *Ansāb al-Ashrāf*, p. 405; *Ṣaḥīḥ al-Bukhārī*, 5: p. 77.

[13] *al-Kāfī* 1: p. 461; *Manāqib*, 3: p. 365.

[14] *Bihar al-Anwar*, 43: p. 183.

who has come to you and is lying under the ground next to you... Fāṭimah's death was a strike that hurt my heart and deepened my sorrow, and scattered us sooner than expected. I take my complaint to God and I leave your daughter to you. She will soon tell you what oppressions your nation did to her after you. Ask whatever you desire from her and say whatever you want to her, so that she opens her heart to you and the pressure she has gone through pours out and God, who is the best judge, judges what went on between her and the oppressors... God knows that your daughter is buried secretly. Not many days have passed since your death and your name has not been forgotten yet but they deprived her of her rights and took away her heritage. I share the pain of my heart with you and I seek calmness in your memory. May God bless you and praise and bless Fāṭimah."[15]

In the morning, the people of Medina found out that the Prophet's daughter had been buried overnight. They thought that Fāṭimah's grave is in Baqī'.

['Umar and his companions] arrived at Baqī' and said, "We will bring women and dig up these graves to see where Fāṭimah's body is, and then we will pray on it." 'Alī (as), who was steaming, went to Baqī' and declared, "If any of you touches these graves, I will stain the ground with his blood." When they saw 'Alī (as) in such conditions, they immediately left.[16]

Aṣbagh ibn Nubāta asked 'Alī (as) why he buried Fāṭimah (sa) during the night? 'Alī (as) replied, "Because Fāṭimah (sa) was angry with those people, she did not want their presence at her funeral; and whoever conforms to them, is forbidden to pray on any of Fāṭimah's descendants."[17]

Indeed the concealment of the Prophet's daughter's grave shows her disapproval of some people, and it is clear that she wanted others to be aware of this disapproval.

---

[15] *al-Kāfi*, 1: pp. 458-459; Also see *Sharḥ Nahj al-Balāgha* by Ibn Abī l-Hadīd 10: p. 265.

[16] *Bihar al-Anwar*, 43: pp. 171-172.

[17] *Bihar al-Anwar*, 43: p. 183.

The Situation in Medina after Fāṭimah's Martyrdom and the Fulfillment of Her Prophecies

After Fāṭimah's martyrdom, the caliphate sent troops to confront those out of Medina who had not pledged allegiance to Abū Bakr, and a group of which were from apostate tribes. In those campaigns, none of the Anṣār was appointed as the leader. The government also completely consisted of people who were Qurayshite.[18]

Quraysh took precedence over the non-Quraysh in everything. In the cities they conquered, commanders of the army and the governors of the cities were all chosen from Quraysh.[19]

---

[18] To consolidate their superiority, Quraysh even forged hadīths and related them to the Prophet (pbuh). Hereby, some of them will be mentioned:

After this [the conquest of Mecca] up until the Doomsday, no Qurayshite shall be killed. (*Ṣaḥīḥ Muslim*, p. 1409; *Sunan al-Darimi*, 2: p. 198; *Musnad Aḥmad ibn Ḥanbal*, 3: p. 412 & 4: p. 213.)

Whoever offends Quraysh will be disdained by God. (*Musnad Aḥmad ibn Ḥanbal*, 1: pp. 64, 171 & 176; *Musnad al-Tayalisi*, hadīth 209.)

People are subject to Qurayshites in governing. The Muslims of this nation are subject to the Muslims of Quraysh and their infidels are subject to their own infidels. (*Ṣaḥīḥ al-Bukhārī*, 2: p. 176; *Ṣaḥīḥ Muslim*, p. 1415; *Musnad Aḥmad ibn Ḥanbal*, 1: p. 101 & 2: pp. 243, 261, 319, 395 & 433; *Musnad al-Tayalisi*, p. 313, hadīth 2380.)

The government belongs to Quraysh. Even if only two people remain on earth, it is Quraysh that must rule them. (*Ṣaḥīḥ al-Bukhārī*, 4: p.155; *Musnad Aḥmad ibn Ḥanbal*, 2: pp. 29, 93 & 128; *Ṣaḥīḥ Muslim*, p. 1452; *Musnad al-Tayalisi*, p. 264, hadīth 1956.)

Obey commands of Quraysh and do not question what they do. (*Musnad Aḥmad ibn Ḥanbal*, 4: p. 260; *Musnad al-Tayalisi*, hadīth 1185.)

[19] Of course, when Alī reached power, he broke the government monopoly among Quraysh. He divided the treasury equally among people and, just like the Prophet (pbuh), did not differentiate between Qurayshite and non-Qurayshite. He himself, similar to other Muslims, took only three dinars and gave three dinars to his slave Qambar. He also used non-Qurayshite people in his assigning positions and appointed Anṣār as governors of provinces and cities. For example, he assigned Uthmān ibn Hunaif to govern Baṣrah and his brother to govern Medina, and Qays Ibn Saʿd ibn

As a result, the Anṣār went poor and fell so behind that they could not even provide food for themselves. What we read in the biography of Imam Sajjād (as), Imam Baqir (as) and Imam Ja'far al-Ṣādiq (as) going to the house of the poor of Medina in the dark of the nights and bringing them bread and money is about poor people who were descendants of those same Anṣār.

Mu'allā ibn Khunays, one of Imam Ṣādiq's companions narrates, "I saw the Imam coming out of his house in the dark of the night carrying a sack on his shoulder. I said: O' son of the Prophet (pbuh), let me help. He said: I have to take this load myself. And so he took off. I followed him. Something dropped out of his sack. The Imam bent down and said: God, help me reach it. He found it and threw it back in the sack on his shoulder. Then he went to Saqīfa Banī Sā'ida[20] and put two loaves of bread next to each of those who were asleep."

When he was returning, Mu'allā ibn Khunays asked the Imam, "O' son of the Prophet (pbuh), do they know the worth (of Imamate)?" He said, "If they were aware of the worth, we would even share the ground salt of our houses with them; No, they do not know the worth."[21]

Imam Sajjād (as) also delivered food to houses. The people of those houses would stand at their doors awaiting the person who visited at nights to receive the food from him. After his death, when Ġusl was being performed on his body, calluses were seen on his back. Imam Baqir (as) was asked about the reason and said, "This is caused by the sacks he carried at nights."[22]

'Ubāda, and after him Mālik al-Ashtar, one to govern Egypt and the other to govern Alexandria. In return, he ousted Mu'awiyah, a Qurayshite man, from the Shām government and rejected Ṭalḥa and Zubayr's request for position. Of course, he did employ one or two Qurayshites, but he abolished the government monopoly among Quraysh. (For more detail see: *Naqsh A'emah Dar Ehya'e Din*, 14: p. 159 and on.)

[20] At the same place Anṣār had assembles to seek allegiance for Sa'd ibn 'Ubadah, later on, the poor of Anṣār would sleep. There was no one but the Anṣār in Saqīfa Banī Sā'ida.

[21] *Bihar al-Anwar*, 47: p. 20, hadīth 17.

[22] *Hilyat al-Awliya'*, 3: p. 136; *Kashf al-Ghumma*, 2: p. 289; *Manāqib*, 4: p. 154; *al-Khisal*, pp. 517-518.

114

When Imam Sajjād (as) passed away, the food delivered to the people at nights was cut off. It was then that they realized the person who brought food to their doors was Imam Sajjād (as).[23]

All these poor people were from the Anṣar. But Qurayshites possessed wealth and prestige and slaves, and lived luxurious lives. When 'Abdur-Rahman ibn 'Awf died (in 'Uthmān's caliphate era), his gold was brought so that 'Uthmān would distribute it among his heirs. There was so much gold piled up in the caliphate's assembly room that it filled the gap between the two groups of people sitting on two sides of the room to such extent that the two group could not see each other![24]

These were some of the cases which Fāṭimah (sa) had predicted at the presence of the women of the Anṣar and conditions she had told them they would be facing some day. And it even got worse. In the Battle of Ḥarrah, when Yazīd's army came to Medina and massacred its people, Yazīd gave his soldiers orders to do as they wished for three whole days.[25] The Anṣar were massacred, blood was even shed in the Prophet's mosque, all the stuff in people's houses were looted, and thousands of unmarried girls got pregnant after the incident.[26]

'Alī's Allegiance[27] after Fāṭimah's Martyrdom and its Reason

In *Ṣaḥīḥ al-Bukhārī*, Zuhrī quotes a hadith from Ā'ishah in which what went on between Fāṭimah (sa) and Abū Bakr regarding the Prophet's heritage is

---

[23] *Kashf al-Ghumma*, 2: p. 289; *Nūr al-abṣār fī Manāqib, Āl Bayt al-Nabī al-mukhtār*, p. 140; *Bihar al-Anwar*, 46: p. 88; *Manāqib*, 4: p. 154; *Kitāb aṭ-Ṭabaqāt al-Kabīr*, Ibn Sa'd 5 :p. 222; Is'af al-Raghibin printed in the margin of *Nūr al-Absār*, p. 219; *Kitāb al-Ithāf*, p. 136. Also see: *Hilyat al-Awliya'*, p. 140; *Bihar al-Anwar*, 46: p. 88; *Taḏkirat al-Khawāṣ*, p. 327.

[24] *Murūj aḏ-Ḏahab*, 2: p. 340.

[25] *Tārīkh al-Ṭabarī*, 7: p. 11; *Al-Kāmil fit-Tārīkh Ibn al-Athir*, 3: p. 47; *Al-Bidaya wa an-Nihaya*, 8: p. 220.

[26] *Al-Bidaya wa an-Nihaya*, 6: p. 234 & 8: p. 32.

[27] Allegiance is that which is voluntary and with consent, otherwise it is not allegiance, and it is only shaking hands, and in other words, it is a fake allegiance. Just as if a sale is made with will and consent, it can be considered a sale; otherwise it is oppression and usurpation. Therefore, Alī's allegiance, which took place six months later and was

discussed and at the end of that story Ā'ishah says, "Fāṭimah (sa) turned her face away from Abū Bakr and never spoke to him again, as long as she lived. She lived six months after the death of the Prophet (pbuh), and when she died, her husband 'Alī (as) prayed on her body and buried her and did not inform Abū Bakr. Fāṭimah (sa) was a source of pride and respect for 'Alī (as). As long as Fāṭimah (sa) was alive, 'Alī (as) was respected by everyone, and when she passed away, people turned away from him."

At this point, someone asked Zuhrī, "Did 'Alī (as) not pledge allegiance to Abū Bakr during these six months?"

Zuhrī answered, "No. Neither he nor any of the people of Banī Hāshim did so, until the time when 'Alī (as) pledged allegiance to Abū Bakr."[28]

Out of Medina, a group opposed to allegiance to Abū Bakr. When the news about the Prophet's death spread, some underwent apostasy and converted from Islām; who, in history, are referred to as the "apostates". The most prominent of them was Musaylimah in Yamāmah, who claimed to be a prophet. Near Yemen, forty thousand people prepared to attack Medina, and if they had, it would've destroyed Medina. That is, the case was a much bigger issue than the Battle of Khandaq, for there were ten thousand prepared soldiers in Khandaq, whereas these were forty thousand. If they had attacked and

---

out of reluctance and only for the preservation of Islām and with no consent, was only a fake allegiance and a shake of hands. This hadīth that has been narrated by Imams is also in this regard, "There is not a single one of us that does not have a rogue's allegiance on his record, except the last Imam." This means none of the allegiances have been real and rather they have just been a shake of hands and forcible.

[28] *Tārīkh al-Ṭabarī*, 2: p. 448 & in the European edition 1: p. 1825; *Ṣaḥīḥ al-Bukhārī*, part the Battle of Khaybar 3: p. 38; *Ṣaḥīḥ Muslim*, 1: p.72& 5: p. 153; *Al-Bidaya wa an-Nihaya*, 5: pp. 285-286; *al-ʿIqd al-Farīd*, 3: p. 63; *Al-Bidaya wa an-Nihaya*, 2: p. 126; *Kifāyat al-Ṭālib fī Manāqib ʿAlī ibn Abī Ṭālib*, pp. 225-226; *Sharḥ Nahj al-Balāgha* by Ibn Abī l-Hadīd 2: p. 122; *Murūj aḏ-Ḏahab*, 2: p. 414; *at-Tanbih wal-'Ishraf*, p. 250; *As-Sawayiq al-Muhriqah*, 1: p. 124; *Tārīkh al-Khamis*, 1: p. 193; *Al-Isti'ab*, 2: p. 244; *Tārīkh Abī al-Fada'*, 1: p. 156; *al-Bad' wa a-Tārīkh*, 5: p. 66; *Ansāb al-Ashrāf*, 1: p. 586; *Usd al-Ġābah*, 3: p. 222; *Tārīkh Yaʿqūbī*, 2: p. 105; *al-Ghadīr*, 3: p. 102 narrated from ibn Hazm pp. 96-97.

116

conquered Medina, there would not have been a trace left of Islām, and they would have even demolished the Prophet's tombstone.

Therefore, 'Uthmān met up with 'Alī (as) and said to him, "O' cousin[29]! As long as you do not pledge allegiance, no one will rise to fight these enemies and…" He rambled on so much until he finally took 'Alī (as) to Abū Bakr and eventually 'Alī (as) pledged allegiance to Abū Bakr. After 'Alī's allegiance to Abū Bakr, Muslims rejoiced and rose to fight against the apostates, and armies were formed everywhere.[30]

Also, in *Nahj al-Balāgha*[31] it is stated that 'Alī (as) said, "So I waited and did not pledge allegiance, although I was convinced that I, indeed, deserved Muḥammad's position more than anyone else and definitely more than those who took power after him. So I waited until God desired. Then I found out that a group of people, who have apostatized and converted from Islām, are calling out for the destruction and abolishment of God's religion and the Prophet's traditions. So I feared if I don't aid Islām and the Muslims, I would see ruination and rupture in Islām and the consequences and sufferings of these two would be much greater on me than the loss of control over your affairs; a government that is nothing more than a few days and what is gained from it vanishes, like a mirage or a cloud that is scattered. Thus, at that time, I went to Abū Bakr and pledged allegiance to him, and at that point, I revolted to destroy falsehood and to preserve God's words [Islām] as it was always superior, even if the disbelievers disapprove."

---

[29] He uses the phrase "cousin" because Alī was from Banī Hāshim and Uthmān was from Banī Umayyah and Hāshim and Umayyah were both sons of Abd Manāf.

[30] *Ansāb al-Ashrāf*, 1: p. 587.

[31] *Sharḥ Nahj al-Balāgha* by Ibn Abī l-Hadīd, Kitab ar-Rasa'il ar-Rasa'il 62: p. 130.

Chapter 8

The Situation in Islāmic Lands and Imams' Policies

The Islāmic lands had several main capitals whose governors were appointed by the caliph. Alexandria was one of them which had all the African countries (that had converted to Islām) under its control. The governor of Alexandria would appoint judges for every part of Africa, assign the governors of all cities, collect all tributes and taxes, and march to cities that had not yet been conquered and conquer them and so on.

Another one of these capitals was Kūfah. When it is said that Walīd was the governor of Kūfah, it does not mean that he only ruled Kūfah. The capital of the government of Kūfah was the city of Kūfah, but lands from Iraq to Madā'in (of those days), from Baghdād to Mosul and Kermanshah and Ray and Khorasan and to some cities in Central Asia, which was called the Islāmic World, were all ruled by him. Walīd would appoint governors for those cities, assign the leaders of the congregational Friday prayers, and send troops to the Islāmic border cities.

The capital of the government of Baṣrah was the city of Baṣrah, but ruling cities in southwestern Iran and the countries that are nowadays located around the Persian Gulf, except for Ḥijāz (present Saudi Arabia), were also under his authority. All the vast land of today's Saudi Arabia except for Mecca and Medina and Jeddah and Riyaḍ, was also governed by the ruler of Baṣrah. In addition, Baṣrah's governor ruled the sea, all the way to India. The Indian cities that were conquered would go under the ruling of Baṣrah. Baṣrah was called the Indian Port because connection to India was through this port.

Shām had two capitals; one was Damascus and the other Ḥimṣ. Shām meant today's Jordan, Lebanon, Palestine and Syria. All these lands were in the territory of those two governments. This area was called Eastern Rome. In all these lands, there were five cities where Muslim army camps were settled: Kūfah, Baṣrah, Damascus, Ḥimṣ, and Alexandria. In addition to being the capital of governments, these cities were also the center of Muslim army camps.

It is noteworthy that our Imams did not take part in any of the battles or wars that took place during the time of Abū Bakr, 'Umar and 'Uthmān. Neither Imam 'Alī (as), nor Imam Ḥassan (as) or Imam Ḥusayn (as) participated in any battles or wars. The next Imams, namely Imam Sajjād (as) all the way to Imam Ḥassan Askari (as), too, followed the same tradition and manners of their righteous predecessors.

Chapter 9

Abū Bakr's Will and 'Umar's Caliphate

Abū Bakr fell ill in Jumādā ath-Thānī in year 13 AH/ 634 CE. On his deathbed, he called for 'Uthmān to write his will. Abū Bakr said, "Write: In the name of god, the beneficent the merciful. This is Abū Bakr ibn Abī Quhāfah's will to the Muslims." After this sentence, he passed out due to the severity of his illness. 'Uthmān concluded the will as follows, "I have chosen 'Umar ibn al-Khaṭṭāb to be my successor and your caliph, and I have not abandoned you from any benevolence in this path."

At that point, Abū Bakr came round and said to 'Uthmān, "Read me what you have written." 'Uthmān read him the will. Hearing 'Uthmān's writing, Abū Bakr said, "I agree to what you have written. May God reward you by Islām and Muslims." Then he signed that same writing.[1]

In the end of this story, al-Ṭabarī writes:

'Umar was sitting in the Prophet's mosque surrounded by people, holding a stick from a palm tree. Shadeed, Abū Bakr's freed slave, showed up holding on to the paper containing the order of 'Umar's substitution. 'Umar turned to people and said, "O' people, listen to what the Prophet's successor has said and obey his command; he says he has not failed you in benevolence."[2]

In the story of the Prophet's death when he had said, "Bring me a quill and a paper. I want to write a letter (a will) for you, which secures you from going astray." It is said that the Prophet's conditions worsened and 'Umar said, "God's book is sufficient for us." Some wanted to get a quill and a paper but

---

[1] *Tārīkh al-Ṭabarī*, 1: p. 2138 & in European edition 3: p. 52.

[2] *Ibid.*

one of the attendees said, "This man has become delirious!"[3] And that person could not have been any of the Companions other than 'Umar. How 'Umar's behavior and what he said when the Holy Prophet (pbuh) was writing a will before his death and his behavior and what he says regarding Abū Bakr's will, which was written while he was unconscious, differs!

---

[3] *Ṣaḥīḥ al-Bukhārī*, part Kitabat al-Ilm min Kitab al-Ilm 1: p. 22; *Musnad Aḥmad ibn Ḥanbal*, hadīth 2992; *Kitāb aṭ-Tabaqāt al-Kabīr*, Ibn Sa'd 2: p. 244. Also see: *Ṣaḥīḥ al-Bukhārī*, 2: p. 120; *Ṣaḥīḥ Muslim*, 5: p. 76 ; *Tārīkh al-Ṭabarī*, 3: p. 193.

Chapter 10

The Government Status in 'Umar's Time

'Umar's government followed the policy of Arab ruling, and so he had prohibited non-Arabs to inhabit the capital of Islām, i.e. Medina. Only two non-Arabs were allowed to stay in Medina; Hormuzan, the former king of Susa and Shūshtar, who had converted to Islām and kept providing war plots for 'Umar to conquer the cities of Iran,[1] and Abū Lu'lu'a who was Mughīra ibn Shu'ba's slave. He was a skilled worker and had achieved mastery of painting, blacksmithing and carpentry. Mughīra asked 'Umar to allow Abū Lu'lu'a to settle in Medina and 'Umar did so.[2] Indeed, Arab prejudice was this tense and non-Arabs did not have permission to remain in the Islāmic capital.[3] 'Umar had also forbidden non-Arabs to ask Arab girls' hands in marriage, or even non-Quraysh Arabs to marry Qurayshite girls.[4] This is how 'Umar changed the Islāmic society into a class society.

In *Muwaṭṭa'* by Mālik, it is stated that 'Umar had dictated - and his dictation was considered the law of Sharia in people's opinion - that if an Arab man marries a non-Arab (Ajam) woman and had a child from her, if born in the Arab land, the child is bound to receive heritage from the father but if born in a non-Arab land, he/she does not inherit anything from the father.[5]

---

[1] For more details on these consultations, see: *Tārīkh al-Khulafā'*, pp.143-144.

[2] *Murūj aḏ-Ḏahab*, 2: p. 322.

[3] *Tārīkh al-Khulafā'*, p. 133. Although, Salmān and Bilāl also lived in Medina, ever since the Prophet lived, and were considered his companions.

[4] *Ma'alim al-Madrasatayn*, 2: p. 364.

[5] *Al-Muwaṭṭa'*, 2: p. 60.

'Umar's government was based on the perspectives and cultures of a Qurayshite-Arab authority. He would never assign a governor or army commander from non-Qurayshite Arabs. However, there was an exception here and that was that he would not appoint anyone from Banī Hāshim, who were among the families of Quraysh, to ruling. In this regard, we will narrate three events from *Tārīkh al-al-Ṭabarī* about 'Umar and Ibn 'Abbās.[6]

Ibn 'Abbās's Conversation with 'Umar

One day 'Umar said to Ibn 'Abbās, "What was the reason the Qurayshites did not let you, Banī Hāshim, govern?" Ibn 'Abbās replied, "I don't know." 'Umar said, "I do. Qurayshites hated for you to rule them." 'Abbās asked, "But Why? We would have been good for them." He said this because the Prophet (pbuh) was from Banī Hāshim. 'Umar responded, "They hated for prophecy and caliphate to be among you so you would be higher in position compared to Qurayshite. You might say it was Abū Bakr's fault. No! I swear to God, Abū Bakr did the wisest thing he could."[7]

In another narration, 'Umar says to Ibn 'Abbās, "Do you know why your people (i.e. Qurayshites) deprived you of government after Muḥammad?" Ibn 'Abbās says: It did not please me to answer 'Umar, therefore I said, "If I don't, will you inform us?" He answered, "The Qurayshites hated for prophecy and Caliphate to be among you."

We have already stated that their policy was to say, "Keep the government among the Qurayshite tribes so that it overtakes everyone." They were right. When the caliphate was expelled from the Prophet's family, it overtook Banī Taym, Banī Adi and Banī Umayya.

---

[6] Arabs were divided into two tribes: 'Adnanite and Qahtanite. Qahtanite were originally from Yemen and Anṣār were from them; 'Adnanite, which Qurayshites were from them, were originally from Mecca and Najd. 'Umar's policy was to bring Ibn 'Abbās closer to himself so that he would superior him versus Alī (as). After Alī (as), Ibn 'Abbās was the first among Qurayshites and Banī Hāshim to be a master in eloquence and oratory. (For more details, see: *Kitāb aṭ-Tabaqāt al-Kabīr*, Ibn Sa'd 2: part 2, p. 120; *Sharḥ Nahj al-Balāgha* by Ibn Abī l-Hadīd.)

[7] *Tārīkh al-Ṭabarī*, 5: p. 276 European edition.

'Umar said, "The Qurayshites chose to do so and they were actually right and successful." Ibn 'Abbās says, "I said, O' Commander of the Faithful, if you allow me and do not get angry, I will speak, otherwise I will remain silent." 'Umar said, "Go on." I said, "O' Commander of the Faithful! Regarding when you say the Qurayshites chose the Caliph and was successful, if the Qurayshites had chosen the one whom God had selected [that is, 'Alī (as)], then they would have succeeded. But regarding when you said that the Qurayshites hated for prophecy and caliphate to be among us, God has actually described people who hated it in the Qur'ān, where he says:

ذَٰلِكَ بِأَنَّهُمْ كَرِهُوا۟ مَآ أَنزَلَ ٱللَّهُ فَأَحْبَطَ أَعْمَٰلَهُمْ

"That is because they disliked what Allāh revealed [which was assigning a successor for the Prophet], so He rendered worthless their deeds."[8]

'Umar said, "I heard some things that were said to be yours but I refused to believe them, lest your dignity be lost to me." Ibn 'Abbās stated, "If I have spoken the truth, it wouldn't be logical for my dignity to be lost to you, and if I have not truly said them and you have heard lies, I can defend myself against any false accusation." 'Umar said, "I have been informed that you have said: the caliphate was taken from us through oppression and jealousy." Ibn 'Abbās responded, "The oppression forced on us is well known by any wise or ignorant person.[9] But what you said about my saying it was out of jealousy, well, Satan was jealous of Adam too and we are all Adam's descendants." 'Umar then raged, "Your hearts are far away, Banī Hāshim! They are filled with jealousy which does not leave your hearts, and resentment and deception that does not fade and will remain for good." Ibn 'Abbās said, "O' Commander of the Faithful, calm down. You said Banī Hāshim are like this. The Prophet is from Banī Hāshim and God has said:

---

[8] Muḥammad 9.

[9] With what Fāṭimah (sa) did up to her burial, the truth was not concealed from anyone in that time, when they heard of it.

إِنَّمَا يُرِيدُ اللَّهُ لِيُذْهِبَ عَنكُمُ الرِّجْسَ أَهْلَ الْبَيْتِ وَيُطَهِّرَكُمْ تَطْهِيرًا

"Allāh intends only to remove from you the impurity [of sin], O' people of the [Prophet's] household, and to purify you with [extensive] purification."[10]

'Umar declared, "Get away from me, Ibn 'Abbās." Ibn 'Abbās replied, "Will do." And he got up to leave. But 'Umar was immediately ashamed and demanded, "Ibn 'Abbās! Sit down.[11] I swear to God, I respect your right and I want and love what pleases you." Ibn 'Abbās said, "O' Commander of the Faithful, I am worthy of being honored by you and every Muslim; whoever honors me achieves happiness, and whoever dishonors me turns miserable." 'Umar could not bear it anymore, so he got up and left.[12]

Another narration is that 'Umar sent for Ibn 'Abbās and when he arrived, he was told, "The governor of Ḥimṣ was a good person and he passed away. I'm willing to send you there, but I'm afraid." Ibn 'Abbās asked, "How come?" He said, "I am afraid I die while you are still there[13] [which is an army campaign] and turn people to be against me and get them on your side [i.e. Banī Hāshim's side]. People should not be your defenders. I need to be relieved of this worry." Ibn 'Abbās responded, "It is better for you to appoint someone whose affairs you take comfort in."[14]

Indeed, 'Umar's general policy in ruling during his life was that the government should be Qurayshite-Arab and that the Banī Hāshim should be kept away from the government.[15]

---

[10] Part of al-Ahzāb 33.

[11] It would have been bad for 'Umar if Banī Hāshim heard about this incident. The Banī Hāshim were a large tribe and the government's policy was not to take issue with them.

[12] *Tārīkh al-Ṭabarī*, 5: pp. 2770-2771 European edition.

[13] Just like Kūfah, Baṣrah, Alexandria, and Damascus, Ḥimṣ had military barracks. That's why, the governor of these cities, who was also the army leader, could have mobilized the army of that area to take over the government after the caliph; as Mu'awiya did after Uthmān, against Alī (as).

[14] *Murūj aḏ-Ḏahab*, 2: pp. 321-322.

[15] In this regard, in the case of the six-member council to appoint a caliph after 'Umar was killed, Alī (as) has said, "People expect Quraysh to do something and the Quraysh

Mu'awiya in 'Umar's Time

When 'Umar went to Shām, Mu'awiyah welcomed and greeted him with the glory of a monarchal system. Seeing his magnificent party in the distance, 'Umar said, "This is the Arab's monarch." And as he came closer, he stated, "This is your status and I hear that the in-need are suspended in your palace; why are you doing so?" Mu'awiyah apologized and replied, "We are in a land where there are many enemy spies (Romans); therefore, it is necessary for us to reveal the glory of our kingdom in order to terrify them."[16]

Mu'awiyah took part in one of the Muslim wars (against the Roman) during 'Umar's caliphate. The battle led to the Muslims' victory and booty was gained. Among the booty and spoils was some silverware that he demanded to be put for sale so that the money would be distributed among everyone. People hurried to buy the silverware. One ounce of these items was traded for two dirhams (i.e. silver coins) which was usury and known a sin. 'Ubādah ibn al-Samit, a great companion of the Prophet who was in Shām, got up and shouted out, "I heard the Prophet (pbuh) forbid the trade of gold for gold and silver for silver, unless it is done in equal value, and I heard him say: Whoever pays or asks for more in such trades, has practised usury." Upon hearing this, people returned whatever they had bought.

When Mu'awiyah was informed of this incident, he disappointedly recited a sermon saying, "How is it that some narrate hadiths from the Prophet (pbuh) that we, who have seen and accompanied him, have never heard of?!" 'Utbah rose and said, "We will repeat what we have heard from the Prophet (pbuh) whether Mu'awiyah likes it or not."

Mu'awiyah expelled him from the army and he returned to Medina. 'Umar asked him why he had returned to Medina (because he had been sent to Shām to teach the Qur'ān). 'Utbah recounted Mu'awiyah's indecent actions toward

---

tribe rethinks its affairs and says: If Banī Hāshim takes the caliphate position, they will never let go of it but if the caliphate is left to any clan from Qurayshite other than Banī Hāshim, it will remain among them and they will all get a chance." (*Tārīkh al-Ṭabarī*, 5: p. 2787 European edition.)

[16] *Al-Isti'ab*, 1: p. 253; *al-Iṣābah*, 3: p. 413; *Al-Bidaya wa an-Nihaya*, 8: p. 120.

him. Then 'Umar demanded, "Go back. May God debase a land where you and people like you cannot live in! Mu'awiyah will never rule over you."[17]

'Umar's Confessions, the Council and Allegiance to 'Uthmān

In the last year 'Umar went to Hajj, 'Ammār ibn Yāsir told his friends in Minā, "Allegiance to Abū Bakr was an aberration that happened anyway; if 'Umar dies, we will pledge allegiance to 'Alī (as)."[18]

This news reached 'Umar in Minā when he was heading for Medina. On the first Friday in the Prophet's Mosque in Medina, at the end of a long, detailed sermon he said that allegiance to Abū Bakr was an aberration and God had taken away Abū Bakr's evil presence from Muslims. He continued by saying, after that, allegiance (to the caliph) should be consulted and if anyone swears allegiance to another person with no consultation, both shall be killed.[19]

When Abū Lu'lu'a stabbed 'Umar in the abdomen and water would pour out of his wound making it clear that his intestines were torn and he was going to die, he was told, "Appoint someone to replace you." He said, "If Abū 'Ubaydah ibn al-Jarāḥ was still alive, I would have chosen him; and if God questioned me on this choice, I would have said your prophet used to say that he is the trustworthy of the nation! And if Sālim, Abī Ḥudayfah's freed slave, still lived, I would undoubtedly have chosen him to be my substitute; and if God questioned me, I would have said I heard your Prophet say that Sālim loves God so much that even if he did not fear God, he would not disobey him."[20] The attendants said to 'Umar, "O' Commander of the Faithful! In any case, appoint someone as your successor." He replied, "I had in mind to elect a man to your government who would undoubtedly lead you to truth and justice [referring to

---

[17] *Ṣaḥīḥ Muslim*, 5: p. 46; *Tahzīb Ibn 'Asākir*, 5: p. 212; Also see: *Musnad Aḥmad ibn Ḥanbal*, 5: p. 319; *Sunan an-Nasa'i*, 20: p. 222.

[18] *Sharḥ Nahj al-Balāgha* by Ibn Abī l-Hadīd 2: p. 123.

[19] *Ansāb al-Ashrāf*, 1: pp. 583-584; *Sirat ibn Hisham*, 4: pp. 336-337. For more information in this field see: *Abdullah ibn Saba'* by Allamah 'Askarī 1: p. 159.

[20] Has any other companion heard these two hadīths, besides 'Umar?

'Alī (as)], but I did not want your affairs to be my responsibilities both in life and after death!"[21]

In *Ansāb al-Ashrāf*, Balādurī writes:

On the day 'Umar was injured, he called out for 'Alī (as), 'Uthmān, Ṭalḥa, Zubayr, 'Abdur-Rahman ibn 'Awf, Sa'd ibn Abī Waqqās. Then he only spoke to 'Alī (as) and 'Uthmān. He said to 'Alī (as), "O' 'Alī! Perhaps this group [the people of the council] will consider your right of kinship with the Prophet (pbuh) and that you were his son-in-law and the abundant knowledge and jurisprudence that God has bestowed on you, and hence choose you as their ruler; in that case, do not forget God!"

Then he turned to 'Uthmān and said, "O' 'Uthmān! Perhaps they will consider you being the Prophet's son-in-law and respect your elderliness [and select you as the caliph]. If you come to power, fear God and do not empower Abū Mu'ayṭ's dynasty over people."

Afterwards he ordered Ṣuhayb to come and when he showed up, 'Umar said to him, "You will perform the congregational prayer among people for three days and meanwhile this group will gather in a house and consult each other on appointing a caliph. So if they unanimously voted for one of them to be the caliphate, behead anyone who opposes!" As the group left 'Umar's side, he said, "If the people elect the bald[22] to be the caliph, he will lead them to the right path."[23]

---

[21] *al-'Iqd al-Farīd*, 4: p. 260.

[22] By using this word, 'Umar meant Alī (as).

[23] *Ansāb al-Ashrāf*, 5: p. 16. Close to this see: *Kitāb aṭ-Ṭabaqāt al-Kabīr*, Ibn Sa'd 1: p. 247. Also see: *Al-Isti'ab*, & *Muntakhab Kanz al-Ummāl*, 4: p. 249. It is worth mentioning that according to *Al-Riaz un-Nazra*, 2: p. 72, this is narrated and it is added that 'Umar said, "How good would they be if they hand over the leadership of the caliphate to that man with the long forehead [i.e. Alī (as)], for then they will see how he will lead them to the right path, even if he always carries a sword." Muḥammad ibn Ka'b said to 'Umar, "I said: You are aware of such a merit record of him [i.e. Alī (as)], so why don't you entrust him with the caliphate?" 'Umar answered, "If I am leaving people's affairs to themselves, it is because that, who was better than me [i.e. Abī Bakr], did the same."

In *Ansāb al-Ashrāf*, Balādurī quotes Waqidi saying:

'Umar asked those around him about his successor and who to choose. They said to him, "How about 'Uthmān?" He replied, "If I choose him, he will empower Abū Mu'ayṭ's dynasty [i.e. Banī Umayya] over people." They said, "How about Zubayr?" He answered, "He is a believer in the state of happiness and a disbeliever in the state of anger!" They asked, "How about Ṭalḥa?" He said, "He is an arrogant, selfish man." They said, "How about Sa'd ibn Abī Waqqās?" He replied, "His leadership of troops is flawless, but managing as little as a village is too much burden for him." They asked, "What do you say about 'Abdur-Rahman ibn 'Awf?" He answered, "It is enough for him to take care of his own family!"[24]

Elsewhere, Balādurī writes:

When 'Umar ibn al-Khaṭṭāb got injured, he ordered Ṣuhayb, 'Abdullāh ibn Jud'ān's freed slave, to go bring the leaders of the Muhājirūn and the Anṣar to assemble around him. When they showed up, he said, "I have entrusted your caliphate and government affair to the a council of you six pioneers of the Muhājirūn, whom the Prophet (pbuh) approved of at the time of his death, in order for you to elect one of yourselves to lead the rest of you and the nation." Then he named the members of the council one by one, and then he turned to Abū Ṭalḥa Zayd ibn Sahl al-Khazrajī and stated, "Choose fifty people from the Anṣar to accompany you. When I die, force these to choose one among them as the leader of the nation in three days and not longer than that." Then he told Ṣuhayb that as long as they haven't come to a decision, to pray with people.

At that time, Ṭalḥa ibn 'Ubaydullāh was not present and was actually in his house in Sorah.[25]

---

[24] *Ansāb al-Ashrāf*, 5: p. 17.

[25] Al-Sorah was the name of a mountain around Ṭa'if, but in addition to that, other places had that name too. (*Kitāb Mu'jam al-Buldān*)

'Umar declared, "If Ṭalḥa shows up during these three days, fine, otherwise do not wait for him and take the election seriously and swear allegiance to the one on whom you agree, and behead anyone who disagrees with your choice."[26]

'Umar ordered the members of the council to consult for three days to elect a caliph. If two agreed with the caliphate of one man and another two with the caliphate of another man, he demanded them to consult again and resume the consultations. But if four people agreed with one and one person disagreed, he should be subject to the votes of those four people. And if the votes were a tie of three to three, they should accept the votes of those in which 'Abdur-Rahman ibn 'Awf is, because 'Abdur-Rahman's religion and goodness are reliable and his opinions are trustworthy and acceptable to Muslims.[27]

In *Kanz al-Ummāl*, al-Muttaqi al-Hindi also narrates from Muḥammad ibn Jubayr who quotes from his father that 'Umar said, "If 'Abdur-Rahman ibn 'Awf holds one of his own hands with his other hand and gives himself a handshake as an allegiance, obey his command and pledge allegiance to him."[28]

These narrations conclude that 'Umar entrusted the ruling of the caliphate to 'Abdur-Rahman ibn 'Awf, following a specific policy, and granted him a special privilege to be used in appointing the caliph. And it shows that he had an agreement with 'Abdur-Rahman ibn 'Awf to include obedience to the manners and behavior of the two sheikhs [the two former caliphs, Abū Bakr and 'Umar] in the conditions of accepting the caliphate, and he already knew that 'Alī (as) will refrain from putting the practice of the two sheikhs in line with God's book and the Prophet's traditions, but 'Uthmān will go along with it and as a result be chosen as the caliph. Therefore, he had already issued a decision not to elect 'Alī (as).

---

[26] *Ansāb al-Ashrāf,* 5: p. 18. It is worth mentioning that Ṭalḥa came to Medina later, which means after the death of 'Umar and the establishment of the council and the allegiance to Uthmān, and eventually pledged allegiance to Uthmān. (*Ansāb al-Ashrāf,* 5: p. 20)

[27] *Ansāb al-Ashrāf,* 5: p. 19. Close to this: *al-ʿIqd al-Farīd,* 3: p. 74.

[28] *Kanz al-Ummāl,* 3: p. 160.

In addition to what has already been pointed out, the reason for this statement, is what Ibn Sa'd has narrated in his book *Kitāb aṭ-Tabaqāt al-Kabīr* quoting Sa'īd ibn al-'Āṣ al-Umawī:

Sa'īd ibn al-'Āṣ asked 'Umar to exceed the land his house was built on so he can expand it. The caliph promises him that his request would be fulfilled the next day after prayer. 'Umar kept his promise and the next morning, joined Sa'īd and...

[Sa'īd says:] The caliph drew a line on the soil using his foot and expanded the size of my house. But I said, "O' Commander of the Faithful, give me more, for I have a large number of family members, young and old." 'Umar said, "For now, this is enough for you. But keep this secret; after me, someone will take power of caliphate who will respect your kinship and meet your needs!" Sa'īd says: When 'Umar's caliphate era came to an end, 'Uthmān was assigned the caliphate in the council 'Umar had formed. From the very beginning, he fulfilled my requests in the most befitting way.[29]

It follows from this dialogue that the charter of 'Uthmān's Caliphate was signed and finalized by 'Umar during his lifetime, and the appointment of a six-member council was only a cover under which the neutrality of the caliphate in electing the next caliph would be presented valid and acceptable by the public.

Furthermore, the plan to incite some to assassinate and eliminate 'Alī (as) is another important matter that Ibn Sa'd also narrates in his book *Kitāb aṭ-Tabaqāt al-Kabīr* quoting this same Sa'īd ibn al-'Āṣ al-Umawī where he writes:

One day, 'Umar ibn al-Khaṭṭāb said to Sa'īd ibn al-'Āṣ, "Why do you turn your face away and distance yourself from me? Perhaps you think that I killed your father. I did not kill your father; your father was killed by 'Alī ibn Abī Ṭālib."[30]

Wasn't 'Umar trying to provoke Sa'īd to take revenge from the murderer of his father, 'Alī ibn Abī Ṭālib?

---

[29] *Kitāb aṭ-Tabaqāt al-Kabīr*, Ibn Sa'd 5: pp. 20-22.

[30] *Kitāb aṭ-Tabaqāt al-Kabīr*, Ibn Sa'd 5: pp. 20-22. Alī (as) had killed Sa'īd's father in the battlefield.

How 'Uthmān was Elected for Caliphate

Balādurī quotes Mikhnaf saying:

On the day of 'Umar's burial, the members of the council did nothing. According to 'Umar's former demand, Abū Ṭalḥa performed congregational prayer for people, and the next day, assembled the six in the treasury room so they can start consultation. 'Umar was buried on a Sunday, the fourth day of his assassination, and Ṣuhayb ibn Sinan prayed over his body.

When 'Abdur-Rahman observed the conversations going on among the members of the council, he said, "Look! Sa'd and I will withdraw, provided that the privilege of choosing one of the four of you is granted to me, because your discussions have taken so long and people are waiting to meet their caliph and Imam. Inhabitants of other cities, who have stayed in Medina to find out about the result, have also been kept for too long and must return to their homelands soon."

Everyone agreed to 'Abdur-Rahman ibn 'Awf's proposal, except 'Alī (as) who said, "Depends." At this point, Abū Ṭalḥa entered and 'Abdur-Rahman informed him of the procedure, his proposal and everyone's agreement minus 'Alī's. Thereby, Abū Ṭalḥa turned to 'Alī (as) and said, "O' Abū al-Ḥasan! 'Abdur-Rahman is trusted by all Muslims. Why do you oppose him? He has withdrawn himself and would never fall under the burden of sin for anyone else!" Here, 'Alī (as) appealed to 'Abdur-Rahman ibn 'Awf for an oath that he would not heed the wish of his heart, consider the truth and strive for the benevolence of the nation, and promise that kinship would not divert him from the right path. 'Abdur-Rahman agreed to all these and swore an oath. Then 'Alī (as) turned to him and said, "Now make your choice."

This event took place in the treasury room or, according to a saying, in Miswar ibn Makhrama's house.[31] Afterwards, 'Abdur-Rahman came forward

---

[31] In the book *Fatḥ al-Bārī, fī Sharḥ Ṣaḥīḥ al-Bukhārī*, 16: pp. 321 & 322 it is stated as follows: Miswar ibn Makhrama says that Abdur-Rahman came to my door and woke me to go inform the members of the council. I did so and those people gathered at the pulpit. Therefore, the place of the council was the Prophet's mosque and this is not in line with what Balādurī writes in *Ansāb al-Ashrāf*, 5: p. 21 & what Ibn Abī l-Hadīd writes

and took 'Alī's hand and said to him, "Make a covenant with God that if I pledge allegiance to you, you will not empower Abd al-Muṭṭalib's dynasty over people and swear that you will not disobey the traditions of the Prophet and the two sheikhs (i.e. Abū Bakr and 'Umar)." 'Alī (as) replied, "I will treat you, according to God's book and His Prophet's traditions, as strongly as I can."

Then 'Abdur-Rahman said to 'Uthmān, "May God bear witness to you in our favor that if you take over the government, you don't empower Banī Umayya over people and may you treat us according to God's book and His Prophet and Abū Bakr and 'Umar's traditions." 'Uthmān replied, "I will treat you according to God's book and His Prophet and Abū Bakr and 'Umar's traditions."

'Abdur-Rahman turned to 'Alī (as) again and repeated his words to him, and 'Alī (as) answered him as he had the first time. Then he pulled 'Uthmān aside and resumed his words and reheard the same favorable answer from him. For the third time, 'Abdur-Rahman made his first offer to 'Alī (as) and this time 'Alī (as) stated, "God's book and His Prophet's traditions do not need any other system or manner. You are trying your best to distance the caliphate from me." 'Abdur-Rahman ibn 'Awf ignored 'Alī's objection and turned to 'Uthmān, repeating his first words for the third time and hearing the same first answer from 'Uthmān. Later, he shook hands with 'Uthmān and pledged allegiance to him.[32]

Furthermore, narrating about the incidents of the year 23 AH/ 644 CE, al-Ṭabarī and Ibn Athir write:

When 'Abdur-Rahman pledged allegiance to 'Uthmān on the third day, 'Alī (as) said to 'Abdur-Rahman, "You gave him the world. This is not the first time that you have risen, allied against us. I swear to God, you only chose 'Uthmān

---

in *Sharḥ Nahj al-Balāgha*, 1: p. 240-241 who say: The place of the council was in the treasury room and in Miswar ibn Makhrama's house.

[32] *Tārīkh Ya'qūbī*, 1: p. 162; with a bit of difference in *Ansāb al-Ashrāf*, 5: p. 21.

for caliphate so that he would assign you the caliph after himself. It is God who destines us every day."[33]

After 'Abdur-Rahman's allegiance to 'Uthman, other members of the council also pledged allegiance to 'Uthman. 'Ali (as) who was watching the process on foot, sat down. 'Abdur-Rahman addressed him and said, "Pledge allegiance, otherwise I will cut your head off!" And on that day, no one was carrying a sword but 'Abdur-Rahman.

It is also said that 'Ali (as) left the council steamed. The other members of the council ran after him and said, "Pledge allegiance or we will fight you." Thus, he returned and pledged allegiance to 'Uthman.[34]

'Ali's Reason for Participating in 'Umar's Council

'Ali (as) knew very well that he would not be given the caliphate, but he participated in the council so as not to be told that he himself did not want the caliphate.

In *Ansab al-Ashraf*, Baladuri has written:[35]

Before the council meeting, 'Ali (as) complained to his uncle 'Abbas and stated, "The caliphate has been taken away from us for good." 'Abbas replied, "Why do you say so?" 'Ali (as) answered, "Sa'd will not oppose his cousin 'Abdur-Rahman, and 'Abdur-Rahman is 'Uthman's son-in-law; these three are allies. Even if Talha and Zubayr stay with me, because 'Umar has said that whomever 'Abdur-Rahman is with should be the caliph, there is no use."

Therefore, 'Ali (as) was aware, and if he had not participated in the council, they would not have pledged allegiance to him after 'Uthman; because the Prophet's words had vanished and 'Umar's words had remained. 'Umar had grown so great that, to them, his position was greater than that of all the prophets. (God forbid!)

---

[33] *Tarikh al-Tabari*, 3: p. 297; *Al-Kamil fit-Tarikh Ibn al-Athir*, 3: p. 73. Also see: *al-'Iqd al-Farid*, 3: p. 76.

[34] *Ansab al-Ashraf*, 5: p. 21 and so on.

[35] *Ansab al-Ashraf*, 5: p. 19.

Chapter 11

'Uthmān's Caliphate Era

Abū Sufyān's Words

On the first day after pledging allegiance to 'Uthmān for the caliphate, Abū Sufyān, who was blind at the time, entered on 'Uthmān and asked, "Is there anyone here except Banī Umayya?" People replied, "No." He said, "O' Banī Umayya! From the very first day the caliphate fell into the hands of the Taym and Adi,[1] I have been looking forward to it reaching you. Now that it has fallen into your hands, just like children who get a hang on the ball in a game, pass the caliphate on to each other and do not let it out of your team; for there is no heaven or hell!" Yes, he swore that there is nothing going on (after death)! 'Uthmān yelled at him, but Banī Umayya followed his advice.[2]

In another narration it is stated:

Abū Sufyān entered on 'Uthmān, while he was old and his eyes had lost sight. When settled, he asked, "Is there any stranger here to convey our words to others?" 'Uthmān replied, "No." Abū Sufyān said, "The issue of caliphate is a worldly matter and this government is of the type of pre-Islāmic [the Ignorance era] governments. Therefore, assign the rulers and governors of this vast Islāmic land from the Banī Umayya."[3]

It was at that time that one day, Abū Sufyān went to the grave of the great martyr of Islām, Ḥamzah, and stamped his foot on the tombstone and said: "O'

---

[1] The two clans of Abī Bakr and 'Umar.

[2] *Kitab al-Aghani,* 6: pp. 355-356; *Al-Isti'ab,* p. 690; Also see: *Kitāb al-nizā' wa-al-takhāṣum fimā bayna banī Umayyah wa-banī Hāshim,* p. 20; *Murūj aḏ-Ḏahab,* 5: pp. 165-166.

[3] *Kitab al-Aghani,* 6: p. 323. *Tahzīb Ibn 'Asākir,* 6: p. 409.

Abū 'Umārah, what we drew our swords for yesterday, has fallen into the hands of our kids today and they are playing with it."[4]

Walīd, the Governor Assigned to Kūfah by 'Uthmān

Walīd was 'Uqba ibn Abī Mu'ayṭ's[5] son. He converted to Islām on the day Mecca was conquered by the Muslims and fell into the hands of the Prophet (pbuh), leaving no other choice for the pagans and the misguided. After a while, in Medina, the Prophet (pbuh) commissioned him to collect Zakāt from the Banī al-Mustaliq tribe. Walīd traveled to their homeland but returned reporting that the people of that tribe had apostatized and refused to pay Zakāt. The reason to this false news was that a group from the Banī al-Mustaliq clan had come out to greet Walīd when they heard he was coming, so they would see the Prophet's envoy up-close and welcome him.

Walīd considered their gathering to be an evil plan and an attempt upon his life, and thus feared them. Without even meeting or talking to them, he hurried back to Medina and delivered that false report.

The Prophet (pbuh) commissioned Khālid ibn al-Walīd to investigate and report the truth by going there himself. In his report, Khālid stressed that the tribe adheres to Islām and has not apostatized in any way. At that point, the following verse was revealed about Walīd and his story, and God declared him a sinner:[6]

---

[4] *Sharḥ Nahj al-Balāgha* by Ibn Abī l-Hadīd 4: p. 51 & another edition 16: p. 136.

[5] 'Uqba ibn Abī Mu'ayṭ was one of the greatest enemies of the Prophet (pbuh), who showed great disrespect and arrogance towards him. For example, see: *Ansāb al-Ashrāf*, 1: pp. 137-138 & pp. 147-148. On the day of the Battle of Badr, he was captured while fleeing and ordered by the Prophet to be killed by Alī (as). Verses 30 to 32 of Surah al-Furqān have been revealed about him. (*Sirat ibn Hisham*, 1: p. 385 & 3: p. 25; *Imta' al-asma'*, pp. 61 & 90 under the interpretation of Surah al-Furqān in *Tafsīr al-Ṭabarī*, *Tafsīr al-Qurtubi*, *al-Kaššāf*, *Tafsīr al-Qur'ān al-Azim* by *Ibn Kathīr*; Also *al-Durr al-Manthur*, *Tafsīr al-Nīsābūrī*, *Tafsīr al-Razi* and others.)

[6] See Walīd's biography in *Kitāb aṭ-Ṭabaqāt al-Kabīr*, Ibn Sa'd, *Al-Isti'ab*, *Usd al-Ġābah*, *al-Iṣābah*, *Kanz al-Ummāl*, and the interpretation of Surah al-Hujurāt in all Tafsīr books.

يَـٰٓأَيُّهَا ٱلَّذِينَ ءَامَنُوٓاْ إِن جَآءَكُمْ فَاسِقُۢ بِنَبَإٍ فَتَبَيَّنُوٓاْ أَن تُصِيبُواْ قَوْمًۢا بِجَهَٰلَةٍ فَتُصْبِحُواْ عَلَىٰ مَا فَعَلْتُمْ نَٰدِمِينَ

"O' you who have believe! If there comes to you a disobedient one with information, investigate, lest you harm people out of ignorance and become regretful over what you have done."[7]

Now, 'Uthmān, the caliph of the Muslims, who considers himself the Prophet's successor, elects such a notorious, wicked governor for Kūfah only because of his closeness and kinship.

Walīd's ruling over Kūfah lasted for five years, during which he fought the polytheists in the regions of Azerbaijan, which were then under the ruling of Kūfah. But since his faith and beliefs were not strong enough, in that sensitive situation and against the enemy, in a moment of aberration he made a mistake that was subject to Hadd![8] The leaders of the army gathered to impose Hadd on him, but Hudayfah opposed the implementation of God's rule against Walīd, because he was the leader of the Islāmic army and was to command the army against the enemy, and therefore, he was dismissed.[9]

The Story of Walīd Drinking while he was Ruling Kūfah

In *Kitab al-Aghani*[10] and *Murūj ad-Dahab*[11] we read:

Walīd would drink all night long joined by his courtiers and personal singers. Once, when the morning Adān was recited, he went to the mosque drunk and dressed as if for a feast. He stood in the altar and prayed the Morning Prayer in four rak'ats and afterwards, said to the worshipers, "Do you want me

---

[7] al-Hujurāt 6.

[8] Walīd's aberration is not named. Although, he was famous for drinking, and once, in Uthmān's caliphate era, he was punished to Hadd by Alī (as) due to being drunk, a story which is famous. (*Ansāb al-Ashrāf*, 5: p. 35; *Kitab al-Aghani*, 4: p. 177; *Murūj ad-Dahab*, 1: p. 449) However, we do not know whether he was drunk or committed any other debauchery in Azerbaijan.

[9] *Ansāb al-Ashrāf*, 5: p. 31.

[10] *Kitab al-Aghani*, 4: pp. 176-177.

[11] *Murūj ad-Dahab*, 2: p. 335.

to add a few more rak'ats to the Morning Prayer?!" Then suddenly, he vomited and threw up whatever he had drunk in the altar of the mosque.

'Attāb Thaqafi, who was among the worshipers in the front row and exactly behind Walīd, yelled at him saying, "May God curse you! What the hell is going on with you? I swear to God that I am not baffled by anyone but the caliph of the Muslims, who has assigned you to be our governor and headman." The people in the Mosque started throwing pebbles at Walīd. Walīd, the caliph's brother and his governor in Kūfah, got frustrated and staggered back to his palace, uttering these verses to him, "I will never quit drinking and no way will I resist beautiful maids and deprive myself of their pleasure. Instead I will drink so vastly until my brain saturates with it and then I will wander among people drunk." People said sadly, "Let's go warn the caliph ('Uthmān)." [Needless to say that] the man who went to Medina and reported this story was beaten by 'Uthmān.[12]

On another occasion, four men dropped in on Walīd at night and snatched his ring while he was drinking.[13] Walīd did not notice because he was drunk. They brought the ring to 'Uthmān. 'Uthmān asked, "How do you know that Walīd drinks?" They answered, "This is the same thing we used to drink in the Ignorance era. He drinks and here is his ring." 'Uthmān, who was now furious, threatened the witnesses and the complainants and swore that he would punish them. Then he hit them on the chest and pushed them away.

Those complainants, who had been beaten and hit by 'Uthmān, appealed to 'Alī (as) and asked him for a solution. 'Alī (as) went to 'Uthmān and defended their rights and protested saying, "Do you neglect God's limits and beat the witnesses who object your brother? Are you trying to change God's rules?"[14]

––––––––––––––––––––

[12] *Kitab al-Aghani*, 4: p. 178.

[13] These four men were: Abū Zaynab, Jundab ibn Zuhayr, Abū Habiba al-Ġaffārī, al-Ṣa'b ibn Juthama, and the rock on one's ring was his stamp and signature at that time, with which he signed his letters.

[14] *Murūj ad-Dahab*, 2: p. 336.

Umm al-Mu'minin Ā'ishah, to whom the witnesses had appealed, called out to 'Uthmān saying, "Have you violated the Shari'a limits and insulted the witnesses?"[15]

That group had taken sanctuary in Ā'ishah's house in fear of 'Uthmān's punishment. In the morning, 'Uthmān heard Ā'ishah in her room burst forth into invective. He lost it and cried out, "Did the rebellious, wicked Iraqis have no shelter other than Ā'ishah's house?" Upon hearing 'Uthmān's insulting and unforgivable offenses, Ā'ishah took the Prophet's shoe, raised it and loudly declared, "Isn't it too soon for you to bypass the Prophet's traditions and manners, he who this shoe belonged to?!" These words quickly spread about and were heard by everyone in the mosque. Some said, "Good for Ā'ishah." Others believed, "What is with women interfering in social affairs?" Arguments heated up to the point where the two groups started throwing rocks at each other and beating one another with their shoes.[16]

This was the first encounter between Muslims after the Prophet (pbuh).[17]

After this incident, Ṭalḥa and Zubayr met up with 'Uthmān and rebuked him and said, "We initially forbade you to appoint Walīd to any of the affairs of the Muslims, but you did not take our word for it and did not comply. It is still not too late. Now that some have witnessed his drinking and drunkenness, it is in your best interest to remove him from his position."

'Alī (as) also said to him: "Dismiss Walīd and also impose the Shari'a limits on him, if the witnesses testify before him."[18]

---

15 *Ansāb al-Ashrāf,* 5: p. 34.

16 *Kitab al-Aghani,* 4: p. 178.

17 *Ansāb al-Ashrāf,* 5: p. 33.

18 *Ibid.,* 5: p. 35.

Dismissing Walīd

'Uthmān was forced to remove Walīd ibn 'Uqba from the governorship of Kūfah and summon him to Medina and appoint Sa'īd ibn al-'Āṣ to govern Kūfah ordering him to send Walīd to Medina.

When Sa'īd entered Kūfah, he did not climb up the pulpit and instead said, "The pulpit of Kūfah's mosque is impure and it must be washed; the palace too must be hosed with water." A group of Umayyad leaders, who had entered Kūfah with Sa'īd, asked him to refrain from washing the pulpit and told him that even if anyone else had decided to do so, it was up to him to prevent it, for this would bring eternal disgrace to Walīd. Sa'īd rejected their request and had the pulpit and the palace hosed with water and told Walīd to go to Medina.

Upon Walīd's arrival and going to 'Uthmān, the witnesses testified that he drinks. 'Uthmān was forced to impose Hadd on him. Accordingly, he covered him with a thick cloak so that the whip would not hurt. Whoever volunteered to whip Walīd would be begged by him not to do so. He would say, "Consider our kinship and do not ruin it by beating me. Beware not to provoke the Commander of the Faithful, 'Uthmān." And that volunteer would throw the whip aside and leave, for he was not willing to upset 'Uthmān.

When 'Alī (as) saw what was going on, he picked the whip up himself, though his son, Ḥusayn was also there.[19] Walīd entreated him saying, "I beg you by God's name and the mercy of our kinship not to hit me!" 'Alī (as) said, "O' Walīd, be quiet! The reason to Banī Isrā'īl's annihilation was that they showed indifference towards God's rules."[20]

Walīd ran around trying to escape from 'Alī (as) but 'Alī (as) caught him and knocked him to the ground. 'Uthmān protested. 'Alī (as) stated, "He has committed a sin. He has drunk and would not allow God's rule of Hadd to be imposed on him."[21]

---

[19] *Ansāb al-Ashrāf*, 5: p. 35.

[20] *Kitab al-Aghani*, 4: p. 177.

[21] *Murūj aḏ-Ḏahab*, 1: p. 449.

142

Then, instead of eighty hits, 'Alī (as) used a double-strip whip and hit him forty times. He was careful not to raise his arm so high that his armpit would be seen,[22] that is, he did not hit hard.

At that time, it was customary to shave the head of a person who has been beaten for Hadd. So 'Uthmān was told, "Shave Walīd's head." But he refused to do so.[23] After that, 'Uthmān commissioned Walīd to be in charge of collecting Zakāt from the two tribes of Banī Kalb and Banī al-Qayn![24]

The Situation in Kūfah during 'Uthmān's Caliphate Era

The Muslims' situation during 'Uthmān caliphate era was very chaotic. 'Uthmān elected his brother[25] Walīd to govern Kūfah. The territory of Kūfah ruled as far as Madā'in, the imperial capital of Iran, to Kermanshah, Ray, Central Iran, that is, Qom and Kashan, and eastern Iran all the way to the countries of Central Asia. Kūfah was one of the five military capitals of Islām. 'Uthmān had handed over the ruling of all these countries to Walīd!

'Uthmān had to remove Sa'd ibn Abī Waqqās from Kūfah's governship. Sa'd was one of the earliest Companions of Islām and one of the first emigrants to Medina. During the reign of the second caliph, it was decided for him to establish an army campaign in that area. Sa'd ibn Abī Waqqās built Kūfah and since then, according to 'Umar's orders, became Kūfah's governor. In addition to that, the second caliph placed Sa'd in the six-member council as one of the candidates to be the next caliph. That is why Sa'd received a huge amount of respect from Muslims. He had well-spirited morals and he treated people well, therefore people of Kūfah were pleased with him and satisfied with his work.

When Walīd arrived at Kūfah and brought along orders of Sa'd's dismissal, Sa'd asked him dumbfounded, "I do not know if you have gotten smart and

---

[22] *Ansāb al-Ashrāf*, 5: p. 35.

[23] *Ibid.*, 5: p. 35.

[24] *Tārīkh Ya'qūbī*, 2: p. 142.

[25] Uthmān and Walīd were half-brothers having the same mother who was Arwa bint Kurayz ibn Rabi'ah

tactful after us or if we have turned gullible?" [Because the Holy Qur'ān introduces Walīd as a transgressor, and says:

$$\text{إِن جَآءَكُمْ فَاسِقٌ بِنَبَإٍ فَتَبَيَّنُوٓاْ}$$

"If there comes to you a disobedient one with information, investigate."[26]

Walīd said, "Don't be upset. This is how government works; some have it for lunch and others for dinner." Sa'd replied, "I swear to God, I see that you will turn this governorship over the Muslims into a kingdom." Then he left Kūfah and returned to Medina.[27]

Ibn Mas'ud's Story

Ibn Mas'ud[28] was the first of the Prophet's Companions to recite the Qur'ān out loud before the Qurayshite polytheists in the house of God. [When he did so,] they asked each other, "What is he reading?" He answered, "The words Muḥammad has brought." They assaulted and beat him. He went to the Prophet (pbuh) and the Prophet (pbuh) told him to go back and keep reciting the Qur'ān.

He was one of the Muslims who immigrated to Abyssinia accompanying Ja'far ibn Abī Talib and also took part in the Battle of Badr. The second caliph sent Ibn Mas'ud to Kūfah for "Iqra'"[29], namely, the teaching and interpretation of the Qur'ān and the teaching of Islāmic rules, as well as to be in charge of Kūfah's treasury. He was the trustee of the treasury and had the key to it. When 'Umar sent him to Kūfah, he wrote to the people there, "I appraised you superior to myself, hence sent you Ibn Mas'ud."[30]

---

[26] Part of al-Hujurāt 6.

[27] *Ansāb al-Ashrāf,* 5: pp. 29 & 31; *Al-Isti'ab,* 2: p. 604.

[28] Abū 'Abdur-Rahman 'Abdullāh ibn Mas'ud ibn Ġafil ibn Habīb al- Huḏallī; his mother Umm 'Abdud Huḏallī and his father was an allegiant to Banī Zuhrah.

[29] Iqra' (recitation), at that time, meant teaching the Qur'ān plus its interpretation and its Islāmic rules. (For more information see: *Qur'ān al-Karīm wa-Riwāyāt al-Madrasatayn,* 1: p. 287 and so on)

[30] *Usd al-Ġābah,* 3: p. 258.

Upon becoming the governor of Kūfah, Walīd took a loan of 100,000 dirhams from the treasury. All the caliphs, except 'Alī (as), did this and the trustee of the treasury would take a receipt from them in exchange. When the time came to repay the loan, Ibn Mas'ud asked Walīd for the money. Walīd reported the matter to 'Uthmān and 'Uthmān wrote to Ibn Mas'ud, "You are our treasurer; leave Walīd alone." Ibn Mas'ud said, "I thought I was the treasurer of the Muslims and the treasury belonged to the Muslims! If the treasury is yours, I will not be your treasurer." And then, dropped the keys.[31]

After that, Ibn Mas'ud remained in Kūfah and began to expose 'Uthmān. Walīd wrote to 'Uthmān that Ibn Mas'ud was defaming them. 'Uthmān ordered him to send Ibn Mas'ud to Medina. When Walīd ordered Ibn Mas'ud to leave Kūfah, people gathered around him and pleaded for him to stay in Kūfah saying, "We will defend you." Ibn Mas'ud stated, "There will be seditions after this and I do not want to be the first to start them." The people of Kūfah saw him off. He advised them to be pious and recite the Qur'ān, and the people prayed for him and said, "You educated our illiterates, you stabilized our elites, and you taught us the Qur'ān."

When Ibn Mas'ud arrived in Medina, he entered the Prophet's Mosque as 'Uthmān was preaching a sermon on the pulpit. There were also Companions in the mosque. When 'Uthmān's eye caught Ibn Mas'ud, he announced, "Just now, a disgusting, worthless insect entered; if he touches your food, you would vomit." In response to 'Uthmān's diatribe, Ibn Mas'ud said, "No, 'Uthmān! I am not like that. In fact, I am one of the Prophet's Companions who had the honor of participating in the Battle of Badr and the Rezvan Allegiance."[32]

Ā'ishah also asserted, "Hey! 'Uthmān! Are you talking like this to Ibn Mas'ud, the Prophet's companion and mate?!" In response to Ā'ishah, 'Uthmān shouted, "Hush!" And then, ordered for Ibn Mas'ud to be expelled from the mosque. Following the orders of the Caliph, Ibn Mas'ud was expelled from the

---

[31] *Ansāb al-Ashrāf*, 5: p. 36.

[32] In this statement, he is actually insulting Uthmān because Uthmān had neither taken part in the Battle of Badr nor been a member of the Bay'ah (Allegiance) of Rizwan.

Prophet's mosque in an offensive, insulting manner. Just then, Yaḥmūm, 'Uthmān's slave, kneeled, put his head between Ibn Mas'ud's legs, lifted him up and dropped him so hard his ribs fractured. 'Alī (as), witnessing the incident, turned to 'Uthmān and said, "O' 'Uthmān! Are you treating the Prophet's Companions like this only based on Walīd's report?!" Then, he took Ibn Mas'ud to his house and took care of him until he recovered and returned to his house.

After that, Ibn Mas'ud settled in Medina and 'Uthmān did not allow him to leave town. When he recovered from that injury and asked for permission to take part in Jihād, fighting against the Romans, once again 'Uthmān did not grant him permission. He also cut Ibn Mas'ud's pension.

Thus, Ibn Mas'ud could not leave Medina as long as he lived and was actually supervised, until he died two years before 'Uthmān was killed. Ibn Mas'ud lived in Medina for three years.

When fell ill, 'Uthmān visited him and asked, "What is bothering you?" Ibn Mas'ud answered, "My sins."

"What do you need?"

"The mercy and forgiveness of my Lord."

"Do you want me to call a doctor to your bedside?"

"It's the doctor who has made me ill."

"Do you want me to order for your salary and pension to be paid?[33] (It had been two years that his salary was cut)."[34]

---

[33] In the time of the Prophet (pbuh) and Abī Bakr, what was gained from the expeditions, tributes and battles, was not kept but distributed the very same day. But 'Umar set an annual stipend; five thousand dirhams for those who participated in the Battle of Badr, four thousand dirhams for those who fought in the Battle of Uhud up to the Ṣalaḥ Al-Hudaybiyyah, three thousand dirhams for those who were part of any battle from Ṣalaḥ Al-Hudaybiyyah until the death of the Prophet (pbuh), and for those who had taken part in any battle after the death of the Prophet (pbuh), he had assigned from two thousand dirhams to two hundred dirhams annually. (*Kitāb al-Futūḥ al-Buldān*, pp. 549 & 550-565; *Sharḥ Nahj al-Balāgha* by Ibn Abī l-Hadīd 3: p. 154. Also see: *Tārīkh Ya'qūbī*, 2: p. 153; *Tārīkh al-Ṭabarī*, 5: p. 33 & 2: pp. 22-23.)

[34] *Al-Bidaya wa an-Nihaya*, 7: p. 163; *Tārīkh Ya'qūbī*, 2: p. 170.

"You did not pay it when I needed it. You want to pay it now that I have no use for it?!"

"It will remain for your heirs."

"God will bless my heir with what they need."

"Ask God to forgive me (for what I have done to you)."

"I will ask God to redeem my rights."

Ibn Mas'ud pleaded that 'Ammār ibn Yāsir pray over his body and for 'Uthmān not to attend his funeral. His wish was granted and he was buried in the Baqī' Cemetery without 'Uthmān knowing about it. When 'Uthmān heard of Ibn Mas'ud's death and his burial, he steamed and angrily said, "Did you do this without informing me?" 'Ammār replied, "He, himself had wanted for you not pray over his body."

In reference to this condition, 'Abdullāh ibn Zubayr composed this verse:[35]

"You praise me and cry for me after my death, whereas you did not pay me what I deserved while I was alive."

This was part of Ibn Mas'ud's story of misery during the reign of Walīd ibn 'Uqba. This was not the only outcome of Walīd's government. During his ruling in Kūfah, lots of seditions and subversions took place, e.g. how he treated Abū Zubayd Naṣrānī, the Christian poet and the Jewish magician.

Walīd Getting Drunk with Abū Zubayd Naṣrānī

Walīd would drink publically. He would hang out with his friend and courtier Abū Zubayd Naṣrānī and they would drink together. Walīd had gifted this friend of his with Aqīl ibn Abī Ṭālib's house, which was close to the door of Kūfah's mosque. Abū Zubayd would leave his house and go to the governor's house, where they would spend the night drinking together. The door to the governor's house opened in the mosque. The Christian drunk staggered through the mosque when leaving.

---

[35] The story told about Ibn Mas'ud in this part is based on *Ansāb al-Ashrāf*, 5: p. 36; and in some cases *Kitāb aṭ-Ṭabaqāt al-Kabīr*, Ibn Sa'd 3: pp. 150-161; *Al-Isti'ab*, 1: 361; *Usd al-Ġābah*, 3: p. 384, biography no. 3177; *Tārīkh Ya'qūbī*, 2: p. 170; Also see: *Tārīkh al-Khamis*, 2: p. 268; *Sharḥ Nahj al-Balāgha* by Ibn Abī l-Hadīd 1: pp. 236-237.

Walīd had also given this alcoholic Christian farm lands named "Red Palaces", located near Kūfah. In return, Abū Zubayd reciprocated by lauding him in his poem.[36]

In *Ansāb al-Ashrāf*, Balādurī writes:[37]

Walīd had set a stipend from the Muslim treasury for Abū Zubayd to buy alcoholic drinks and pork on a monthly basis. Walīd was then the governor of the Muslims. Abū Bakr and 'Umar hadn't done any such things during their caliphate eras, thereby, Muslims got very upset. Inevitably, Walīd crunched up the cost of the drinks and pork and added the amount to Abū Zubayd's monthly salary so it would be him buying them and not the Muslims paying for it.

Jundab al-Khayr's Story

Walīd was informed that a Jewish man named Zurārah, who had mastery in all kinds of magic, lived in a village near the Babylon Bridge. He demanded the man be brought to Kūfah so he can watch his magic shows up-close. The magician was brought to Walīd. Walīd ordered him to perform his magic shows in Kūfah's mosque.

In one of his shows, in the dark of the night, he showed everyone a large elephant sitting on a horse. In another he himself turned into a camel walking on a rope. In the next, he showed them a donkey with himself crawling into its mouth and crawling out of its anus. In the end, he called one of the spectators up and recklessly beheaded him with a sword! But then, the dead man rose to his feet unscathed before the astonished audience.

In Kūfah, there was a person named Jundab ibn Ka'b al-Azadi who was known for staying up all night worshiping. When Jundab saw this, he went to the market where they made and sold swords, borrowed a sword, came back and killed the magician with it and declared, "Let's see you revive yourself if you can!"

Walīd was very disappointed and demanded Jundab be killed taking revenge for Zurārah, the Jewish victim. But Jundab's relatives from the Azad

---

[36] *Kitab al-Aghani*, 4: p. 181.

[37] *Ansāb al-Ashrāf*, 5: pp. 29 & 31.

tribe rose to his defense and prevented him from being killed. Having no other choice, Walīd resorted to trickery and imprisoned Jundab in order to kill him covertly. In prison, the jailer saw him praying and worshiping all night long so he did not want the blood of such an ascetic, faithful man on his hands. Therefore, he suggested leaving the prison door unlocked for him to escape. Jundab said, "If I do so, Walīd will not leave you alone and will definitely kill you." The jailer replied, "Giving my life for the sake of God and the rescue and salvation of one of his saints is nothing."

When Jundab's escape was reported to Walīd, he ordered the jailer to be beheaded. Jundab secretly left Kūfah and reached Medina, where he remained until 'Alī (as) spoke to 'Uthmān about him and interceded for him. 'Uthmān agreed and wrote a letter to Walīd not to hurt Jundab, and thus Jundab returned to Kūfah.[38]

Such was Walīd's story and his ruling in Kūfah. And now, the story of another governor related to the caliph.

'Abdullāh ibn Sa'd ibn Abī al-Sarḥ's Story

'Abdullāh was 'Uthmān's foster brother who converted to Islām before the conquest of Mecca and immigrated to Medina. He was also one of the Prophet's writers, but after a while, he apostatized and returned to Mecca and said to the Qurayshites: "Muḥammad was obedient to my will and desire. He would say: Write "Azizun Hakim" in the verse of the Qur'ān. But I would say: Can I write "Alimun Hakim"? And he would reply: No problem. They are both good!" Therefore, God revealed this verse about him:

وَمَنْ أَظْلَمُ مِمَّنِ ٱفْتَرَىٰ عَلَى ٱللَّهِ كَذِبًا أَوْ قَالَ أُوحِيَ إِلَيَّ وَلَمْ يُوحَ إِلَيْهِ شَيْءٌ وَمَن قَالَ سَأُنزِلُ مِثْلَ مَا أَنزَلَ ٱللَّهُ وَلَوْ تَرَىٰ إِذِ ٱلظَّالِمُونَ فِي غَمَرَٰتِ ٱلْمَوْتِ وَٱلْمَلَـٰئِكَةُ بَاسِطُوٓاْ أَيْدِيهِمْ أَخْرِجُوٓاْ أَنفُسَكُمُ ٱلْيَوْمَ تُجْزَوْنَ عَذَابَ ٱلْهُونِ بِمَا كُنتُمْ تَقُولُونَ عَلَى ٱللَّهِ غَيْرَ ٱلْحَقِّ وَكُنتُمْ عَنْ ءَايَٰتِهِ تَسْتَكْبِرُونَ

"And who is more unjust than one who invents a lie about Allāh or says: It has been inspired to me; while nothing has been inspired to him, and one who says: I will reveal [something] like what Allāh revealed. And if you could but

---

[38] *Ansāb al-Ashrāf,* 5: pp. 29 & 31. Also see: *Kitab al-Aghani,* 4: p. 183.

see when the wrongdoers are in the overwhelming pangs of death while the angels extend their hands [saying]: Discharge your souls! Today you will be awarded the punishment of [extreme] humiliation for what you used to say against Allāh other than the truth and [that] you were, toward His verses, being arrogant."[39]

When Mecca was conquered by the Muslims, the Prophet (pbuh) issued a general amnesty for the people of Mecca, but ordered for 'Abdullāh to be killed, even though he was clinging to the drapes covering Ka'bah. 'Abdullāh feared for his life and took sanctuary in 'Uthmān. 'Uthmān hid him for a while and then brought him to the Prophet (pbuh) and sought forgiveness for him. The Prophet (pbuh) remained silent for a long while and did not raise his head, until he finally agreed. When 'Uthmān left, the Prophet (pbuh) turned to those who were in his company and said, "I remained silent to create a chance so one of you would get up and behead him." In response, they said, "We wish you had signaled us in some way giving us a hint." The Prophet (pbuh) replied, "It is inappropriate for a prophet to signal or wink."

When 'Uthmān became the caliph, based on their brotherhood, he appointed such a person to the government of Egypt in year 25 AH/ 646 CE,[40] and dismissed 'Amr ibn al-'Āṣ, who was the ruler there.[41]

'Abdullāh conquered parts of Africa and 'Uthmān awarded him with one fifth of the war spoils.[42]

---

[39] al-An'ām 93. See the interpretation in *Tārīkh al-Ṭabarī*.

[40] Egypt of that time means all Africa.

[41] It is true that Amr ibn al-'Āṣ is known as a bad person to us, but he was the conqueror of Egypt. He was respected by people and he had not yet done what he did during Mu'awiyah's time.

[42] *Al-Isti'ab*, 2: pp. 367-370; *al-Iṣābah*, 2: pp. 309-310 & 1: pp. 11-12; *Usd al-Ġābah*, 3: pp. 173-174; *Ansāb al-Ashrāf*, 5: p. 49; *al-Mustadrak*, 3: p. 100; and the Tafsīr books including *Tafsīr al-Qurtubi* under the verse no. 93 Surah al-An'ām; *Sharḥ Nahj al-Balāgha* by Ibn Abī l-Hadīd 1: p. 68.

150

The Story of Ḥakam ibn Abī al-'Āṣ, the Caliph's Uncle

'Uthmān had made a throne for the caliph and only allowed four people to sit next to him on the throne; 'Abbās, the Prophet's uncle, Abū Sufyān, Ḥakam ibn Abī al-'Āṣ, his uncle, and Walīd ibn 'Uqba. Ḥakam ibn Abī al-'Āṣ was known for his hypocrisy in the time of the Prophet (pbuh).

In Medina, he would walk behind the Prophet (pbuh) and mock him. He would shake his arms, his head, stick out his tongue, and role his eyes. Once the Prophet (pbuh) turned around and said to him, "Stay like this." For the rest of his life, Ḥakam remained that way, walking around shaking his arms and legs and rolling his eyes.

One day, the Prophet (pbuh) was sitting with 'Alī (as), in one of his houses. Ḥakam was secretly looking through the peephole and eavesdropping on their conversation. The Prophet (pbuh) told 'Alī (as), "Go bring him." 'Alī (as) went out and took his ear as if a goat's and dragged him inside. There, the Prophet (pbuh) cursed him[43] and exiled him to Ṭa'if.

The verse:

$$وَٱلشَّجَرَةَ ٱلْمَلْعُونَةَ فِي ٱلْقُرْءَانِ$$

"As was the accursed tree [mentioned] in the Qur'ān."[44] is either about Ḥakam ibn Abī al-'Āṣ ibn Umayya and his family[45] or all the Umayyad.[46] In the time of the Prophet (pbuh), 'Uthmān had asked permission for Ḥakam and his family to be allowed to return to Medina and the Prophet (pbuh) had not agreed. During the caliphate of Abū Bakr, 'Uthmān made the same request, but Abū Bakr declined. During 'Umar's time, 'Uthmān went to 'Umar and asked him to allow Ḥakam and his family to come back, but 'Umar did not accept. When 'Uthmān himself became the caliph, he returned him to Medina.[47] Ḥakam

---

[43] *Ansāb al-Ashrāf,* 5: pp. 27&225.

[44] Part of al-Isrā' 60.

[45] *al-Durr al-Manthur,* 4: p. 191; *al-Mustadrak,* 4: pp. 479-481.

[46] *al-Durr al-Manthur,* 4: p. 191.

[47] *Ansāb al-Ashrāf,* 5: p. 27.

entered 'Uthmān's house wearing a worn, threadbare outfit, holding on to the ear of a goat that was his only possession. But when he left 'Uthmān's house, he was dressed in fur.[48] 'Uthmān would seat him next to himself on the throne of the caliphate. One day, Ḥakam walk in on 'Uthmān. The caliph pushed Walīd away and seated his uncle next to himself. When Ḥakam left, Walīd said to 'Uthmān, "Some poem verses just came to my mind. I want to recite them to you." 'Uthmān said, "Go on." Walīd composed:

"When I saw that a man's uncle is so close to him and has such respect that his brother does not, unlike the past, I wished for your two sons, Khālid and 'Amr, to grow up and call me uncle on the Doomsday."

'Uthmān took pity on Walīd and in compensation for his brother's broken heart, said to him, "I will make you the governor of Kūfah."[49] Thus, Walīd, who was condemned in the Qur'ān, became the governor of the Muslims.

The Story of Sa'īd ibn Ḥakam ibn Abī al-'Āṣ and Mālik al-Ashtar

After removing Walīd from Kūfah following the story of his drinking, as his replacement, 'Uthmān appointed Sa'īd ibn al-'Āṣ as the governor of Kūfah, and ordered him to treat the people well. When Sa'īd arrived at Kūfah, he had the pulpit and the palace washed,[50] and unlike Walīd, who was a drinker and hung out with the alcoholic Christian man, chose to spend his spare time and night gatherings with the "Qurrā"[51] including Mālik al-Ashtar, Adi ibn Ḥatim a'ṭ-Ṭā'iyy, and about fourteen seniors and headmen of the tribes of Kūfah. In addition to being one of the Qurrā of Kūfah, they were also headmen of the clans.

---

[48] *Tārīkh Ya'qūbī*, 2: p. 164.

[49] *Kitab al-Aghani*, 14: p. 177.

[50] *Tārīkh al-Ṭabarī*, 5: p. 188 & in the European edition 1: p. 2951.

[51] At that time, Qurrā were those who were scholars of the interpretation of the Qur'ān and were in fact Muslim scholars.

One day, Sa'īd's constable said, "I wish these Iraqi lands[52] belonged to the governor and you had better farms and gardens." Mālik al-Ashtar commented, "If you are wishing something for the governor, wish him obtaining something better than our farms and gardens; do not wish him our properties and leave them for us." The man replied, "What harm did this wish do to you that resulted in you scowling like this? I swear to God, if he (Sa'īd ibn al-'Āṣ) wills and demands, he can take over all these farms and gardens." Mālik al-Ashtar said, "By God if he intends to take them, he won't be able to do so."

Sa'īd got very angry with what Mālik al-Ashtar said and turned to the audience and declared, "The fields and gardens of Iraq belong to the Qurayshite. [By Qurayshite he meant the Umayyad seniors and the tribes of Taym and Adi and others like them who were in Mecca, and not the Anṣār who were originally from Yemen and Mālik al-Ashtar and most of the people of Kūfah were from those tribes].

In response to him Mālik al-Ashtar said, "Do you want to take what we have earned from battles and what God has blessed us with, for yourself and your relatives? I swear to God, if anyone is coveting the lands and farms of these areas, they will be beaten so hard that they would be frightened and contemptible." Following this, he tried to attack the constable but was stopped by others.

Sa'īd ibn al-'Āṣ wrote to 'Uthmān, "I am not the ruler of Kūfah, while Mālik al-Ashtar and his companions are all around. They are called the Qurrā, but in fact they are fools." 'Uthmān wrote back, "Exile them."

Sa'īd, in a letter, wrote to Mālik al-Ashtar, "There is something in your heart that if you say out loud, you will deserve to be killed. Go to Shām." And he sent them to Shām.

Mālik al-Ashtar along with the other Qurrā of Kūfah went to Shām. Mu'awiyah honored them [at first]. After a while, a heated conversation arose

---

[52] The term used refers to Iraqi villages and farms that were conquered during 'Umar's lifetime and were abundant of trees and crops so much that they looked black. This area started in Mosul and ended in Ābādān, and from Qādisiyeh to Hulwan. (*Kitāb Mu'jam al-Buldān*)

between Mālik al-Ashtar and Mu'awiyah. Mu'awiyah said, "If all human beings were descendants of Abū Sufyān, they would all be wise and brilliant." Mālik al-Ashtar replied, "Adam was better than Abū Sufyān, however, Adam's descendants didn't turn out like that."

Following that conversation, Mu'awiyah imprisoned Mālik al-Ashtar. Later, there was another conversation between Mu'awiyah and 'Amr ibn Zurārah. As a result, he imprisoned all of the Qurrā. 'Amr apologized to Mu'awiyah and Mu'awiyah forgave him and released everyone from prison.

The people in Shām knew Islām from what they had seen from Mu'awiyah's life. They had not seen the Prophet's life or the Ahl al-Bayt or the Prophet's Companions; therefore, their lives did not differ much from that before Islām. Mu'awiyah's governorship was similar to that of the Roman emperor who ruled Shām before Mu'awiyah. Whereas, the Prophet's Companions, such as Abū Darr and 'Ubādah ibn al-Samit, and besides these two, the followers and the Qurrā who lived in Kūfah, would spend time with people and preach about the Prophet's manners and traditions.

Mu'awiyah wrote to 'Uthmān that, "With them in Shām, the people in Shām will be misguided. They teach people things they are not familiar with and this will corrupt the people of Shām!" 'Uthmān replied that he should send them to Ḥimṣ. And Mu'awiyah sent them to Ḥimṣ.[53]

Khālid ibn al-Walīd's son ruled Ḥimṣ. He would mount a horse and have them follow him on foot and he would say, "I will show you that you cannot do to me what you did to Sa'īd and Mu'awiyah!" After harassing them violently, he said to them, "O' sons of Satan!" And they eventually bowed their heads and expressed regret. Thus, he sent them back to Kūfah.[54]

---

[53] *Ansāb al-Ashrāf,* 5: pp. 39-43. What we have written here is just a summary.

[54] *Tārīkh al-Ṭabarī,* 1: p. 2914 the European edition; *Sharḥ Nahj al-Balāgha* by Ibn Abī l-Hadīd 1: p. 160 & 2: p. 134.

Apart from them, other seniors of Kūfah were also dissatisfied with their governors. In fact, all the tribes of Kūfah were dissatisfied with 'Uthmān's governorship and his governors![55]

'Abdullāh ibn Āmir, Governor of Baṣrah

'Abdullāh ibn Āmir was 'Uthmān's cousin.

One day, Shibl ibn Khālid, who was the half-brother of Ziyād ibn Abīhi, both sons of the famous Sumayah,[56] entered the assembly while the Umayyad leaders were gathered around 'Uthmān and said, "Is there not a poor person among you who you wish wealth for? Is there not an unknown person among you whom you wish fame for? How is it that you have given Iraq as a gifted land to Abū Mūsa al-Ash'arī (who is not from the Quraysh and the Muḍar tribe and is from the Yemeni tribes)?" 'Uthmān, who was influenced by Shibl's statements, dedicated the ruling of Baṣrah to his sixteen-year-old cousin, 'Abdullāh ibn Āmir ibn Kurayz, and dismissed Abū Mūsa al-Ash'arī from his position!

'Abdullāh was a generous, giving person. One day, he could not recite the Friday sermon on the pulpit. [So instead,] he said, "There are two attributes that cannot be found in me; inability to recite sermons and stinginess. Go to the sheep market and take one sheep each; my treat." And he paid for them all from the treasury. Then he wrote to 'Uthmān that the money in the treasury was not enough. Thus, 'Uthmān allowed him to go and conquer other places and use up the spoils of the conquests.[57] When 'Uthmān was killed, 'Abdullāh took the

---

[55] *Ansāb al-Ashrāf*, 5: pp. 39-43; Also see: *Tārīkh al-Ṭabarī*, 5: pp. 88-90; *Al-Kāmil fit-Tārīkh Ibn al-Athir*, 3: pp. 57-60; *Sharḥ Nahj al-Balāgha* by Ibn Abī l-Hadīd 1: pp. 158-160. There were two groups of people living in Kūfah at that time; a group of Iranians who were captured and later released, and several Arab clans, most of whom were from Yemen.

[56] [Sumayah was famous for sleeping with men and so the fathers of her sons weren't always known, hence called "ibn Abihi" meaning son of his father.]

[57] *Tārīkh Dimashq Ibn 'Asākir*, 9, part 2 p. 231 & 233.

treasury of Baṣrah and brought it to Mecca and Medina and distributed it among the people.[58]

Mu'awiyah's Biography in 'Uthmān's Caliphate Era

In 'Uthmān's time, 'Ubādah ibn al-Samit, a companion of the Prophet (pbuh) was in Shām. One day, he saw a camel train loaded with full waterskins going to Mu'awiyah's palace. He asked what they were filled with and if its olive oil; [since there were many olive groves in Shām]. He was told, "No. These are alcoholic drinks that are being delivered to Mu'awiyah." He got a knife from the market, tore the waterskins and the drinks all spilled to the ground. Abū Hurayrah was in Shām. He said to 'Utbah, "What do you care what Mu'awiyah does? It's him who is responsible for his sins." 'Utbah replied, "You were not there at the time when we pledged allegiance to the Prophet (pbuh)[59] to enjoin what is goodness and forbid what is evil, and we do not fear blame when we stick to our oath." Abū Hurayrah chose to remain silent.

Mu'awiyah wrote to 'Uthmān, "Either take 'Utbah away from Shām, or I will leave Shām to him and come to you." Due to 'Uthmān's demand, he was returned to Medina. Upon reaching Medina, 'Utbah gave a speech and stated, "I heard the Prophet (pbuh) say that after him, your affairs and governorship will be upon those who enjoin the evil and forbid the goodness. They do not have obedience; he who commits a sin against God has no obedience." 'Uthmān did not say a word.[60]

Another companion was 'Abdur-Rahman ibn Sahl ibn Zayd Anṣārī, who participated in Jihād during 'Uthmān's caliphate era. At that time, they would leave from Shām for conquests.

---

[58] See also: *Ansāb al-Ashrāf*, 5: p. 30; *Al-Kāmil fit-Tārīkh Ibn al-Athir*, 3: p. 73; *Al-Bidaya wa an-Nihaya*, 7: pp. 153-154.

[59] What 'Utbah means is Anṣār swearing allegiance to the Prophet (pbuh) in Minā, which lead to the Prophet (pbuh) immigrating to Medina and establishing an Islāmic government.

[60] *Tahzīb Ibn 'Asākir*, 7: 214; *Siyar A'lam al-Nubala*, 2: p. 10; *Musnad Aḥmad ibn Ḥanbal*, 5: p. 325.

He was too, in Shām and saw the camel train carrying waterskins full of alcoholic drinks to Mu'awiyah. 'Abdur-Rahman pierced them one by one with a spear and spilled the drinks to the ground and got into a fight with Mu'awiyah's agents. Mu'awiyah said, "Release him for he is insane." When he heard what Mu'awiyah had said, he announced, "I have heard the Prophet (pbuh) say something about Mu'awiyah that,[61] if I see him, I swear to God, I will not rest unless I tear him apart."[62]

Indeed, towards the end of 'Uthmān's caliphate era, people treated his appointed governors like this.

'Uthmān's Behavior towards 'Ammār

Towards the end of 'Uthmān's time in caliphate, the Companions including Miqdād, 'Ammār ibn Yāsir, Ṭalḥa and Zubayr and some other Companions of the Prophet (pbuh) gathered around and wrote a letter to 'Uthmān pointing out his behavior and manners and in it, said, "If you do not stop doing these, we will mutiny against you."

No one dared to take the letter to 'Uthmān except 'Ammār. 'Uthmān read the letter and then asked, "Among all, is it just you who has revolted against me?!" 'Ammār answered, "I am advising you." 'Uthmān ordered his slaves to push 'Ammār to the ground, and then he himself kicked him in the private area. 'Ammār was an old, feeble, weak man so he fainted from the pain.[63]

---

[61] What Abdur-Rahman had heard from the Prophet (pbuh) about Mu'awiyah is mentioned in *Sharḥ Nahj al-Balāgha* by Ibn Abī l-Hadīd 4: p. 108 narrated from al-Qārat Thaqafī: The Prophet (pbuh) said, "Soon, a man from my nation will reveal to these people, who has huge buttocks, the gullet from his throat to his stomach is wide, he eats a lot and is never full, he carries the burden of sins of jinn and mankind, and he will request ruling one day. So, if you find him, tear him apart." At that time, the Prophet (pbuh) was holding a stick from a tree, one end of which he placed on Mu'awiyah's stomach. (Also see: *al-Iṣābah,* 2: p. 394.)

[62] *al-Iṣābah,* 2: p. 394; *Usd al-Ġābah,* 3: p. 299; *Al-Isti'ab,* p. 400; *Tahdīb al-Tahdīb,* 6: p. 192.

[63] *Ansāb al-Ashrāf,* 5: pp. 49 & 54; *al-'Iqd al-Farīd,* 2: p. 272. Also see: *Al-Imāma wal-Siyāsa & Tārīkh Ya'qūbī,* 2: p. 150.

'Uthmān's Performance Regarding the Treasury Money

'Uthmān used to say, "If I had the keys to Heaven, I would give them to Banī Umayya so that their last person would enter Heaven."[64]

Instead of the keys to Heaven, the keys of the treasury were in 'Uthmān's hands, and he opened its doors to Banī Umayya limitlessly and gifted them with its money and belongings. Some of the gifts 'Uthmān, who was the caliph of the Muslims, gave to his relatives are as follows:

1. Abū Sufyān ibn Ḥarb: 200,000 dirhams[65]
2. Marwān ibn al-Ḥakam: 500,000 dinars[66]
3. 'Abdullāh ibn Khālid: 300,000 dirhams[67] (and for each of his relatives: 1,000 dirhams)
4. Sa'īd ibn al-'Āṣ: 100,000 dirhams[68]
5. Ḥārith ibn Ḥakam ibn Abī al-'Āṣ: 300,000 dirhams (for Marwan)[69] in addition to the alms of Medina market, which was a land that was the Prophet's property which he had entrusted to the Muslims. 'Uthmān gave this market to his cousin, and he would collect rent from whoever used that land which had become part of the market.[70]
6. Ḥakam ibn Abī al-'Āṣ: 300,000 dirhams[71]
7. Walīd ibn 'Uqba: 100,000 dirhams[72]

---

[64] *Musnad Aḥmad ibn Ḥanbal*, 1: p. 62.

[65] *Sharḥ Nahj al-Balāgha* by Ibn Abī l-Hadīd 1: p. 67.

[66] *Kitāb al-Ma'ārif*, p. 84; *Sharḥ Nahj al-Balāgha* by Ibn Abī l-Hadīd 1: p. 66; *al-'Iqd al-Farīd*, 4: p. 283; *Ansāb al-Ashrāf*, 5: pp. 25 & 88; *Tārīkh Dimashq Ibn 'Asākir*, 11: 1. p. 140.

[67] *Ansāb al-Ashrāf*, 5: p. 285.

[68] *Ansāb al-Ashrāf*, 5: p. 285.

[69] *Ansāb al-Ashrāf*, 5: pp. 28 & 52.

[70] *As-Sirat al-Halabiah*, 2: p. 87; *al-'Iqd al-Farīd*, 2: p. 261.

[71] *Ansāb al-Ashrāf*, 5: p. 28.

[72] *Ansāb al-Ashrāf*, 5: pp. 30-31.

8. 'Abdullāh ibn Khālid ibn Usayd: 300,000 dirhams once and 600,000 dirhams a second time[73]

9. Zayd ibn Thabit Ansārī: 100,000 dirhams[74]

10. Zubayr: 59,800,000 dirhams[75]

11. Ṭalḥa: 200,000 dinars[76]

12. Sa'd ibn Abī Waqqās: 250,000 dirhams[77]

13. 'Uthmān (the Caliph): 3,500,000 dirhams[78]

14. 'Abdullāh ibn Sa'd ibn Abī al-Sarḥ: 100,000 dinars, which was one fifth of the spoils of Africa.[79]

---

[73] *Tārīkh Ya'qūbī*, 2: p. 168; *Sharḥ Nahj al-Balāgha* by Ibn Abī l-Hadīd 1: p. 66; *al-'Iqd al-Farīd*, 4: p. 283.

[74] *Ansāb al-Ashrāf*, 5: pp. 54 & 55; *Murūj ad-Dahab*, 1: p. 434.

[75] *Ṣaḥīḥ al-Bukhārī*, book Bab al-Qazi 5: p. 21. al-Bukhārī estimated the total amount of Zubayr's assets to be two hundred million and two hundred thousand dirhams. But the commentators of *Ṣaḥīḥ al-Bukhārī*, have considered this incorrect and have mentioned the correct amount to be two hundred and fifty million and eight hundred thousand dirhams. (See: *Fatḥ al-Bārī, fī Sharḥ Ṣaḥīḥ al-Bukhārī, Al-Irshad, as-Sārī fī Sharḥ Ṣaḥīḥ al-Bukhārī; Umdat al-Qari; Shadarāt al-Dahab fī Akhbār man Dahab*, 1: p. 43.) Of course, *Ṣaḥīḥ al-Bukhārī*, and other sources do not contain the word "dirham" and have only written the amounts, but in *Al-Bidaya wa an-Nihaya*, 7: p. 249 the term "dirham" is mentioned.

[76] *Ansāb al-Ashrāf*, 5: p. 7. Apart from this, other gifts were also given to Ṭalḥa so much that his heritage was estimated to be millions of dirhams. (For more information, see: *Kitāb aṭ-Tabaqāt al-Kabīr*, Ibn Sa'd 3: p. 158; *Murūj ad-Dahab*, 1: p. 434, *al-'Iqd al-Farīd*, 2: p. 279; *Al-Riaz un-Nazra*, 2: p. 258; *Duwal al-Islām*, 1: p. 18; Khulasa p. 152.)

[77] *Kitāb aṭ-Tabaqāt al-Kabīr*, Ibn Sa'd 3: p. 105; *Murūj ad-Dahab*, 1: p. 434.

[78] *Kitāb aṭ-Tabaqāt al-Kabīr*, Ibn Sa'd 3: p. 53; *Murūj ad-Dahab*, 1: p. 332. It is worth mentioning that according to Ibn Sa'd, in *Kitāb aṭ-Tabaqāt al-Kabīr*, 3: p. 53, on the day of Uthmān's assassination, he had thirty million and five hundred thousand dirhams in the hands of his treasurer. In *Murūj ad-Dahab*, 1: p. 433, al-Mas'ūdī also writes that Uthmān had a huge fortune at the time of his death, including his lands in Wadi al-Qura and Hunayn, which were worth 200,000 dinars. Also see: *Ansāb al-Ashrāf*, 5: p. 49.

[79] *Al-Isti'ab*, 2: pp. 367-370; *al-Isābah*, 2: pp. 309; *Al-Kāmil fit-Tārīkh Ibn al-Athir*, 3: p. 38.

15. 'Abdur-Rahman ibn 'Awf: 2,560,000 dinars[80]

During 'Umar's caliphate time, in one of the conquests in Iran, a basket of royal jewels was brought and placed in the treasury by 'Umar's orders. 'Uthmān took that basket of jewelry and distributed it among his wife and daughters.[81]

Abū Mūsa al-Ash'arī was the governor of Baṣrah. The spoils of gold and silver he brought back with him from his battles were taken by 'Uthmān and distributed among his wife and children too.[82]

This was a summary of the squandering and lavishness of the Muslims' treasury done by 'Uthmān.[83]

---

[80] *Kitāb aṭ-Tabaqāt al-Kabīr*, Ibn Sa'd 3: p. 96; *Tārīkh Ya'qūbī*, 2: p. 146.

[81] *Ansāb al-Ashrāf*, 5: p. 85.

[82] *As-Sawayiq al-Muhriqah*, p. 68; *As-Sirat al-Halabiah*, 2: p. 78.

[83] This was all at the same time the Aṣḥāb of Badr were being paid only 5000 dirhams per year. (*Sharḥ Nahj al-Balāgha* by Ibn Abī l-Hadīd 3: p. 154; *Kitāb al-Futūḥ al-Buldān*, pp. 550-565.) Consider the difference!

<h1 style="text-align:center">Chapter 12</h1>

People's Insurrection against 'Uthmān and 'Alī's Role in Reconciling the Two Parties

The Egyptian Revolt

Muslims were in severe misery. In order to complain about their governor, 'Abdullāh ibn Sa'd ibn Abī al-Sarḥ, a group of Muslims from Egypt, came to see 'Uthmān and so entered the Prophet's mosque.

'Uthmān would not allow anyone to complain about his governors. A group of the Muhājirūn and the Anṣār who were in the mosque asked them, "What brought you here from Egypt?" They answered, "We are here to complain about the oppression of our governor." 'Alī (as) said to them, "Do not rush in judgment. Present your complaint to the caliph and inform him of what is going on for it is possible that the governor of Egypt has treated you in contrast with the caliph's wills. Go to the caliph and tell him your issues; if 'Uthmān takes it hard on him and dismisses him from his position, then you have achieved your goal, and if not, you can always come back for more complaint." The Egyptians asked 'Alī (as) to accompany them, but he said, "You don't need me to go with you." The Egyptians continued, "Although, this is the case, but we want you to be with us and witness everything." 'Alī (as) replied, "He who is stronger than me, more dominant over all creatures and more compassionate towards His servants, will be with you and witness and observe you."

The Egyptian seniors went to 'Uthmān's door and asked for permission to enter. 'Uthmān protested, "Why have you left Egypt and come here without asking me first?" They said, "We have come to complain about you and your actions, as well as your governor's actions!" The argument between them heated and was dragged to the mosque. Ā'ishah and Ṭalḥa intervened and from then on took the leadership of 'Uthmān's opponents.[1]

Afterwards, 'Alī (as) interfered and after discussing the matter with 'Uthmān,[2] 'Uthmān wrote this letter:

In the name of God, the Beneficent, the Merciful

This is a covenant that the servant of God, 'Uthmān, the Commander of the Faithful, writes for those believers and Muslims who are disappointed in him. 'Uthmān vows to henceforth act in accordance with the God's Book and the Prophet's traditions, restore the salaries and pensions of those who have been cut off, spare those who fear his wrath and secure their freedom, return those who have been exiled to their families, and distribute the spoils from battles among the soldiers (Mujahids) without any out of order consideration or exception. On behalf of 'Uthmān, 'Alī ibn Abī Ṭālib (as) guarantees the fulfillment of all these obligations to the believers and Muslims. The following witnesses also testify to the validity of these obligations:

Zubayr ibn al-Awām, Sa'd ibn Mālik Abī Waqqās, Zayd ibn Thabit, Ṭalḥa ibn 'Ubaydullāh, 'Abdullāh ibn 'Umar, Sahl ibn Ḥunayf, Abū Ayyub Khalid ibn Zayd.

(Dated, Ḏū al-Qa'dah, year 35 AH/ 656 CE)

The groups that had come from Kūfah and Egypt each took a copy of the treaty and left.[3] 'Alī (as) said to 'Uthmān, "It is good for you to go out and recite a sermon and silence the people and bear witness to God that you have repented."

'Uthmān delivered the following sermon:

---

[1] *Kitāb al-Futūḥ*, pp. 46-47.

[2] This discussion is mentioned in historical resources, including: *Ansāb al-Ashrāf*, 5: p. 60; *Tārīkh al-Ṭabarī*, 5: pp. 96-97; *Al-Kāmil fit-Tārīkh Ibn al-Athir*, 3: p. 63; *Sharḥ Nahj al-Balāgha* by Ibn Abī l-Hadīd 1: p. 303; *Al-Bidaya wa an-Nihaya*, 7: p. 167; *Tārīkh Abī al-Fada'*, 1: p. 168.

[3] *Ansāb al-Ashrāf*, 5: pp. 63-64.

...O' people! I swear to God, I already knew everything you criticized me about, and all that I have done in the past was all by knowledge and awareness; but in the meantime, my ego and inner desires deceived me sorely and misguided me from seeing facts accurately. Eventually I was misled and went astray and distanced from the path of truth.

I myself heard the Prophet (pbuh) say, "Whoever makes a mistake in a moment of aberration must repent and whoever commits a sin must seek forgiveness, not drown himself more and more in obliquity, and if he continues to oppress, he will be one of those who have completely deviated from the path of truth."

I am the first to take advice from this command. Hereby, I seek forgiveness from the Almighty God for what I have done and I turn to Him. It is better for someone like me to renounce sin and seek repentance and forgiveness. Now, as I descend from the pulpit, let your leaders and nobles come to me and share their suggestions with me. I swear to God, if I deserve to be redeemed as a servant, I will do the best a servant of God can do, and I will be contemptible and degraded just like them.

At this point, 'Uthmān burst into tears. The narrator says:

I saw that he wept so intensely his tears wet his beard and people started pitying and feeling sorry for him due to his statements. Some even cried for him and were affected by his misery, helplessness and repentance. Just then, Sa'īd ibn Zayd said to 'Uthmān, "O' Commander of the Faithful! No one is more sympathetic to you than you yourself. Think about yourself and commit to what you have promised."

Marwān's Sabotage

When 'Uthmān descended the pulpit and entered his house, he found Marwān, Sa'īd and a group of Umayyads there. After 'Uthmān took a seat, Marwān turned to him and said, "Shall I speak?" 'Uthmān replied, "Go ahead." Marwān said, "If you had expressed what you just expressed at a time when you were strong, it would have been good. But now that you are weak and contemptible, saying these words means you are defeated. You should not have done this and should not have humiliated yourself in front of all those people."

People came to 'Uthmān's door expecting him to attend to their affairs and look into their complaints, taken him at his word. Marwān said to 'Uthmān, "People have gathered in crowds like mountains." 'Uthmān said, "I am ashamed to confront them, you go out." Marwān went out and exclaimed, "What the hell is going on? Are you here to plunder? Shame on you! Wherever I look, I see a person accompanied by a friend except for those whom I am looking forward to see. What is it that you have your eyes on? Is the way you have attacked us supposed to tell us that you intend to steal our properties? You idiots! Return to your homes. You've made a huge mistake. We never retreated and we will not let go of our power and government."

People Taking their Complaint to 'Alī and his Ceding

After this occurrence, a group took their complaint to 'Alī (as). 'Alī (as) angrily walked in on 'Uthmān and exclaimed, "Have you not given up on Marwān yet? He will not give up on you unless he turns you away from religion and consciousness altogether. And just like a despicable, contemptible camel that is dragged around, you submissively follow him! Marwān has neither an opinion nor a religion. I see that he will destroy you. I will no longer do anything for you."

When Imam 'Alī (as) left, 'Uthmān's wife, Nā'ila, said to him, "'Alī (as) will not visit you anymore. You heard Marwān, he has dragged you wherever he has wanted." 'Uthmān asked, "What should I do?" Nā'ila answered, "Fear God who has no partner and follow the traditions of your two friends who preceded you.[4] If you obey Marwān, he will lead you to death, for Marwān is not respected, honored, or liked by people. You have lost people's support because of Marwān. Send someone after 'Alī (as) and reconcile with him. Indeed, you are related to him and he is accepted and cherished by people and no one disputes with him."

---

[4] She meant Abī Bakr and 'Umar

'Uthmān sent someone after 'Alī (as), but 'Alī (as) refused to go back and said, "I told him I will not go to him anymore."[5]

After this incident, on the Friday of that week, 'Uthmān ascended the pulpit and started praising God. Before starting his speech, someone from the audience got up and said, "O' 'Uthmān! Follow God's Book." 'Uthmān replied, "Sit down." This quarrel was repeated three times. Eventually, those who were in the mosque divided into two groups; one against 'Uthmān and the other on his side. The dispute heated and people started throwing rocks at each other. Some even threw pebbles to the top of the pulpit at 'Uthmān, so much that he passed out. He was taken home. 'Alī (as) went to visit him.

The Umayyads were surrounding 'Uthmān when 'Alī (as) entered. They scolded 'Alī (as) saying, "This is all on you; you did this! We swear to God, if you achieve what you want (i.e. the governorship), we will have people revolt and commit munity." Therefore 'Alī (as) angrily got up and left.[6]

This was the situation in Medina.

Groups that Had Come from Other Cities

A crowd of 'Uthmān's opponents from Dākhushub, outside Medina, had come to see what would happen. Mughīra ibn Shu'ba said to 'Uthmān, "Let me go and bring back those who are out of Medina." 'Uthmān agreed. When Mughīra reached them, they shouted at him, and the groups that had come from other cities said, "O' lecher! Go back; O' debauchee! Go back;[7] O' blind! Go back!" Mughīra, inevitably, returned.

---

[5] *Tārīkh al-Ṭabarī*, 5: p. 112 & in the European edition pp. 2977-2979; *Al-Kāmil fit-Tārīkh Ibn al-Athir*, 3: p. 96. Balādurī has also mentioned part of what we have narrated. See: *Ansāb al-Ashrāf*, 5: p. 65.

[6] *Tārīkh al-Ṭabarī*, 5: p. 113 & in the European edition 1: pp. 2979-2990.

[7] These terms were used for Mughīra because when he was the governor of Baṣrah, he was accused of sleeping around but 'Umar did not agree for him to be punished and imposed to Hadd. (*Kitab al-Aghani*, 14: pp. 139-142; *Sharḥ Nahj al-Balāgha* by Ibn Abī l-Hadīd 2: p. 161; *Tārīkh al-Ṭabarī*, *Al-Kāmil fit-Tārīkh Ibn al-Athir*, and *Tārīkh Abī al-Fada'*, narrating events of the year 17 AH; *Tārīkh al-Ṭabarī*, 1: p. 2529, the European edition; *Ansāb al-Ashrāf*, 1: p. 423; *Tārīkh Ya'qūbī*, 2: p. 124.)

Then, 'Uthmān called out for 'Amr ibn al-'Āṣ and said to him, "Go to the people and invite them to God's Book and tell them I will do whatever they want me to."

'Amr ibn al-'Āṣ went and greeted them as soon as he approached them. They said, "O' enemy of God! Go back![8] O' Son of Nābiġah! Go back![9] Neither are you trustworthy nor do we feel safe around you."

'Abdullāh ibn 'Umar and others who were in the company of 'Uthmān said, "No one can calm this crowd down except 'Alī (as)." 'Uthmān summoned 'Alī (as). 'Alī (as) showed up. 'Uthmān said to him, "Preach these people to God's Book and the Prophet's traditions." 'Alī (as) said, "Provided that you make a covenant and bear witness to God that you will do whatever I tell them." 'Uthmān agreed, so 'Alī (as) made a pact with 'Uthmān and he swore to do whatever 'Alī (as) promised the rebels 'Uthmān would do. 'Alī (as) left him and went to Dākhushub, where the rebels had assembled. When they saw 'Alī (as) they asked him to return. But 'Alī (as) said to them, "I am approaching you. Your wishes will be granted." The rebels accepted. 'Alī (as) repeated 'Uthmān's words to them. They asked, "Do you guarantee that he will do all these?" 'Alī (as) replied, "Yes." They said, "We are satisfied." And then the seniors and nobles accompanied 'Alī (as) and went to visit 'Uthmān.[10] They were Egyptians who had complaints about their governor, 'Abdullāh ibn Sa'd ibn Abī al-Sarḥ. The last time they had sent a letter, when they delivered 'Uthmān's reply letter to him, he had killed one of them.[11]

Apart from 'Alī (as), Ṭalḥa, Zubayr and Ā'ishah also intervened. They said to 'Uthmān, "Change the governor of Egypt." He said, "Who do you recommend?" They answered, "Assign Muḥammad ibn Abū Bakr." And so

---

[8] Amr ibn al-'Āṣ's record was that when he hadn't converted to Islām yet, he composed a sixty-verse poem vilifying the Prophet (pbuh).

[9] Nābiġah, Amr ibn al-'Āṣ's mother was known for immorality.

[10] *Ansāb al-Ashrāf*, 5: pp. 63-64.

[11] *Ibid.*, 5: pp. 25-26.

Muḥammad, together with the Egyptians, and a letter from 'Uthmān, headed for Egypt.[12]

This was the story of the Egyptian rebellion.[13]

The Caliph's Trick

There was also a riot inside Medina. Once again, 'Alī (as) intervened and they were told that this time 'Uthmān will fulfill his promises. 'Uthmān claimed, "Time is needed to establish justice and restore people's rights." 'Alī (as) said, "There is no need of time in Medina, and regarding out of Medina, you have until your letters reach them." He repeated, "I need time." And so 'Alī (as) said, "You have got three days."[14]

After Muḥammad ibn Abū Bakr was appointed by 'Uthmān to govern Egypt, he joined the Egyptians and headed for Egypt with them. On the way, they suddenly saw 'Uthmān's servant riding a camel and passing by them very quickly. They stopped him and asked, "Where are you going?" He answered, "I am going to Egypt." They asked, "What do you have with you?" He replied, "I have nothing with me." They said, "That's impossible." So they had him descend the camel and then they searched him. He was carrying an empty waterskin. They tore it apart and found a lead tube in which there was a letter from 'Uthmān to 'Abdullāh ibn Sa'd ibn Abī al-Sarḥ, the governor of Egypt, with 'Uthmān's seal on it. In that letter, he wrote to the governor of Egypt, "When these people arrive, hang Muḥammad ibn Abū Bakr and this and that, and remain in your position (and imprison all those who came to me to complain about you, and wait for my next order)."

When they read the letter, they returned to Medina with Muḥammad ibn Abū Bakr, and went to 'Alī (as) and gave him 'Uthmān's letter.[15] 'Alī (as) went up to 'Uthmān and asked him, "What is this letter?" 'Uthmān claimed, "I have

---

[12] *Ibid.*, 5: pp. 63-65.

[13] The Egyptian rebellion had taken place before Uthmān's sermon in the mosque.

[14] *Tārīkh al-Ṭabarī*, 5: pp. 116-117 & in the European edition 1: pp. 2987-2989; *Al-Kāmil fit-Tārīkh Ibn al-Athir*, 3: pp. 71-72; *Sharḥ Nahj al-Balāgha* by Ibn Abī l-Hadīd 1: p. 166.

[15] *Ansāb al-Ashrāf*, 5: pp. 67-68.

not written it." People said, "*Your* official courier was riding *your* camel and the letter is in the handwriting of *your* writer and it has *your* seal on it." He said, "The camel has been stolen. The handwriting is similar to my writer's. The seal may be a replica of mine!" He was told, "Resign from the caliphate, otherwise you will either be dismissed or killed." 'Uthmān did not see eye to eye with them. They told him, "You have done many wrong things. When you are warned, you repent, but you do not keep your promises. Last time you repented, you said you would not backslide, and Muḥammad ibn Maslamah guaranteed us, but you did it again. Now, you have to either dismiss yourself or you will be killed." 'Uthmān said, "I will not resign from the caliphate. I swear to God, I will never take off the clothes that God has dressed me in![16]

Ā'ishah Sentencing 'Uthmān to Death

Ā'ishah, Umm Al-Mu'minin, who was extremely upset with 'Uthmān and had hopes for her cousin, Ṭalḥa, to reach a position in the government, took advantage of the people's revolt and their sieging 'Uthmān and, in a historical move, sentenced him to death.

Ā'ishah said, "O' 'Uthmān, you have possessed the treasury of Muslims and you have allowed the Umayyads to own people's properties and lives and you have given them guardianship and governorship and by all these things, you have caused the Prophet's nation troubles? May God take his blessing away from you. If it weren't for your daily prayers five times a day just like other Muslims, they would have beheaded you as they would a camel."[17]

When 'Uthmān heard Ā'ishah's statements, he recited the tenth verse of Surah at-Taḥrīm, which was revealed about Ā'ishah and Ḥafṣah:

ضَرَبَ ٱللَّهُ مَثَلًا لِّلَّذِينَ كَفَرُواْ ٱمْرَأَتَ نُوحٍ وَٱمْرَأَتَ لُوطٍ كَانَتَا تَحْتَ عَبْدَيْنِ مِنْ عِبَادِنَا صَٰلِحَيْنِ فَخَانَتَاهُمَا فَلَمْ يُغْنِيَا عَنْهُمَا مِنَ ٱللَّهِ شَيْئًا وَقِيلَ ٱدْخُلَا ٱلنَّارَ مَعَ ٱلدَّٰخِلِينَ

---

[16] *Tārīkh al-Ṭabarī*, 5: pp. 120-121 & in the European edition 1: pp. 2995-2997.

[17] Apparently, these were said before the revealing of Uthmān's letter to the governor of Egypt in which he had given orders for Muḥammad ibn Abī Bakr's to be killed, because after this event, Ā'ishah sentenced Uthmān to death with no fear regarding his prayers.

168

"Allāh presents an example of those who disbelieved; Noah's wife and Lot's wife. They were under two of Our righteous servants but betrayed them, so they [i.e., those prophets] did not avail them from Allāh at all, and it was said: Enter the Fire with those who enter it."

Ā'ishah had a harsh, brusque, rebellious temperament. She found out about the letter her brother Muḥammad had received on his way to Egypt, in which he and his Companions had been ordered to be murdered in the handwriting of 'Uthmān's writer and sealed by him. This made Ā'ishah, Umm Al-Mu'minin, who would die for her relatives, so furious that she recklessly and explicitly sentenced the Caliph to death and issued him as an infidel. She exclaimed, "Kill Na'thal, for he has turned to an infidel!"[18] She described 'Uthmān as Na'thal[19] and by this, she violated the sanctity of the caliphate.

Of course, the wrongdoings of the leaders and governors of the Umayyads, Marwān and Ḥakam ibn Abī al-'Āṣ and Walīd and Sa'id and 'Abdullāh ibn Sa'd ibn Abī al-Sarḥ, have all been effective in their place. Persecuting the Muslims and looting the treasury all had a great impact on these uprisings. However, Ā'ishah's sentence to death left no respect for the caliph, and it incited the Muslims against him, and thereby, occurred what will be told.

The Words of Jahjāh Ġifārī

Once, when 'Uthmān was reciting a sermon, leaning on the cane which Abū Bakr and 'Umar once leaned on, Jahjāh Ġifārī, who was one of the Anṣār, got up and said, "Get up Na'thal, and climb down from this pulpit."[20] And in

---

[18] *Tārīkh al-Ṭabarī,* 4: p. 474 & in the European edition p. 3112; *Kitāb al-Futūḥ,* p. 155; *Al-Kāmil fit-Tārīkh Ibn al-Athir,* 3: p. 87; *Sharḥ Nahj al-Balāgha* by Ibn Abī l-Hadīd 2: p. 77; *An-Nihāya,* 4: p. 156.

[19] Na'thal means a Jew; although, there are other meanings to the word i.e. a gullible old man and a male hyena. It is also been said that Na'thal was the name of a man from Egypt who had a long beard. (See: *An-Nihāya, al-Qāmus al-Muḥīṭ, Tāj al-'Ārūs, Lisan al-'Arab* under the term Na'thal.)

[20] *Tārīkh al-Ṭabarī,* 5: p. 114 & in the European edition 1: p. 2982; *Ansāb al-Ashrāf,* 5: pp. 47-48; *Al-Riaz un-Nazra,* 2: p. 123; *Al-Kāmil fit-Tārīkh Ibn al-Athir,* 3: p. 70; *Sharḥ Nahj al-*

another narration, he said, "Let me ride you on a camel and take you to a volcano and throw you in it!" No one said anything to him. The Umayyads pulled 'Uthmān down from the pulpit and took him home.[21] As a result, the oppressed revolted against 'Uthmān and besieged him.

Sieging 'Uthmān's House

Most of the people besieging 'Uthmān's house were Egyptians. The Anṣār also helped. The Egyptians, who had come to perform Hajj, had arranged to join the people of Kūfah and Baṣrah going to Mecca. They reached outside Medina and with the help of the people of Medina besieged 'Uthmān's house. In the meantime, Ā'ishah's letters reached different cities and had a significant effect on people revolting against 'Uthmān.[22] They surrounded the caliph and deprived him access to water, according to Ṭalḥa's command.[23]

Ā'ishah, who believed the damage was done, did not want to be in Medina while 'Uthmān was being killed; so she prepared to go to Hajj. 'Uthmān said to Marwān and 'Abdur-Rahman ibn 'Attāb, "Go ask Ā'ishah to stay. She may stop people from killing me." They came to Ā'ishah and said to her, "Do not go to Hajj. Stay. God may repel this rebellion from this man ('Uthmān) by you."[24] Ā'ishah said, "No, I have packed my bags and obligated myself to go to Hajj. I can't stay." They suggested, "We will pay you twice the amount you have spent." She still refused to accept.[25] Marwān recited this poem:

Balāgha by Ibn Abī l-Hadīd 1: p. 165; *Al-Bidaya wa an-Nihaya*, 7: p. 175; *al-Iṣābah*, 1: p. 253; *Tārīkh al-Khamis*, 2: p. 260.

[21] *Tārīkh al-Ṭabarī*, 5: p. 114 & in the European edition 1: p. 2982; *Ansāb al-Ashrāf*, 5: pp. 47-48; *Al-Riaz un-Nazra*, 2: p. 123; *Al-Kāmil fit-Tārīkh Ibn al-Athir*, 3: p. 70; *Sharḥ Nahj al-Balāgha* by Ibn Abī l-Hadīd 1: p. 165; *Al-Bidaya wa an-Nihaya*, 7: p. 175; *al-Iṣābah*, 1: p. 253; *Tārīkh al-Khamis*, 2: p. 260.

[22] *Ansāb al-Ashrāf*, 5: p. 103

[23] *Ibid.*, 5: p. 90.

[24] *Ibid.*, 5: p. 81.

[25] *Tārīkh Ya'qūbī*, 2: p. 142.

Qays set the city on fire and abandoned me as the flames rose and engulfed me.[26]

In response to Marwān, Ā'ishah said, "O' Marwān! Do you think I have doubts about your owner?[27] By God I wish I could fit him into one of my boxes and carry him so I could throw him into the sea."[28] After that, Ā'ishah headed for Mecca.

In that year, 'Abdullāh ibn 'Abbās was the leader of the pilgrims of Hajj assigned by 'Uthmān. He reached Ā'ishah in the land of Ṣulṣul[29]. Ā'ishah told him, "I beg you in the name of God not to scatter the people who have revolted against this man ('Uthmān) using the convincing and attracting fluency that you have, and do not make them doubt themselves about this selfish, rebellious man. People are aware of what they are doing and they have recognized the right path, and they have gathered from the cities in crowds to be a part of what has started. I saw with my own eyes how Ṭalḥa found access to the treasury keys. If he takes over, he will undoubtedly, follow in his cousin's footsteps; Abū Bakr!" In response to Ā'ishah, Ibn 'Abbās said, "Mother![30] If a calamity befalls this man and he gets killed, people will not bow down to anyone other than our leader, 'Alī (as)." Ā'ishah hurriedly said, "I do not want to argue with you."[31]

Ṭalḥa Having the Treasury Keys

Ṭalḥa had found access to the treasury keys, and because of that, people had gathered in his house. So, his house was so full of people and there was no

---

[26] *Ansāb al-Ashrāf,* 5: p. 75.

[27] *Tārīkh Ya'qūbī,* 2: p. 124.

[28] *Ansāb al-Ashrāf,* 5: p. 75; *Kitāb al-Futūḥ,* p. 155; *Kitāb aṭ-Ṭabaqāt al-Kabīr, Ibn Sa'd,* 5: p. 25.

[29] The name of a place a few miles away from Medina (*Kitāb Mu'jam al-Buldān*). The correct word is actually "ḌalḌal" but historians have always narrated it Ṣulṣul. (*Mu'jam mā Ista'jam*)

[30] The wives of the Prophet (pbuh) were called "Mother".

[31] *Ansāb al-Ashrāf,* 5: p. 75; *Tārīkh al-Ṭabarī,* 5: p. 140 & in the European edition 1: p. 3040; *Kitāb al-Futūḥ,* p. 156.

more room left. As the state of siege worsened for 'Uthmān, he sent someone to 'Alī (as) to deliver this message, "If I am destined to be eaten up, I want you, my cousin to come and eat me otherwise rush to my rescue before I tear apart."

Earlier, 'Alī (as) had told 'Uthmān that he would not go to him anymore; nevertheless he did. 'Uthmān said to 'Alī (as), "There are several reasons to why you need to be on my side; our Islāmic brotherhood and kinship and being the Prophet's son-in-law. Even if you ignore all these and assume that we are in the Ignorance era, it is still a disgrace for the Abd Manāf dynasty to seize power and ruling from one of the sons of the Taym clan [Ṭalḥa]." In response to him, 'Alī (as) said, "You will be posted." Then he left 'Uthmān's house and went to the Prophet's mosque. There he saw Usama (Zayd's son, the Prophet's freed slave), tapped him on the shoulder and together, they went to Ṭalḥa's house. When they reached Ṭalḥa, 'Alī (as) said to him, "Ṭalḥa! What is this turmoil that you have started?!" Ṭalḥa replied, "O' Abū al-Ḥasan! You are too late. Everything is over."[32]

'Alī (as), seeing that it was useless to talk to Ṭalḥa, said nothing and left his house and went to the treasury. He said, "Open the treasury." They said, "We do not have the keys. Ṭalḥa has them." He ordered the treasury to be broken and he himself began to distribute the gold and silver coins as well as the rest of the gold and silver accumulated in the treasury. Those who had surrounded Ṭalḥa, left his house one by one and went to 'Alī (as) and got something from the treasury. Ṭalḥa was left alone. He went to 'Uthmān and said, "O' Commander of the Faithful! I ask God for forgiveness for what I have done. I had a dream, but God did not destine it for me and built barriers between me and my wish." 'Uthmān replied, "By God you are not here to repent. You are only here because you found yourself defeated in this case! I will not take revenge and leave it to God."[33]

---

[32] Which means don't meddle because my becoming the next caliph is certain.

[33] *Ansāb al-Ashrāf*, 5: p. 78; *Tārīkh al-Ṭabarī*, 5: p. 154; *Al-Kāmil fit-Tārīkh Ibn al-Athir*, 3: p. 64; *Kanz al-Ummāl*, 6: p. 389 hadīth 5965. Also see: *Al-Mubarrad*, p. 11; *Zahr al-Ādāb*, 1: p. 75; *Kitāb al-Futūḥ*, pp. 156-157; *Tārīkh al-Ṭabarī*, & in the European edition 1: p. 3071.

Ṭalḥa Deprives 'Uthmān's Access to Water and 'Alī Delivers Water to Him

al-Ṭabarī writes:

'Uthmān was under siege for forty days and during this time, Ṭalḥa prayed with people.[34]

None of the Prophet's Companions were as determined as Ṭalḥa in terms of opposition to 'Uthmān.[35] Ṭalḥa and Zubayr had taken charge. Ṭalḥa prevented 'Uthmān's house from getting water and would not allow them to have access to drinking water. 'Alī (as) said to Ṭalḥa, "What are you doing? Let this man draw water from his well." Ṭalḥa said, "No." and refused to agree.[36]

al-Ṭabarī writes:

Because the besiegers intensified their actions and prevented water from reaching 'Uthmān's house, 'Uthmān sent someone to 'Alī (as) and asked him for help to provide supplies and bring some water to his house. 'Alī (as) talked to Ṭalḥa but only saw his refusal, so he got so angry that Ṭalḥa had no choice but to agree with him and finally brought some water to 'Uthmān.[37] However, they deprived him from drinking water once again. This time 'Uthmān went to the roof and spoke to the public and said, "Is 'Alī (as) amongst you?" They said, "No." He then asked, "How about Sa'd?" They answered, "No." 'Uthmān remained silent for a while. Then he dropped his head and said, "Is there anyone who would tell 'Alī (as) to bring us water?" When the news reached 'Alī (as), he sent three waterskins full of water to 'Uthmān's house. The Banī Hāshim and Banī Umayya servants held on to the waterskins tightly to protect them from being damaged by the insurgents. Nevertheless, by the time the water reached 'Uthmān's house, some of them were harmed.

In the middle of all this chaos, Mujame' ibn Jārieh Anṣārī was passing by Ṭalḥa. Ṭalḥa asked him, "How is your lord 'Uthmān doing?" He answered, "I

---

[34] *Tārīkh al-Ṭabarī*, 5: p. 117 & in the European edition 1: p. 2989.

[35] *Ansāb al-Ashrāf*, 5: p. 81.

[36] *Ansāb al-Ashrāf*, 5: p. 90.

[37] *Tārīkh al-Ṭabarī*, 5: p. 113.

swear to God, I think you will kill him in the end." Ṭalḥa replied sarcastically, "Even if so, it's not like a messenger of God or a beloved angel will be killed."[38]

'Abdullāh ibn 'Abbās ibn Abī Rabi'ah says:

When 'Uthmān was under siege, I went to him one day and talked with him for an hour. While we were talking, 'Uthmān took my hand and made me listen to the words of those behind his door. At that time, I heard someone say, "What are you waiting for?" And another answer, "Wait, he may change." As 'Uthmān and I were eavesdropping, Ṭalḥa ibn 'Ubayd passed by. He paused and asked, "Where is Ibn 'Udayss[39]?" He was told, "He is here." Ibn 'Udayss appeared and Ṭalḥa whispered something in his ear. Then Ibn 'Udayss returned and gave these orders to his Companions, "From now on, do not let anyone enter or exit 'Uthmān's house." 'Uthmān said, "Dear God! Rescue me from the evilness of Ṭalḥa, for he incited and provoked people against me... He was the one who started disrespect against me whereas I did not deserve it!"

'Abdullāh says:

When I wanted to leave the caliph's house, they wouldn't let me out due to Ibn 'Udayss's orders. Until Muḥammad ibn Abū Bakr, who was passing by, said, "Leave him alone." And so I was released.

'Uthmān's Assassination and 'Alī's Reaction

'Alī (as) was informed that they were going to kill 'Uthmān. He gave these orders to his sons, Ḥasan and Ḥusayn, "Pick up your swords and guard 'Uthmān's door and do not allow anyone to get his hand on the caliph." 'Alī's sons went to 'Uthmān's house in obedience to their father. There was a strange chaos going on around the Caliph's palace and people insisted on ending 'Uthmān's life. Eventually, fighting broke out and Ḥasan and Ḥusayn got injured defending 'Uthmān. Ḥasan's face turned red covered in blood and Qambar, 'Alī's servant, ended up with a broken head and severely injured.

Muḥammad ibn Abū Bakr feared Banī Hāshim getting angry at the sight of 'Alī's sons in such conditions and later can start sedition. So, he pulled two of

---

[38] *Ansāb al-Ashrāf,* 5: p. 74.

[39] Ibn Udayss was the head of the Egyptian rebellions.

the attackers aside and said to them, "If Banī Hāshim see this situation, especially the blood on Ḥasan's face, it is possible that they will drive the people away from around 'Uthmān swaying their swords and hence ruin our plans. It is better for us to get into 'Uthmān's house climbing the wall and kill him quietly."[40]

Ibn Abī l-Ḥadīd writes:

Ṭalḥa, who had covered his face with a piece of cloth and thus kept himself hidden from the public, was shooting arrows at 'Uthmān's house.[41] Muḥammad ibn Abū Bakr and two other people climbed the walls of 'Uthmān's neighbors' houses and reached 'Uthmān. Muḥammad ibn Abū Bakr said to those two, "I will hold 'Uthmān and you kill him." When the three reached 'Uthmān, Muḥammad ibn Abū Bakr sat on his chest. 'Uthmān said to him, "If your father, Abū Bakr, would have seen you sitting on my chest he would've been disappointed in you." Muḥammad ibn Abū Bakr started getting cold feet but the other two killed 'Uthmān.[42]

When 'Uthmān was killed, the news was brought to Ṭalḥa as good news. However, when 'Alī (as) heard the news, he angrily stormed out. Ṭalḥa's eye caught 'Alī (as) and he asked, "O' Abū al-Ḥasan, what has enraged you?" 'Alī (as) replied to Ṭalḥa, "God Damn you! Shall a companion of the Prophet (pbuh) be killed?!" Ṭalḥa answered, "If he had kept Marwān away from himself, he would not have been killed."[43] In another narration, it is stated that he said, "He was neither a beloved angel nor a messenger of God."[44]

---

[40] *Ansāb al-Ashrāf,* 5: p. 69; *Tārīkh al-Ṭabarī,* 5: p. 118 & in the European edition 1: p. 3021; *Al-Kāmil fit-Tārīkh Ibn al-Athir,* 3: pp. 68-70.

[41] *Sharḥ Nahj al-Balāgha* by Ibn Abī l-Ḥadīd 2: p. 404.

[42] *Ansāb al-Ashrāf,* 5: p. 69; *Tārīkh al-Ṭabarī,* 5: p. 118 & in the European edition 1: p. 3021; *Al-Kāmil fit-Tārīkh Ibn al-Athir,* 3: pp. 68-70

[43] *Ansāb al-Ashrāf,* 5: pp. 69-70.

[44] *Ansāb al-Ashrāf,* 5: p. 74.

People's Allegiance to 'Alī and 'Uthmān Burial

'Uthmān's corpse was left on the ground and no one was allowed to bury it until people pledged allegiance to 'Alī (as). The Umayyads then asked 'Alī (as) to allow 'Uthmān's family to do so. 'Alī (as) gave the permission and ordered that he be allowed to be buried. After the Sunset prayers, five people, including Marwān, 'Uthmān's daughter and three of his servants, picked the body up and took it to be buried.

When people heard about this, they filled their pockets with pebbles and sat in the way. When 'Uthmān's corpse reached them, they pelted his coffin with stones and attacked to overthrow it. The incident was reported to 'Alī (as). He ordered some to repel the disturbance and protect 'Uthmān's body. They performed according to the order, surrounded the body and took it to its destination, and thus, 'Uthmān was buried in "Ḥashshu Kawkab" Garden, next to Baqī', where the Jews buried their dead.

At her father's funeral, 'Uthmān's daughter raised her voice in mourning and lamentation and even then, a crowd pelted them with pebbles and stones and kept shouting, "Na'thal! Na'thal!"[45]

After Mu'awiyah obtained the caliphate, he ordered that the walls of "Ḥashshu Kawkab" Garden be demolished and that piece of land be attached to Baqī' Cemetery, and he also ordered the Muslims to bury their dead around 'Uthmān's grave, so that his tomb would join Muslims tombs. Nowadays, 'Uthmān's grave is at the end of al-Baqī.

The End of Saqīfa

Saqīfa, which was planned by several people in the Prophet's era, ended after 'Uthmān was killed. In Saqīfa, the plan was for them to become the caliph one after the other. If 'Uthmān had not been killed, he would have appointed someone from the Umayyads like Mu'awiyah, and so 'Alī (as) would not have become the caliph. However, the pact they had made in Saqīfa was broken by the revolt of the people against 'Uthmān and his assassination, and therefore

---

[45] *Tārīkh al-Ṭabarī*, 5: pp. 143-144 & in the European edition 1: p. 3046; *Kitāb al-Futūḥ*, p. 159; *Al-Riaz un-Nazra*, 2: pp. 131-132.

people were liberated. When the Muslims were released from Saqīfa, the Muhājirūn, the Anṣār and the Companions rushed to 'Alī's house, brought him to the Prophet's Mosque and pledged allegiance to him.[46]

*****

One day in the last days of his caliphate, while delivering a sermon known as "Shaqshaqiya",[47] 'Alī (as) briefly mentioned the period when Abū Bakr came to power until how people pledged allegiance to him and the events that followed. At the end of this book, we saw fit to narrate this sermon.

---

[46] *Tārīkh al-Ṭabarī*, 5: pp. 152-153 & in the European edition 1: p. 3066; *Kanz al-Ummāl*, 3: p. 161 hadīth 2471; *Kitāb al-Futūḥ*, pp. 160-161; *Ansāb al-Ashrāf*, 5: p. 70; *al-Mustadrak*, 3: p. 114.

[47] *Nahj al-Balāghah*, sermon 3.

'Alī's Sermon also known as Shaqshaqiya

"Beware! By Allah, the son of Abu Quhafah (Abu Bakr) dressed himself with it (the caliphate) and he certainly knew that my position in relation to it was the same as the position of the axis in relation to the hand-mill. The flood water flows down from me and the bird cannot fly upto me. I put a curtain against the caliphate and kept myself detached from it.

Then I began to think whether I should assault or endure calmly the blinding darkness of tribulations wherein the grown up are made feeble and the young grow old and the true believer acts under strain till he meets Allah (on his death)..

I found that endurance thereon was wiser. So I adopted patience although there was pricking in the eye and suffocation (of mortification) in the throat. I watched the plundering of my inheritance till the first one went his way but handed over the Caliphate to Ibn al-Khattab after himself."

After this statement, 'Alī (as) recited a poem by Al-A'sha the poet:

"My days are now passed on the camel's back (in difficulty) while there were days (of ease) when I enjoyed the company of Jabir's brother Hayyan?!"

It is strange that during his lifetime he wished to be released from the caliphate but he confirmed it for the other one after his death. No doubt these two shared its udders strictly among themselves. This one put the Caliphate in a tough enclosure where the utterance was haughty and the touch was rough. Mistakes were in plenty and so also the excuses therefore. One in contact with it was like the rider of an unruly camel. If he pulled up its rein the very nostril would be slit, but if he let it loose he would be thrown. Consequently, by Allah people got involved in recklessness, wickedness, unsteadiness and deviation.

Nevertheless, I remained patient despite length of period and stiffness of trial, till when he went his way (of death) he put the matter (of Caliphate) in a group4 and regarded me to be one of them. But good Heavens! What had I to do with this "consultation"? Where was any doubt about me with regard to the first of them that I was now considered akin to these ones? But I remained low when they were low and flew high when they flew high.

One of them turned against me because of his hatred and the other got inclined the other way due to his in-law relationship and this thing and that thing, till the third man of these people stood up with heaving breasts between his dung and fodder. With him his children of his grand-father, (Umayyah) also stood up swallowing up Allah's wealth like a camel devouring the foliage of spring, till his rope broke down, his actions finished him and his gluttony brought him down prostrate.

At that moment, nothing took me by surprise, but the crowd of people rushing to me. It advanced towards me from every side like the mane of the hyena so much so that Hasan and Husayn were getting crushed and both the ends of my shoulder garment were torn. They collected around me like a herd of sheep and goats. When I took up the reins of government one party broke away and another turned disobedient while the rest began acting wrongfully as if they had not heard the word of Allah saying:

$$تِلْكَ ٱلدَّارُ ٱلْآخِرَةُ نَجْعَلُهَا لِلَّذِينَ لَا يُرِيدُونَ عُلُوًّا فِي ٱلْأَرْضِ وَلَا فَسَادًا وَٱلْعَٰقِبَةُ لِلْمُتَّقِينَ$$

"That abode in the hereafter, We assign it for those who intend not to exult themselves in the earth, nor (to make) mischief (therein); and the end is (best) for the pious ones. (Qur'an, 28:83)"[1]

Yes, by Allah, they had heard it and understood it but the world appeared glittering in their eyes and its embellishments seduced them. Behold, by Him who split the grain (to grow) and created living beings, if people had not come to me and supporters had not exhausted the argument and if there had been no pledge of Allah with the learned to the effect that they should not acquiesce in the gluttony of the oppressor and the hunger of the oppressed I would have cast the rope of Caliphate on its own shoulders, and would have given the last one

---

[1] al-Qasas 83.

the same treatment as to the first one. Then you would have seen that in my view this world of yours is no better than the sneezing of a goat."

(It is said that when Amir al-mu'minin reached here in his sermon a man of Iraq stood up and handed him over a writing. Amir al-mu'minin began looking at it, when Ibn 'Abbas said, "O' Amir al-mu'minin, I wish you resumed your Sermon from where you broke it." Thereupon he replied, "O' Ibn 'Abbas it was like the foam of a Camel (Dulla)[2] which gushed out but subsided." Ibn 'Abbas says that he never grieved over any utterance as he did over this one because Amir al-mu'minin could not finish it as he wished to.)

'Alī (as) expressed the pain he had endured for nearly twenty-eight years of the three caliphs' rulings, as the organ that hangs from a male camel's mouth when it is excited and then said, "It calmed down after the excitement." Due to this similitude, this sermon has been called the Shaqshaqiya Sermon.

---

[2] A male camel has an organ called "Dulla" in its mouth that enlarges and hangs out of its mouth when aroused to attract female camels, which in Arabic is called Shaqshaqiya, and so the name of this sermon is taken from this similitude.

The Battle of Ḥarrah

Envoys of the People of Medina in Yazīd's Palace

The governor of Medina, 'Uthmān ibn Muḥammad ibn Abī Sufyān ibn Muḥammad ibn Abī Sufyān, chose envoys from the people of Medina, including 'Abdullāh ibn Ḥanẓala, son of Ġasīl al-Malā'kah from the Anṣār, 'Abdullāh ibn Abī 'Amr al-Makhzūmī, and Munḏir ibn Zubayr, and a group of many aristocrats and nobles of Medina to be sent to Yazīd.

These envoys went to Yazīd. Yazīd welcomed them and gifted them with considerable presents. He gave one hundred thousand dirhams to 'Abdullāh ibn Ḥanẓala, who was an honorable, scholarly, devout, respected man, and rewarded ten thousand dirhams, as well as clothes and shoes, to each of his eight sons who were with him!

When this group of envoys went back to Medina, they started badmouthing and defaming Yazīd and stated that, "We have returned from a place where its host has no religion, drinks and plays a musical instrument and is friends with singers. He takes pleasure in keeping dogs and spends his time with corrupt young men. O' people! Know that we do not consider him worthy of the caliphate and so we will remove him from this position."

'Abdullāh ibn Ḥanẓala, Ġasīl al-Malā'kah's son, rose and said, "I have come from a place where I would have rebelled against its host even if I had no friends or helpers other than my sons."

People said to him, "We have been told that he has exalted and cherished you and honored you with presents and kindness!" 'Abdullāh ibn Ḥanẓala said, "Yes, he has done so and I have accepted his gifts in order to obtain power by them and prepare an army and weapons to fight him."

Therefore, the people deposed Yazīd from the caliphate, and in result, pledged allegiance to 'Abdullāh ibn Ḥanẓala and made him their governor and ruler.

When Mundir ibn Zubayr, who had received a reward of one hundred thousand dirhams from Yazīd during their meeting, came to Medina, he said, "Although Yazīd has given me a reward of one hundred thousand dirhams, this amount will not prevent me from telling the truth about him. I swear to God that Yazīd drinks up to the point where he gets wasted and does not pray." He, like his other Companions, and even more severely, rebuked Yazīd.[1]

The Uprising of the Companions and their Followers

The Uprising of People of Medina and their Allegiance to 'Abdullāh ibn Ḥanẓala

In *Tārīkh al-Islām al-Kabir*, ad-Dahabī writes:

People of Medina gathered around 'Abdullāh ibn Ḥanẓala and made a pact with him to obey him until his death. 'Abdullāh addressed them and said, "O' people! Fear God. We are revolting against Yazīd only because we feared the sky would rain stones over our heads. This man rapes maids who have been impregnated by his father and sleeps with his own daughters and sisters! He drinks and does not perform his prayers."[2]

Ya'qūbī also writes in his history book:

Ibn Mīnā, Mu'awiyah's agent keeping hold of his personal agricultural tax incomes, came to 'Uthmān ibn Muḥammad, who had been appointed governor of Medina by Yazīd, and informed him that when he wanted to collect the annual load of wheat and dates to be sent to Shām, people of Medina obstructed his work. 'Uthmān summoned a group of them and when they showed up, he snapped at them. In result, they revolted against him and anyone from the Umayyads who was in Medina, and eventually drove them out of Medina, and pelted them with pebbles and stones as they were leaving.[3]

According to *Kitab al-Aghani*, 'Abdullāh ibn Zubayr attempted to overthrow Yazīd and many supported him. 'Abdullāh ibn Muṭī' and 'Abdullāh ibn

---

[1] *Tārīkh al-Ṭabarī*, 7, pp. 3-13; *Al-Kāmil fit-Tārīkh Ibn al-Athir*, 4, pp, 40-41; *Al-Bidaya wa an-Nihaya*, 8, p 216; *al-'Iqd al-Farīd*, 4, p. 388.

[2] *Tārīkh Ya'qūbī*, 2, p. 250.

[3] *Ibid.*, 2, p. 250.

Ḥanẓala and a group of people from Medina entered Mecca, walked in on 'Abdullāh ibn Zubayr in the Prophet's mosque, and announced the ousting of Yazīd everywhere on the pulpit.

'Abdullāh ibn Abī 'Amr ibn Ḥafḍ ibn al-Mughīrah al-Makhzūmī declared the ousting of Yazīd as, "I oust Yazīd from the caliphate just like I would remove the turban from my head." He said this and he took the turban off his head. Then he continued, "I am saying this while Yazīd himself has shown me hospitality and given me decent presents. Indeed, this man is the enemy of God and is always drunk and wasted!"

Someone else stated, "I remove Yazīd from the caliphate, just as if I'm taking my shoes off." Another announced, "I will oust him like I take off my clothes." And another said something similar, until a bunch of turbans, clothes and shoes of all colors were piled up in the mosque, thus revealing their disgust towards Yazīd, and allying in removing him from his position.

But 'Abdullāh ibn 'Umar and Muḥammad ibn 'Alī ibn Abī Ṭālib refused to coordinate with them. Therefore, many conversations and discussions took place between Muḥammad ibn 'Alī ibn Abī Ṭālib, especially with 'Abdullāh ibn Zubayr's Companions and friends in Medina, to the extent where they wanted to force him to fulfill their desire which inevitably led him to leave Medina and return to Mecca. This was the very first unfortunate encounter that occurred between him and 'Abdullāh ibn Zubayr.

After that, the people of Medina decided to expel the Umayyads from their town. Hence, they induced them to agree to a covenant that after leaving Medina, they would not aid any enemy troops against the people of Medina, and instead chase them away and if they didn't succeed in that, at least not join them in entering Medina.

The Umayyads's Families under the Protection of Imam Sajjād

In *Kitab al-Aghani*, Abū al-Faraj writes:

Marwān went to 'Abdullāh ibn 'Umar and said, "O' Abū 'Abdur-Rahman! You see that people are revolting against us. So protect our families." 'Abdullāh ibn 'Umar replied, "I have nothing to do with you or them."

Receiving this answer, Marwān got up to leave and said, "Curse on you and this situation and your religion and beliefs!" Then he went to 'Alī ibn al-Ḥusayn (as) and asked him to protect his family. Imam Sajjād (as) accepted his request and took Marwān's family including his wife, Umm Abān, 'Uthmān's daughter, in his support and sent them to Ṭa'if with his two sons Muḥammad and Abdullāh.

Al-Ṭabarī and Ibn al-Athir have both narrated:

When the people of Medina expelled the governor and representative of Yazīd and the Umayyads from Medina, Marwān went to 'Abdullāh ibn 'Umar and asked him to protect his family. But 'Abdullāh ibn 'Umar did not agree to Marwān's request. Later, he turned to 'Alī ibn al-Ḥusayn (as) and said, "O' Abū al-Ḥassan! I deserve your consideration due to our kinship. Protect my family and keep them next to yours." Imam Sajjād (as) replied, "Will do." So Marwān sent his family to Imam Sajjād (as) and he sent them out of Medina with his own family and placed them in Yanbu.[4]

In *Al-Kāmil fit-Tārīkh* Ibn al-Athir it is stated that:

Marwān sent his wife Ā'ishah, who was 'Uthmān ibn 'Affān's daughter, and other members of his family to 'Alī ibn al-Ḥusayn (as), and he sent Marwān's family with his family to Yanbu.

It is also stated in *Kitab al-Aghani* that:

People expelled the Umayyads from Medina. Marwān wanted to pray with his Companions, but he was prevented from doing so, and they said, "We swear to God he has no right to pray with the people, but he can pray with his family." It was then that Marwān performed his prayers with them and then left.[5]

The Umayyads Seeking Help from Yazīd

al-Ṭabarī and others have said that:

The Umayyads left their homes and entered Marwān's house and gathered there, and the people of Medina almost sieged them. When the Umayyads saw this, they wrote a letter to Yazīd and asked him for help and to rescue them.

---

[4] *Tārīkh al-Ṭabarī,* 7: p. 7; *Al-Kāmil fit-Tārīkh Ibn al-Athir,* 4: p. 45.

[5] *Kitab al-Aghani,* 1: p. 36.

Yazīd said to their herald, "Doesn't the number of the Umayyads and their followers in Medina reach one thousand?!" The herald said, "It does. And I swear to God it is even more than that!" Yazīd said, "So this number of people could not stand against the attackers for even a few hours?!"

Hence, Yazīd summoned 'Amr ibn Sa'īd and when he showed up, read him the letter from the Umayyads and informed him of the incident and then ordered him to suppress the people of Medina. But 'Amr did not give in and did not accept such a mission.

Therefore, this time Yazīd wrote a letter to 'Ubaydullāh ibn Ziyād, ordering him to go to Medina and suppress the people there, and after that go to Mecca and suppress 'Abdullāh ibn Zubayr. 'Ubaydullāh ibn Ziyād did not accept this mission and said, "I swear to God that I will not do these two stigmas and scandals for this wicked person; one killing the Prophet's daughter's son, and the other fighting the house of God!"

It is worth mentioning that Marjānah, 'Ubaydullāh ibn Ziyād's mother, blamed and scolded her son for killing Imam Ḥusayn (as) and reminded him of the vastness of what he had done and said, "Woe to you! What have you done?! How could you bear the hugeness and the shame of such an accountability?!"[6]

When Yazīd was disappointed by 'Ubaydullāh ibn Ziyād, he sent after Muslim ibn 'Uqba al-Murrī because Mu'awiyah had once told him, "One day, you will finally clash with the people of Medina. In that case, order Muslim ibn 'Uqba to suppress them because he is a man who has proven his loyalty and courtesy to me!" When Muslim came to Yazīd, he was an old, ill, weak man.[7]

In *Kitab al-Aghani*, Abū al-Faraj writes:

Muslim claimed to Yazīd, "Whoever you assigned to fight Medina did not give in and did not take responsibility. But I am the one for you for I dreamed that the thorn tree of Medina is screaming, "Only by the hands of Muslim!" I

---

[6] *Al-Amalī*, p: 164.

[7] *Tārīkh al-Ṭabarī*, 7: pp. 5-13; *Al-Kāmil fit-Tārīkh Ibn al-Athir*, 4: pp. 44-45; *Al-Bidaya wa an-Nihaya*, 8: p. 219; *Kitab al-Aghani*, 1: pp. 35-36.

turned to the voice and heard it say, "Muslim! Take revenge on the people of Medina who are 'Uthmān's killers!"

The Caliph's Orders to the Commander of the Army

al-Ṭabarī writes:

When Yazīd commissioned Muslim to suppress the uprising of the people of Medina, he said to him, "If a calamity befell you, appoint Ḥaṣīn ibn Numayr al-Sakūnī as your successor in the army." Then he added, "Give people three days. If in that time they declared their obedience then let them go, otherwise after that period, fight them. And when you beat them, leave your troops free for three days to plunder and loot their belongings and possessions, so that whatever they gain including wealth, jewels, money, weapons and food would belong to them! After three days, leave them alone and pay attention to 'Alī ibn al-Ḥusayn and have mercy on him and do not hurt him in any way. Order your troops to respect him as well. Bring yourself closer to him because he had no role in the behavior and tumult of the people of Medina."

Thus, Muslim ordered his harbinger to mobilize the people. The harbinger shouted, "Towards Ḥijāz; by receiving an award and one hundred dinars in cash for personal expenses!" And that was how twelve thousand armed fighters prepared to leave.

In the book *At-Tanbih wal-'Ishraf*, al-Mas'ūdī says:

Yazīd ordered Muslim ibn 'Uqba saying, "When you reach Medina, fight anyone who prevents you from entering the city or guards it. Bring their swords down with your swords. Do not have mercy on them, and leave your troops free to plunder the belongings of the people of Medina for three days. Kill their wounded and chase their fugitives. But if they sought peace, forgive them and go to Mecca and fight 'Abdullāh ibn Zubayr."

In *Murūj aḏ-Ḏahab*, al-Mas'ūdī also mentions that:

Yazīd commissioned Muslim ibn 'Uqba to suppress the uprising of the people of Medina. Unlike the Prophet (pbuh), who used to call Medina "Tayyiba" (i.e. fragrant), Muslim called Medina "Netnah" (i.e. rotten)! al-Dīnawarī has also narrated this same thing.

188

The Caliph of the Muslims' Poem

When the army was getting ready to move to Medina, Yazīd saw it and addressed the following poem to 'Abdullāh ibn Zubayr:

When the night is over and the army lands in Wadi al-Qura, tell Zubayr's son, "Do you see the twenty thousand young and old fighters drunk and wasted or all awake and sharp?!"

'Abdullāh ibn Zubayr's nicknames were Abū Bakr and Abū Khabīb and he called Yazīd the "wasted drunk". al-Mas'ūdī writes that Yazīd sent the following poems to Ibn Zubayr:

Call on God for help because I have sent the warriors of 'Ak and Ash'ar to your battle. In such a situation, O' Abū Khabīb! How will you survive? Now think about saving your life before my army reaches you![8]

Al-Ṭabarī and Ibn al-Athir have also narrated:

When 'Abdul Malik ibn Marwān heard that Yazīd had sent troops (with such orders) to Medina, in objection to the vastness of such a decree and its offensiveness he stated, "I wish the sky would fall to the ground!"

But it was not long before he himself, at the beginning of his caliphate, did something more insolent. And that was when he commissioned Ḥajjāj ibn Yūsuf to besiege Mecca and to both smash the Ka'bah (the house of God and the Qibla of the Muslims) with a catapult, and to kill 'Abdullāh ibn Zubayr.

Caliphate Troops on the Way to Mecca and Medina

When the news of Muslim and his troops heading for Medina reached the people there, they increased the intensity of their siege on the Umayyads in Marwān's house and said, "We swear to God we will not let go of you, and we will behead you unless you covenant not to rebel against us, not to take part in any conflict, not to take advantage of our weaknesses, and not to aid our enemies. In this case, we will not hurt you and will only kick you out." The Umayyads agreed and promised to do so. Later, the people of Medina freed

---

[8] *at-Tanbih wal-'Ishraf*, P: 263; *Murūj aḏ-Ḏahab*, 3: pp. 68-69; *Al-Akhbar al-Tuwal*, p. 265 where these verses are; we have narrated the first poem from *Tārīkh al-Ṭabarī*, 8: p.6 & *Al-Kāmil fit-Tārīkh Ibn al-Athir*; Also see: *Tārīkh al-Islām al-kabir aḏ-Ḏahabī*, 2: p. 355.

them and they packed up and emigrated from Medina. However, on their way to Wadi Al-Qura, they encountered Muslim ibn 'Uqba.

In this confrontation, Muslim called one of them, who was 'Umar ibn 'Uthmān, and said to him, "Tell me what is going on and inform me about the situation in Medina and give me your opinion." 'Umar ibn 'Uthmān replied, "I can't say anything; they made us promise not to say anything about them." Muslim said, "I swear to God if you were not 'Uthmān's son, I would have decapitated you! And I swear to God that after you, I will not leave any Qurayshite person alone."

'Uthmān's son left Muslim and returned to his Companions, informing them of what had been said between him and Muslim. So Marwān ibn al-Ḥakam said to his son 'Abdul Malik, "Go meet Muslim before me because that may be enough for him so he wouldn't ask me for anything." So 'Abdul Malik went to Muslim and Muslim asked him, "What have you brought me?" 'Abdul Malik answered, "OK. In my opinion, move with your troops to Dī Nakhla (the groves) and settle there and have your troops rest in the shades of the palm trees there so that they can eat nectarous, sweet dates; dates so nutritious they are used for milking. The next day, move around Medina and go until the city is located on your left and you reach the desert of Ḥarrah, which is located on the east side of Medina. From there, appear to the people of Medina, so that they can see the sunrise beyond your soldiers' shoulders and the sharpness of the sun doesn't dazzle your troops' eyes. Also, if you do so, the beams of light caused by the collision of the sun rays with their helmets, bayonets and armors will have people stunned and aghast, rather than if you enter on them from the west. Then, fight them and ask God for victory over them!" Muslim said to him, "Good for your father for raising such a son!"

After that, Marwān walked in on him and Muslim asked, "Well! What do you have to say?!" Marwān replied, "Didn't 'Abdul Malik already talk to you?" Muslim said, "He did. And what a great man he is. I have never talked to any Qurayshite like 'Abdul Malik." Marwān said, "Now that you have talked to 'Abdul Malik, it is as if you have spoken to me."

Muslim followed 'Abdul Malik's orders wherever he stepped, until they finally settled in the east of Medina. He gave the people there a respite of three days, and at the end of that period of time, he asked them, "O' people of Medina! What are you going to do? Will you surrender or fight?" They answered, "We will fight." He said, "Don't do that. Give in to obedience so that we can unite and combine our power and strength and attack this atheist, who has been surrounded by a bunch of impious, libertine lowborn people who are his followers." (He meant 'Abdullāh Ibn Zubayr) In response, they said, "O' enemies of God! If you have plans to attack him, you have to get over your fantasy. Do you really think we would allow you to attack Mecca and the House of God, and disturb its people, and dishonor it?! No way! We swear to God, we will not let you do so."[9]

Al-Mas'ūdī and Al-Dīnawarī also report:

The people of Medina dug up the Prophet's moat that had been dug in the Battle of Ahzab, and built walls around Medina. Their poet addressed Yazīd, reciting:

Our proud moat is a joyous state. Neither are you, Yazīd, one of us nor is your uncle. O' ruiner of prayers for lusts! When we get killed, convert to Christianity and turn into a Christian. Then drink and forget the Friday prayers.[10]

Ad-Dahabī says:

'Abdullāh ibn Ḥanẓala spent his nights in the mosque. He did not eat or drink and he fasted every day and he would break his fasts with a little syrup. In addition, he was never seen taking his eyes off the ground and looking up.

When Muslim and his helpers and friends arrived, 'Abdullāh ibn Ḥanẓala gave a speech among his Companions and encouraged and motivated them to fight and battle and stay brave and determined, and at the end he said, "O Mighty Lord! We are counting on you."

In the morning, the people of Medina prepared for battle and showed face when suddenly, from behind, they heard the outcry of Takbīr (Allāhu Akbar).

---

[9] *Tārīkh al-Ṭabarī*, 7: pp. 6-8; *Al-Kāmil fit-Tārīkh Ibn al-Athir*, 4: pp. 45-46.

[10] *at-Tanbih wal-'Ishraf*, :p. 264; *al-Akhbar al-Tuwal*, : p. 265.

Banū al-Ḥārith unexpectedly attacked them from Ḥarrah, and as a result of this sudden attack, the fighters of Medina quickly retreated.

'Abdullāh ibn Ḥanẓala, who was leaning on one of his sons and had fallen asleep, was awakened by his son and informed of the incident. Seeing this, 'Abdullāh ordered his eldest son to confront them. And so to carry out his father's orders, he fought up to when he was killed.

'Abdullāh ibn Ḥanẓala sent his sons one after the other to fight the invaders until they were all killed in battle and he was left alone among a group of his Companions. Then, he turned to one of his servants and said, "Protect me from behind so that I can perform the noon prayer." When he had finished his prayer, that servant said to him, "There is no one left, why should we stay?" And he said this to 'Abdullāh while he was still waving his flag with only five people remaining around them. 'Abdullāh replied, "Because we have risen up to fight until we die. Shame on you!"

The narrator writes:

The people of Medina fled around like fleeing ostriches and the people from Shām hit them with swords of hatred. When people were defeated, 'Abdullāh took off his armor and with no armor or helmet, rushed to the enemy and kept fighting until he was killed. Then, Marwān ibn al-Ḥakam appeared at 'Abdullāh ibn Ḥanẓala's corpse, whose index finger was still pointed, and addressed him saying, "In life, your index finger was always working too!"[11]

Caliphate Troops Plundering the Prophet's Shrine

Al-Ṭabarī and others have reported that:

Muslim left his troops free to plunder Medina. Hence, they killed defenseless people and looted their belongings.[12]

Ya'qūbī writes:

Many people were killed in the fall of Medina and there were few who survived. Muslim left his troops free to kill, loot and desecrate the people of that

---

[11] *Tārīkh al-Islām al-kabir aḏ-Ḏahabī,* 2: pp. 356-357.

[12] *Tārīkh al-Ṭabarī,* 7: p. 11; *Al-Kāmil fit-Tārīkh Ibn al-Athir,* 3: p. 47; *Al-Bidaya wa an-Nihaya,* 8: p. 220.

192

region. Their rapes resulted in impregnating virgin girls who gave birth to children whose fathers were unknown.[13]

In his history book, Ibn Kathīr states that:

In the Battle of Ḥarrah, seven hundred memorizers of the Qur'ān, three hundred of whom were Companions of the Prophet (pbuh) and had comprehended his words, were killed. Elsewhere, he says:

So many people were killed in this incident that there was the fear that Medina would become empty of inhabitants.[14] He has also said:

Women were raped, so much that it was said that in those days thousands of unmarried women got pregnant! And he narrates from Hishām ibn Ḥassān who said, "After the Battle of Ḥarrah, a thousand unmarried women gave birth to children in Medina!" And he quotes Zuhrī, who said, "Seven hundred leaders from the Muhājirūn and the Anṣār were killed, and the number of servants killed and those who could not be identified to be slaves or freed, reached ten thousand!"[15]

In his history book, Al-Suyūṭī states that:

The Battle of Ḥarrah[16] started from the gate of Ṭayyebah and many groups of Companions and others were killed and Medina was looted and a thousand virgins were raped.[17]

Al-Dīnawarī and Ad-Dahabī have quoted that Abū Hārun al-'Abdī said:

I saw Abū Sa'īd al-Khudrī, whose white beard was very short on both sides and long on the chin. I asked him, "O' Abū Sa'īd! What happened to your beard?" He answered, "This is a calamity that the oppressors from Shām brought upon me in the Battle of Ḥarrah. They broke into my house and looted what I had, even my water-drinking bowl, and then left the house. After them,

---

[13] *Tārīkh Ya'qūbī*, 6: p. 251.

[14] *Al-Bidaya wa an-Nihaya*, 6: p. 234.

[15] *Ibid.*, 8: p. 22.

[16] For detailed account of the Battle of Harrah, please see: *Battle of Harrah* by Mohammad Ali Chenarani. Islamic Research Foundation Astan-e Quds Razavi (2008).

[17] *Tārīkh al-Khulafā'*, p. 209; *Tārīkh al-Khamis*, 2: p. 302.

ten other people invaded my house, while I was performing my prayers. They searched all over the house and found nothing, and so pitied me for this situation. Then, they dragged me from my prayer position and knocked me to the ground, and each separately, brought this calamity upon me as you can see. They cut off my beard on the sides, and turned me into this, and what is left is the part that was buried in dirt and debris and they couldn't reach. I haven't touched it so I would meet my God as is."[18]

Indeed, this is what went on in the city of the Prophet (pbuh) on those three days.

Allegiance Based on the Servitude of the Caliph!

Al-Ṭabarī and others have reported that:

Muslim ibn 'Uqba asked people to pledge allegiance on the basis that Yazīd ibn Mu'awiyah be free to encroach on their lives, belongings and families![19]

Al-Mas'ūdī says:

Muslim asked those who remained to pledge allegiance on the basis that they are slaves and bondmen of Yazīd. In this rule, he excluded 'Alī ibn al-Ḥusayn (as) because he had not interfered in the uprising of the people of Medina, and also 'Alī ibn 'Abdullāh ibn 'Abbās, whose uncles from the Kinda tribe, who were in Muslim's army, supported him. Al-Mas'ūdī says:

Whoever did not swear to such allegiance would need to deal with the sword of the executioner (i.e. be killed).[20]

In *Kitāb aṭ-Tabaqāt al-Kabīr* by Ibn Sa'd, it is stated that:

When Musrif ibn 'Uqba (he means Muslim ibn 'Uqba) started killing people, he went to the 'Aqīq region and settled there and then asked those around him, "Is 'Alī ibn al-Ḥusayn here?" They said, "Yes." He said, "Then how come I don't see him?" Just then, 'Alī ibn al-Ḥusayn (as) and his cousins, who were Muḥammad ibn al-Ḥanafiyyah's sons, came forward and when Muslim's

---

[18] *al-Akhbar al-Tuwal,* : p. 269; *Tārīkh al-Islām al-kabir aḏ-Ḏahabī,* 2: p. 357.

[19] *Tārīkh al-Ṭabarī,* 7: p. 13.

[20] *at-Tanbih wal-'Ishraf,* : p. 264; *Murūj aḏ-Ḏahab,* 3: p. 71.

eyes caught him, he welcomed him and seated him on the throne next to himself.[21]

Additionally, in the history book, *Tārīkh al-Ṭabarī*, it is written that:

Muslim welcomed him and placed him next to himself on the small futon that was spread on the throne. Then he said, "The Commander of the Faithful has asked me to keep an eye on you, but these filthy people preoccupied me and prevented me from attending you." Then he continued, "It seems that your family is concerned and worried about your coming here?" 'Alī ibn al-Ḥusayn (as) replied, "God knows yes." Therefore, Muslim ordered his horse to be saddled and he be returned to his family respectfully and will much honor.[22]

Al-Dīnawarī also writes:

On the fourth day, Muslim ibn 'Uqba sat on the throne and called people to pledge allegiance to Yazīd. The first to emerge was Yazīd ibn Abdullāh, one of Rabi'ah ibn al-Aswad's descendants, whose grandmother was Umm Salamah, the Prophet's wife. Muslim said to him, "Take allegiance." Yazīd ibn 'Abdullāh replied, "I swear allegiance according to the God's Book and His Prophet's traditions." Muslim said, "No. Swear allegiance that you are fully a slave to the Commander of the Faithful who can encroach on your belongings and children as he wishes." Yazīd ibn 'Abdullāh did not take such allegiance. Later, Muslim ordered that he be decapitated.[23]

Al-Ṭabarī says:

Muslim ibn 'Uqba called people to swear allegiance to Yazīd in the Quba region, and one day after the Battle of Ḥarrah, two leaders of the Quraysh named Yazīd Ibn 'Abdullāh ibn Zam'ah and Muḥammad ibn Abī al-Jahm, who had both asked for aegis after the Battle of Ḥarrah and had received it, came to Muslim. Muslim told them to take allegiance. They said, "We pledge allegiance to you according to God's Book and His Prophet's traditions." Muslim said, "God no! I will neither accept such allegiance from you nor let you go." Then

---

[21] *Kitāb aṭ-Tabaqāt al-Kabīr*, Ibn Sa'd 5: p. 215.

[22] *Tārīkh al-Ṭabarī*, 7: pp. 11-12; *Kitāb al-Futūḥ*, 5: p. 300.

[23] *Tārīkh al-Ṭabarī*, 7: pp. 11-12.

he ordered them to be decapitated! At this point, Marwān said, "Glory be to God! Did you just behead two Qurayshite men who were under your aegis?!" Muslim hit him on the buttocks with his cane and said, "I swear to God, if you speak like those two, you will not survive either."

Then he says:

After that, Yazīd Ibn Wahhāb ibn Zam'ah was brought and Muslim said to him, "Take allegiance." Yazīd said, "I will pledge allegiance to you according to 'Umar's traditions." Muslim ordered, "Kill him!" Yazīd, who was terrified, said, "I'll pledge allegiance!" Muslim replied, "No! I swear to God, I will not exonerate this mistake!"

Hereby, Marwān interceded and pointed out their relationship to Muslim. Upon hearing this, Muslim ordered Marwān to be taken by his neck and forced to lower his head. Then he declared, "Both of you! Pledge allegiance for you are both tiny, worthless servants of Yazīd." And then he ordered Yazīd Ibn Wahhāb to be decapitated![24]

Severed Heads Before Caliph Yazīd!

Ibn Abd al-Barr writes:

Muslim ibn 'Uqba sent the severed heads of the people of Medina to Yazīd. When these heads were placed on the ground in front of him, Yazīd referred to the poems of Ibn Ziba'rā on the day of the Battle of Uhud, which said:

I wish my elders who were killed in the Battle of Badr were present to see the cries of Banū Khazraj from the blowing of swords and spears! Then, they would scream with great joy and say, "O Yazīd, well done."

At that point, one of the Prophet's Companions turned to Yazīd and said, "O Commander of the Faithful! Have you apostatized from Islām?" Yazīd replied, "Yes. We apologize to God!" The companion said, "I swear to God I will not stay with you in this land." He announced this and left Yazīd's palace.[25]

---

[24] *al-Akhbar al-Tuwal*, p. 265.

[25] *al-'Iqd al-Farīd*, 4: p. 390.

196

In the narration by Ibn Kathīr, after the first verse, comes the following poem:

When the front line formed in the Quba region and the quarrel with the 'Abdul al-Ashal tribe heated, we killed their elders and seniors in revenge for our killed ones in the Battle of Badr.

Ibn Kathīr says that one of the deniers of the first Caliphs has added to these poems as follows:

Banī Hāshim considered ruling and governorship an entertainment, because the truth is that there was nothing going on and there were no divine revelations.

Letter Equivalence

Ā	ā	آ
Ḥ	ḥ	ح
Kh	kh	خ
Ḏ	ḏ	ذ
Ṣ	ṣ	ص
Ḍ	ḍ	ض
Ṭ	ṭ	ط
Ẓ	ẓ	ظ
ʾA/ʾU/ʾI	aʾ/uʾ/iʾ	ع
Ġ	ġ	غ
Q	q	ق
Ū	ū	و
Ī	ī	ي

List of Names

1	Abān and ʿAmr (brothers of Khālid ibn Saʿīd)	ابان و عمرو
2	ʿAbbās ibn ʿAbd al-Muṭṭalib (Prophet's uncle)	عباس
3	Abul-Faḍl	ابو الفضل
4	ʿAbd Manāf [al-Mughīrah ibn Quṣayy]	عبد مناف [المغيرة بن قصي]
5	ʿAbdullāh ibn ʿAbbās ibn Abī Rabiʿah	عبدالله بن عباس بن ابي ربيعه
6	ʿAbdullāh ibn Abī ʿAmr ibn Ḥafḍ ibn al-Mughīrah al-Makhzūmī	عبدالله بن ابي عمرو بن حفض بن المغيرة المخزومي
7	ʿAbdullāh ibn Āmir ibn Kurayz	عبدالله بن عامر بن كُريز
8	ʿAbdullāh ibn Ḥanẓala, Ġasīl al-Malāʾkah	عبدالله بن حنظلة / غسيل الملائكة
9	ʿAbdullāh ibn Judʿān	عبدالله بن جدعان
10	ʿAbdullāh ibn Khālid ibn Usayd	عبدالله بن خالد بن أسيد
11	ʿAbdullāh ibn Muṭīʿ	عبدالله بن مطيع
12	ʿAbdullāh ibn Saʿd ibn Abī al-Sarḥ	عبدالله بن سعد بن ابي سرح
13	ʿAbdullāh ibn ʿUmar	عبدالله بن عمر
14	ʿAbdullāh ibn Zubayr aka Abū Khabīb	عبدالله بن زبير / ابو خبيب
15	ʿAbdul al-Ashal	عبد الاشل
16	ʿAbdul Malik ibn Marwān	عبدالملک مروان
17	ʿAbdur-Rahman ibn ʿAwf	عبد الرحمان بن عوف
18	ʿAbdur-Rahman ibn Sahl ibn Zayd Anṣārī	عبدالرحمن بن سهل بن زيد انصارى
19	ʿAbdur-Rahman ibn ʿAttāb	عبدالرحمن بن عتّاب

20	Abū 'Abdur-Rahman 'Abdullāh ibn Mas'ud ibn Ġafil ibn Ḥabīb al- Huḏallī	ابو عبدالرحمن عبدالله بن مسعود بن غفيل بن حبيب الهُذَلِّي
21	Abū Ayyub Khalid ibn Zayd	ابو ايوب خالد بن زيد
22	Abū Bakr 'Abdullāh ibn Abī Quhāfah	ابو بكر عبدالله بن ابي قحافة
23	Abū Ḏarr	ابوذر
24	Abū Ḏarr al-Ghifārī	ابوذر الغفاري
25	Abū Dujana Simak ibn Kharasha Sā'idī	ابو دُجانة
26	Abū Ḥabiba al-Ġaffārī	ابو حبيبة الغفاري
27	Abū Hārun al-'Abdī	ابو هارون العبدي
28	Abū Hurayrah	ابو هريرة
29	Abū Lu'lu'a	ابو لؤلؤ
30	Abū Mu'ayṭ	ابو معيط
31	Abū Mūsa al-Ash'arī	ابو موسى اشعري
32	Abū Qatāda	ابو قتادة
33	Abū Rāfi'	ابو رافع
34	Abū Sa'īd al-Khudrī	ابوسعيد الخدري
35	Abū Sufyān	ابوسفيان
36	Abū Ṭalḥa	ابو طلحة
37	Abū Ṭalḥa Zayd ibn Sahl al-Khazrajī	ابو طلحة زيد بن سهل الخزرجي
38	Abū 'Ubaydah ibn al-Jarāḥ	ابو عبيدة جراح
39	Abū Zubayd Naṣrānī	ابو زبيد نصراني
40	Abū Zaynab	ابو زينب
41	Adi ibn Ḥātim a'ṭ-Ṭā'iyy	عَدِىّ بن حاتم طايي
42	Ā'ishah [bint Abū Bakr]	عايشه [بنت ابي بكر]
43	Aminah bint Wahb	امينه بنت وهب
44	'Ammār ibn Yāsir	عمار بن ياسر

45	Anas ibn Malik	انس بن مالک
46	'Alī, Amīr al-Mu'minīn / Abū al-Ḥasan /'Alī ibn Abī Ṭālib	علي امير المؤمنين / ابوالحسن علي بن ابی‌طالب
47	'Alī ibn 'Abdullāh ibn 'Abbās	علي بن عبدالله بن عباس
48	'Alī ibn al-Ḥusayn aka Imam Sajjād	علي بن الحسين / إمام سجاد
49	'Amr ibn al-'Āṣ	عَمْرو ابْنِ الْعَاصِ
50	'Amr ibn Abd al-Wud	عمرو بن عبد الود
51	'Amr ibn Sa'īd	عمرو بن سعيد
52	'Amr ibn Zurārah	عمرو بن زُرارة
53	Aqīl ibn Abī Ṭālib	عقيل بن ابي طالب
54	Arwa bint Kurayz ibn Rabi'ah	آروى بنت کُريز بن ربيعه
55	Aṣbagh ibn Nubāta	أصبغ بن نباتة
56	Al-A'sha	الاعشى
57	'Asim ibn 'Adi	عاصم بن عدي
58	'Attāb Thaqafi	عتّاب ثقفى
59	'Awāna ibn al-Ḥakam	عوانة بن حكم
60	Aws ibn Khawlī	اوس بن خولى
61	Bara' ibn 'Azib	براء بن عاذب
62	Bashir ibn Sa'ad	بشير بن سعد
63	Bilāl	بلال
64	Ḍiraar ibn al-Azwar	ضِرار ابْن أَزوَر
65	Faḍl ibn Abbas [Abul-Faḍl]	فضل بن عباس [ابوالفضل]
66	Fāṭimah aka Fāṭimat az-Zahrā	فاطمة / فاطمة الزهراء
67	Gabriel	جبرئيل
68	Ḥafṣah bint 'Umar	حفصة بنت عمر
69	Ḥajjāj ibn Yūsuf	حجاج بن يوسف

70	Ḥakam ibn Abī al-ʾĀṣ	حكم بن ابي العاص
71	Ḥamzah	حمزة
72	Ḥamzah ibn Nuʾmān Udrī	حمزة بن نعمان عُذري
73	Ḥārith ibn Ḥakam ibn Abī al-ʾĀṣ	حارث بن حكم بن ابي العاص
74	Ḥaritha ibn Suraqah	حارثة بن سُراقة
75	Ḥasan [ibn ʾAlī ibn Abī Ṭālib[	حسن [بن علي بن ابي طالب]
76	Ḥasan ibn Thabit	حسن بن ثابت
77	Ḥaṣīn ibn Numayr al-Sakūnī	حصين بن نمير السكوني
78	Hishām ibn Ḥassān	هشام بن حسّان
79	Hubab ibn al-Munḏir	حباب بن المنذر
80	Huḏayfah	حذيفة
81	Ḥusayn [ibn ʾAlī ibn Abī Ṭālib]	حسين [بن علي بن ابي طالب]
82	Ḥayyān	حيان
83	Ibn ʾAbbās	ابن عباس
84	Ibn Abd al-Barr	ابن عبد البر
85	Ibn Mīnā	ابن مينا
86	Ibn ʾUdayss	ابن عُديس
87	Ibn Zibaʾrā	ابن زبعرى
88	Imam Baqir	امام باقر
89	Imam Jaʾfar al-Ṣādiq	امام جعفر الصادق
90	Imam Mahdī	مهدي
91	Imam Sajjād aka ʾAlī ibn al-Ḥusayn	إمام سجاد / علي بن الحسين
92	Jābir	جابر
93	Jaʾfar ibn Abī Talib	جعفر بن ابي طالب
94	Jahjāh Ġifārī	جَهجاه غِفاري

95	Jundab al-Khayr [Jundab ibn Ka'b Al-Azadi]	جندب الخير [جندب بن كعب الأسدي]
96	Jundab ibn Zuhayr	جندب بن زهير
97	Khadija	خديجة
98	Khālid ibn Sa'īd ibn al-'Aṣ	خالد بن سعيد بن العاص
99	Khālid ibn al-Walīd	خالد بن الوليد
100	Mālik al-Ashtar	مالك الأشتر
101	Malik ibn Nuwayrah	مالك بن نويرة
102	Marjānah	مرجانة
103	Maria	مارية
104	Marwān ibn al-Ḥakam	مروان بن الحكم
105	Mikhnaf	مكناف
106	Miqdād ibn 'Amr	مقداد بن عمرو
107	Miqdād ibn al-Aswad	مقداد بن الأسود
108	Miswar ibn Makhrama	مسوار بن مخرمة
109	Mu'allā ibn Khunays	مُعَلّى بن خُنَيس
110	Mughīra ibn Shu'ba	مغيرة بن شعبه
111	Mujame' ibn Jārieh Anṣārī	مجمّع بن جاريه انصارى
112	Mundir ibn Zubayr	منذر بن زبير
113	Mundir ibn Abī'l-Arqam	منذر بن أبي الأرقم
114	Muḥammad ibn Abī Bakr	محمد بن ابي بكر
115	Muḥammad ibn Abī al-Jahm	محمد بن ابي الجهم
116	Muḥammad ibn 'Alī ibn Abī Ṭālib aka Muḥammad ibn al-Ḥanafiyyah	محمد بن علي بن ابي طالب / محمد بن أبي حنيفة
117	Muḥammad ibn Jubayr	محمد بن جُبير
118	Muḥammad ibn Ka'b	محمد بن كعب

119	Muḥammad ibn Maslamah al-Anṣārī	محمد بن مَسلَمَه الانصاري
120	Muḥammad ibn Zakariyyā	محمد بن زكريا
121	Mu'awiya aka Mu'āwiya ibn Abī Sufyān	معاوية بن أبي سفيان
122	Musaylimah al-Kaḏḏāb	مسيلمة الكذّاب
123	Muslim ibn 'Uqba al-Murrī	مسلم بن عقبه مرى
124	Nābiġah	نابغة
125	Nā'ila	نائلة
126	Noah and Lot	نوح و لوط
127	Nu'man ibn 'Ajlan	نعمان بن عجلان
128	Qambar	قنبر
129	Qays ibn Sa'd ibn 'Ubāda	قيس بن سعد بن عبادة
130	Quṣayy	قُصي
131	Qutham	قُثم
132	Rabāḥ	رباح
133	Rabi'ah ibn al-Aswad	ربيعة بن الأسود
134	al-Ṣa'b ibn Juthama	الصعب بن جُثامة
135	Sa'd ibn 'Ubadah	سعد بن عُبادة
136	Sa'd ibn Mālik Abī Waqqās	سعد بن مالك ابي وقّاص
137	Sahl ibn Ḥunayf	سهل بن حُنَيف
138	Sa'īd al-Umawī	سعيد الأموي
139	Sa'īd ibn Ḥakam ibn Abī al-'Āṣ	سعيد ابن حكم ابن ابي العاص
140	Sa'īd ibn al-'Ās al-Umawī	سعيد بن العاص
141	Sa'īd ibn Zayd	سعيد بن زيد
142	Salamah ibn Salāma ibn Waqash	سلمة بن سلامة بن وقش
143	Salamah ibn Aslam	سلمة بن أسلم

144	Ṣāliḥ	صالح
145	Sālim Mawlā Abī Ḥudayfah	سليم مولى ابي حذيفة
146	Salmān al-Fārisī	سلمان فارسي
147	Shibl ibn Khālid	شبل بن خالد
148	Shuqran	شُقران
149	Ṣuhayb ibn Sinan	صُهيب بن سنان
150	Sulaimān	سليمان
151	Sumayah	سميه
152	Thabit ibn Qais ibn Shammās	ثابت بن قيس بن شمّاس
153	Ṭalḥa ibn 'Ubaydullāh	طلحة بن عبيدالله
154	'Ubādah ibn al-Samit	عُبادة بن صامت
155	'Ubaydullāh ibn Ziyād	عبيدالله بن زياد
156	Ubayy ibn Ka'b	أُبي بن كعب
157	Uḥayḥa	أُحَيحة
158	'Umar ibn al-Khaṭṭāb	عمر بن الخطّاب
159	Umm Abān	أم ابان همسر مروان
160	Umm Ayman	أم أيمن
161	Umm Salamah	أم سلمة
162	Umm Mistah ibn al-Uthātha	أم مِسطَح بن أثاثة
163	Usama ibn Zayd	اسامة بن زيد
164	Usayd ibn Huḍair	أُسيد بن حُضَير
165	'Utbah ibn Abū Lahab	عتبة بن ابولهب
166	'Uthmān ibn 'Affān	عثمان بن عفّان
167	'Uthmān ibn Hunaif	عثمان بن حنيف
168	'Uthmān ibn Muḥammad ibn Abī Sufyān	عثمان بن محمد بن ابي سفيان

169	'Uwaym ibn Sā'ideh	عُوَيم بن ساعدة
170	Walīd ibn 'Uqba	وليد بن عُقبه
171	Yaḥmūm	يحموم
172	Yaḥyā ibn Zakarīyā	يحيى بن زكريا
173	Yazīd [ibn Mu'āwiya ibn Abī Sufyān]	يزيد [بن معاوية بن ابي سفيان]
174	Yazīd Ibn 'Abdullāh ibn Zam'ah	يزيد بن عبدالله بن زمعه
175	Yazīd Ibn Wahhāb ibn Zam'ah	يزيد بن وهاب بن زمعه
176	Zayd ibn Thabit Anṣārī	زيد بن ثابت
177	Zaynab	زينب
178	Ziyād ibn Abīhi	زياد ابن ابيه
179	Ziyād ibn Labīd	زياد بن لبيد
180	Zubayr ibn al-Awām	زبير بن العوام
181	Az-Zubayr ibn Bakkār	زبير بن بگار
182	Zuhrī	زُهري
183	Zurārah	زُراره

Bibliography

1.   *Abha al-Midad fi Sharh Mu'tamar 'Ulama' Baghdād, Muhawarah Hawl al-Imamah wa-al-Khilafah*. Atiyah, Muqatil. Beirut: Dār al-Balāq Publication.

2.   *'Abdullāh ibn Saba'*. Allamah 'Askarī, Sayyid Murtadā Sharif 'Askarī. Offset Publication, 1393 AH/ 1973 CE; & the translation in 3 volumes: 5th Edition. Tehran: Majma' Ilmi Islāmi Publication, 1375 SH/ 1997 CE.

3.   *Al-Adab al-Mufrad*. Al-Bukhārī, Muhammad ibn Ismā'īl. Cairo, 1379 AH/ 1960 CE.

4.   *Ahadith Umm al-Mu'minin Ā'ishah* (Saying from Ā'ishah and Roles from her Life). Allamah 'Askarī, Sayyid Murtadā Sharif.

5.   *Al-Ahkam al-Sultania by al-Qādī al-Māwardī w'al-Wilayat al-Diniyya* (The Ordinances of Government). Al-Māwardī, Abū al-Hasan 'Alī ibn Muhammad ibn Habīb al-Basrī.

6.   *Al-Ahkam al-Sultania by al-Qādī Abū Ya'lā*. al-Qādī Abū Ya'lā, Abū Ya'lā Muhammad ibn al-Husayn Ibn al-Farrā'. Edited by Muhammad Hāmed al-Faqī. Eqypt: Mustafā Halabi Publication, 1356 AH/ 1937 CE.

7.   *Al-Akhbār al-Tuwal*. Dīnawarī, Abū Hanīfah Ahmad ibn Dāwūd. Egypt: Ministry of Culture and National Guidance.

8.   *Al-Akhbār al-Muwaffaqīyāt*. Bakkār, Az-Zubayr ibn Bakkār.

9.   *Al-Amalī* (The Dictations). Al-Shaykh al-Mufīd, Abū 'Abd Allah Muhammad ibn Muhammad ibn al-Nu'man al-'Ukbari al-Baghdādi. Edited by Husayn Ustad Vali under supervision of 'Alī Akbar Ghaffari. Tehran: Saduq Publication, 1403 AH/ 1983 CE.

10.   *Ansāb al-Ashrāf* (Genealogies of the Nobles). Al-Balādurī, 'Ahmad ibn Yahyā ibn Jabir al-Bagdādī. Eqypt: Dār al-Ma'arif Publication, 1959 CE; Jerusalem University, 1936 CE.

11. *Aqā'id al-Islām min al-Qur'ān al-Karīm* (The Beliefs of Islām from the Qur'ān). Allamah 'Askarī, Sayyid Murtaḍā Sharif. 1ˢᵗ Edition. Majma' Ilmi Islāmi, 1414 AH/ 1994 CE.

12. *Asbāb al-Nuzūl* (Occasions or Circumstances of Revelation). Al-Wahidi, Abū l-Hasan 'Alī ibn Ahmad. Lebanon: Dār al-Kutub al-Ilmieh publication, n.d.

13. *Asrār Saqīfah* (Translation of *al-Saqīfa* by Muḥammad Riḍā Muẓaffar). Hujjati Kermani, Muḥammad Javad.

14. *Al-Bad' wa at-Tārīkh*. Maqdisī, Mutahhar ibn Tahir. Under supervision of Clément Huart. Paris, 1901-1903 CE.

15. *Balāghāt al-Nisā'*. Ibn Abī Tahir Tayfur, Ahmad ibn Abī Tahir Marwazi. Najaf, 1361 AH/ 1942 CE.

16. *Bihar al-Anwar* (Seas of Lights). Majlesi, Muḥammad Baqer ibn Muḥammad Taqi. Isfahan: Company Publication, 1303-1314AH/ 1886-1896 CE; 3ʳᵈ Edition. Beirut: Dār Ihya at-Turath al-Arabi Publication 1403 AH/ 1983 CE.

17. *Dakhā'ir al-Uqbā fī Manāqib Dawī al-Qurbā*. Ṭabarī Shāfi'ī, Abū Jafar Aḥmad ibn 'Abdullāh Muḥibb al-Dīn. Cairo, 1356 AH/ 1937 CE.

18. *Dalā'il al-Imāma*. al-Ṭabarī, Abū Ja'far Muḥammad ibn Jarīr ibn Yazīd.

19. *Dīwān Ḥāfiẓ Ibrāhīm*. Ibrāhīm, Ḥāfiẓ. Cairo, 1987 CE.

20. *Dow Maktab dar Islām* (Two Schools of Thought in Islām) (The translation of *Ma'alem al-Madrasatain*). Allamah 'Askarī, Sayyid Murtaḍā Sharif. Translated by Sardarnia. 1ˢᵗ Edition. Bontad Be'sat Publication.

21. *Ḍuha al-Islām*. Amin, Ahmad. Lebanon: Dār al-Kitab al-Arabi Publication, n.d.

22. *Al-Durr al-Manthur fi Tafsir Bil-Ma'thur* (The Scattered Pearls Intertextual Exegesis). As-Suyūṭī, Jalāl al-Dīn 'Abd al-Raḥmān ibn Abī Bakr ibn Nasir ad-Din Muḥammad al-Shāfi'ī. Cairo, 1314 AH/ 1896 CE.

23. *Duwal al-Islām* (The Islāmic Nations). Aḏ-Ḏahabī, Shams ad-Dīn Abū 'Abdullāh Muḥammad ibn Aḥmad ibn 'Uthmān ibn Qāymāẓ ibn 'Abdullāh at-Turkumānī Misri Shafi'ī. Research by Fahim Muḥammad Shaltut & Muḥammad Muṣṭafā Ibrahim. Cairo, 1974 CE.

24. *Fatḥ al-Bārī fī Sharḥ Ṣaḥīḥ al-Bukhārī*. Al-'Asqalānī, Ibn Ḥajar. Egypt: Shirkat al-Muṣṭafā al-Babi al-Halabi, 1378-1382 AH/ 1959-1962 CE.

25. *Fatḥ al-Qadir*. Shawkani, Muḥammad ibn 'Alī.

26. *Al-Fath al-Kabir fi Damm az-Ziyadah ila al-Jami' al-Saghir*. As-Suyūṭī, Jalāl al-Dīn 'Abd al-Raḥmān ibn Abī Bakr ibn Nasir ad-Din Muḥammad al-Shāfi'ī. Research by Yusif al-Nabhani. Beirut, n.d.

27. *Fawat al-Wafiyat*. Al-Kutubī, Muḥammad ibn Shakir. Research by Dr. Ihsan Abbas. Beirut, 1973 CE.

28. *Al-Ghadīr fi l-kitāb wa al-Sunna wa al-Adab*. 'Allāma Amīnī, 'Abd al-Ḥusayn ibn Ahmad. 1ˢᵗ Edition. Tehran: Dār al-Kutub al_Islāmieh Publication, 1366 SH/ 1988 CE.

29. *Hadith al-Kisā fi Kutub Madrasat al-Khulafa was Madrasat Ahl al-Bayt*. Allamah 'Askarī, Sayyid Murtaḍā Sharif 'Askarī.

30. *Hazrat Muḥammad's Successor*. Āstān-e Qods-e Razavi Publication.

31. *Hilyat al-Awliya'*. Isfahānī al-Ahwal al-Ash'arī al-Shāfi'ī, 'Abdullāh ibn Ahmad ibn Ishāq ibn Mūsā ibn Mahrān al-Mihrānī. Egypt: as-Sa'adeh Publication, 1351-1357 AH/ 1932-1938 CE.

32. *Ihraq beyt Fāṭimah fi al-kutub al-mutabarah inda ahl al-Sunnah*. Gholami, Hussein Gheib. 1417 AH/ 1996 CE.

33. *Al-Iḥtijāj*. Mash'had. al-Ṭabrisī, Abū Manṣūr Aḥmad ibn 'Alī ibn Abī Ṭālib. 1403 AH/ 1983 CE.

34. *Al-Ijāba li-Īrād mā Istadrakathu 'Ā'isha 'alā al-Sahaba* (The Corrective: 'Ā'isha's Rectification of the Aṣḥāb). az-Zarkashī, Abū 'Abdullāh Badr ad-Dīn Muḥammad ibn 'Abdullāh ibn Bahādir. Research by Sa'id Afqani. Damascus, 1358 AH/ 1939 CE.

35. *'Ilal al-Sharāyi'*. Al-Shaykh al-Ṣaduq, Abū Ja'far Muḥammad ibn 'Alī ibn al-Ḥusayn ibn Mūsā al-Qummī.

36. *I'lam al-Nisa fi Alamey Al-Arab wa al-Islām* (Women's Media in the Arab and Islāmic Worlds). Kaḥḥāla, 'Umar ibn Reḍa ibn Muḥammad Rāghib ibn 'Abdul Ghani. 1397 AH/ 1977 CE.

37. *I'lam al-Wara bi A'lam al-Huda*. Al-Ṭabrisī, Abū 'Alī al-Faḍl ibn al-Ḥasan ibn al-Faḍl. Edited by 'Alī Akbar Ghaffari. Beirut: Dār al-Ma'rafa li-Tiba'a wa an-Nashr, 1399 AH/ 1979 CE.

38. *Al-Imāma wal-Siyāsa* (Imamat and Politics). Ibn Qutaybah al-Dīnawarī, Abū Muḥammad Abd-Allāh ibn Muslim ibn Qutayba al-Dīnawarī al-Marwazī. Egypt, 1900 CE.

39. *Imta' al-Asma'*. Al-Maqrīzī, Aḥmad ibn 'Alī ibn Abdul Ghadīr ibn Muḥammad Shafi`ī. Egypt: Lujnat at-Ta'lif Publication, 1941 CE.

40. *Al-'Iqd al-Farīd* (The Unique Necklace). Ibn `Abd Rabbih, Ahmad ibn Muḥammad. Research by 'Alī Shiri. 1st Edition. Beirut: Dār at-Turath A-Arabi Publication, 1409 AH/ 1989 CE; Egypt: Muḥammad Sa'id al-'Uryan, 1372 AH/ 1989 CE.

41. *Al-Irshad* (Book of Guidance into the Lives of the Twelve Imams). Al-Shaykh al-Mufīd, Abū 'Abd Allah Muḥammad ibn Muḥammad ibn al-Nu'man al-'Ukbari al-Baghdādi. Translated by Sayyid Hashim Rasūlī Mahallātī. Islāmic Theological Publications.

42. *Al-Irshad as-Sārī fi Sharḥ Ṣaḥīḥ al-Bukhārī*. Al-Qasṭallānī al-Qutaybī al-Shāfi'ī, Shihāb al-Dīn Abū'l-'Abbās Aḥmad ibn Muḥammad ibn Abī Bakr.

43. Al-Iṣābah fī Tamyīz al-Ṣahābah. Al-'Asqalānī, Ibn Ḥajar.

44. Is'af al-Raghibin fi Sirat al-Muṣṭafā wa Fada'in Ahlubaytihi (Printed in the margin of Nūr al-Abṣār). Surūr al-Ṣabbān, al-shaykh Muḥammad.

45. *Al-Isti'ab*. Ibn Abdul Barr, Yusuf ibn Abdallah ibn Muḥammad ibn Abdul Barr, Abū 'Umar al-Namari al-Andalusi al-Qurtubi al-Maliki. Egypt, 1358 AH/ 1939 CE & Heydarabad, 1336 AH/ 1918 CE.

46. *Al-Itqan al-Itqan fi Ulum al-Qur'ān*. As-Suyūṭī, Jalāl al-Dīn 'Abd al-Raḥmān ibn Abī Bakr ibn Nasir ad-Din Muḥammad al-Shāfi'ī. Egypt, n.d.

47. *Al-Jamal*. Al-Shaykh al-Mufīd, Abū 'Abd Allah Muḥammad ibn Muḥammad ibn al-Nu'man al-'Ukbari al-Baghdādi. 2nd Edition. Lebanon: Dār al-Mufīd, 1414 Ah/ 1994 CE.

48. *Jami' al-Usul fi Ahadith al-Rasul*. Ibn Athir al-Jazari, Majd al-Din. Edited by Muḥammad Ḥāmed al-Faqī. 1st Edition. Eqypt, 1368 AH/ 1949 CE.

49. *Al-Kāfī* (The Sufficient). Al-Kulaynī ar-Rāzī, Abū Ja'far Muḥammad ibn Ya'qūb ibn Isḥāq. Research by 'Alī Akbar Ghaffari. 3rd Edition. Tehran: Dār al-Kutub al-Islāmieh Publication, 1388 AH/ 1968 CE.

50. *Al-Kāmil* (The Complete). Al-Mubarrad, Abū al-'Abbās Muḥammad ibn Yazīd. Leiden.

51. *Al-Kāmil fit-Tārīkh Ibn al-Athir* (The Complete History). Ibn al-Athir al-Jazari, Abū al-Ḥasan 'Alī ibn Muḥammad ibn Muḥammad al-Shaybani. Cairo, 1348-1356 AH/ 1929-1937 CE; European Edition, 1290-1303 AH/ 1873-1886 CE.

52. *Kanz al-Ummāl fī Sunan al-Aqwāl wal Af'āl* (Treasure of the Workers in the Traditions of Words and Deeds). Al-Hindi, Aladdin 'Alī ibn Hussam al-Din Abdul Malik al-Muttaqi. Heydarabad, 1364 AH/ 1945 CE.

53. *Al-Khasa'is al-Kubra (Kifayat al-Talib al-Labib fī Khasa'is al-Habib.* As-Suyūṭī, Jalāl al-Dīn 'Abd al-Raḥmān ibn Abī Bakr ibn Nasir ad-Din Muḥammad al-Shāfi'ī. Heydarabad, 1319 AH, 1901 CE.

54. *Kashf al-Ghumma fī Ma'rifat al-A'imma.* Al-Irbilī, Abū l-Ḥasan 'Alī ibn 'Isā Hakkārī.

55. *Al-Kashshāf 'an Haqā'iq at-Tanzil* (The Revealer). Al-Zamakhshari, Abū al-Qasim Maḥmūd ibn 'Umar.

56. *Al-Khiṣāl.* Al-Shaykh al-Ṣaduq, Abū Ja'far Muḥammad ibn 'Alī ibn al-Ḥusayn ibn Mūsā al-Qummī.

57. *Khulasa Tahdīb al-Tahdīb al-Kimal fī Asma' al-Rijal.* Al-Khazrajī, Safi al-Din Ahmad ibn 'Abdullāh.

58. *Khāstgāh Khilāfat* (The Origin of the Caliphate) (Translation of *al-Saqīfa wa-al-Khilāfah*). Iftikharzadeh, Sayyid Ḥasan.

59. *Kifāyat al-Ṭālib fī Manāqib 'Alī ibn Abī Ṭālib.* Al-Ganji al-Shāfi'ī, Abū 'Abdullāh Muḥammad ibn Yusuf Gharashi. Najaf, 1356 AH/ 1937 CE.

60. *Kitab al-Aghani* (The Great Book of Songs). Abū al-Faraj al-Iṣfahānī, 'Alī ibn al-Ḥusayn ibn Muḥammad ibn Aḥmad ibn al-Ḥaytham al-Umawī. Eqypt, 1323 AH/ 1905 CE; Beirut: Dār al-Thaqafa; & Dusasi publication.

61. *Kitab al-Amwal* (The Book of Revenue). Abū 'Ubayd, al-Qāsim ibn Sallām al-Khurāsānī al-Harawī. Edited by Muḥammad Ḥāmed al-Ghafiqi. 1934 CE; 3rd Edition. Beirut: Dār Ihya at-Turath al-Arabi Publication, 1403 AH/ 1983 CE.

62. *Kitāb al-Futūḥ* (Book of Conquests). A'tham al-Kūfī al-Kindī, Abū Muḥammad Aḥmad. Beirut: Dār al-Kutub al-Ilmieh Publication, n.d.; Offset in Heydarabad, 1388 AH/ 1968 CE.

63. *Kitāb Futūḥ al-Buldān* (Book of the Conquest of the Countries/Lands). Al-Balāḏurī, 'Aḥmad ibn Yaḥyā ibn Jabir. Research by al-Munjid. 1st Edition. Cairo, 1319 AH/ 1901 CE.

64. *Kitāb al-Ithāf bi-ḥubb al-ashrāf, wa-bi-hāmishihi kitāb Ḥusn al-Tawassul fī Adāb Ziyārat Afḍal al-Rusul.* Shubrāwī, 'Abdullāh ibn Muḥammad.

65. *Kitāb al-Ma'ārif*. Ibn Qutaybah, Abū Muḥammad Abd-Allāh ibn Muslim ibn Qutayba al-Dīnawarī al-Marwazī. Research by Isma'il 'Abdullāh as-Sawi. 2nd Edition. Lebanon, 1390 AH/ 1970 CE.

66. *Kitāb al-Milal wa al-Nihal* (The Book of Sects and Creeds). Al-Shahrastānī, Abū al-Fath Muḥammad ibn 'Abd al-Karīm Ash'ari. Leiden.

67. *Kitāb Mu'jam al-Buldān*. Al-Ḥamawī ar-Rumi al-Baghdādi, Yāqūt Shihāb al-Dīn ibn Abdullāh. Tehran: Asadi offset Publication, 1965 CE; Leiden, 1286 AH/ 1869 CE.

68. *Kitab Sulaym ibn Qays* (The Book of Sulaym ibn Qays). Al-Hilālīy, Sulaym ibn Qays. Research by Muḥammad Baqir Anṣāri Zanjani. Qum: al-Hadi Publication, 1415 AH/ 1373 SH/ 1994 CE.

69. *Kitāb aṭ-Tabaqāt al-Kabīr Ibn Sa'd* (The Book of the Major Classes). Ibn Sa'd, Abū 'Abdullāh Muḥammad ibn Sa'd ibn Manī' al-Baṣrī al-Hāshimī. Leiden; Beirut.

70. *Kitab al-Tārīkh wa al-Maghazi*. Al-Waqidi, Abū 'Abdullāh Muḥammad Ibn 'Umar Ibn Waqid al-Aslami. Research by Dr. Marsden Jones. London: Oxfor University, 1966 CE.

71. *Lisan al-'Arab*. Ibn Manẓūr, Muḥammad ibn Mukarram ibn 'Alī ibn Ahmad ibn Manzūr al-Anṣārī al-Ifrīqī al-Misrī al-Khazrajī. Beirut: Dār Ṣadir Publication, 1374-1376 AH/ 1955-1957 CE.

72. *Lisān al-Mizan*. Ibn Ḥajar al-'Asqalānī, Shihābud-Dīn Abul-Faḍl Aḥmad ibn Nūrud-Dīn 'Alī ibn Muḥammad. 1st Edition. Heydarabad, 1329 AH/ 1911 CE.

73. *Ma'alem al-Madrasatain*. Allamah 'Askarī, Sayyid Murtaḍā Sharif. 2nd Edition. Tehran: Bunyad Be'sat Publication, 1406 AH/ 1986 CE.

74. *Ma'alem al-Madrasatain*. Allamah 'Askarī, Sayyid Murtaḍā Sharif. Translated by Muḥammad Javad Karami. 1st Edition. Qum: Usul Din Faculty Publication, 1379 SH/ 2001 CE.

75. *Ma'ānī l-'Akhbār*. Al-Shaykh al-Ṣaduq, Abū Ja'far Muḥammad ibn 'Alī ibn al-Ḥusayn ibn Mūsā al-Qummī.

76. *Mafatih al-Asrar wa Masabih al-Abrar fi Tafsir al-Qur'ān*. Al-Shahrastānī, Tāj al-Dīn Abū al-Fath Muḥammad ibn 'Abd al-Karīm. Manuscript in the Iranian Parliament Library NO. 78.

77. *Mājarāye Saqifa* (The Story of Saqifah). Sayyid Ġulām Riḍā Sa'īdī.

78. *Majmau' az-Zawa'id wa Manba' al-Fawa'id.* Al-Haythami, Nur al-Din 'Alī ibn Abī Bakr ibn Sulayman. 2nd Edition. Beirut, 1967 CE.

79. *Man lā Yaḥḍuruhu al-Faqīh.* Al-Shaykh al-Ṣaduq, Abū Ja'far Muḥammad ibn 'Alī ibn al-Ḥusayn ibn Mūsā al-Qummī. Edited by 'Alī Akbar Ghaffari. 2nd Edition; Research by al-Sayyid Hasan al-Khurasan. 5th Edition.

80. *Manāqib 'Āle 'Abī Ṭālib.* Ibn-e Shahr-Āshūb, Abū Jafar Muḥammad Ibn 'Alī Mazandarani. Qum: Ilmieh Publication.

81. *Maqātil al-Ṭālibiyyīn.* Al-Isfahāni, Abū al-Faraj. Cairo, 1323 AH/ 1905 CE; Translated by Sayyid Hashim Rasuli Mahallati & Edited by 'Alī Akbar Ghaffari. Tehran: Saduq Bookshop Publication.

82. *Maqtal al-Ḥusayn* aka *Maqtal al-Khwārizmī.* Al-Khwarizmi, Abū al-Mu'ayid Al-Muwaffaq ibn Ahmad Akhtab. Najaf, n.d. & Qum: Anwar al-Huda Publication, 1418 AH/ 1997 CE.

83. *Ma'rifat al-Qurrā' al-Kibār 'alā Ṭabaqāt wal A'ṣār.* Ad-Dahabī, Abū 'Abdullāh Shams ad-Din. Research by Muḥammad Sayyid Jad al-Haq. 1st Edition. Egypt, n.d.

84. *Mir'at az-Zamān fi Tawarīkh al-'Ayān.* Sibṭ ibn al-Jawzi, Shams al-din Abū al-Muẓaffar Yusuf ibn Kizoghlu ibn 'Abdullāh Baghdādi Hanafi. Research by Dr. Ihsan Abbas. 1st Edition. Beirut: Dār al-Shuruq Publication, 1405 AH/ 1985 CE.

85. *Mizan al-I'tidal fi Naqd ar-Rijal.* Ad-Dahabī, Abū 'Abdullāh Shams ad-Din. Research by 'Alī Muḥammad al-Bajawi. Cairo: Dār Ihya' al-Kutub al-Arabi Publication, 1382 AH/ 1962 CE.

86. *Al-Mufakhirat.* (Narrated by Ibn Abī l-Ḥadīd in *Sharḥ Nahj al-Balāgha*). Bakkar, Zubayr ibn Bakkar ibn 'Abdullāh ibn Mas'ab ibn Thabit ibn 'Abdullāh ibn Zubayr ibn al-Awwam. 1st Edition.

87. *Al-Mufradat fi Gharib al-Qur'ān.* Raghib Isfahani, Abul-Qasim al-Hussein ibn Mufaddal ibn Muḥammad.

88. *Al-Muhajjal Samaratal Muhajja.* Ibn Ṭawūs, Sayyid Raḍi ud-Deen 'Alī ibn Musa ibn Ṭawūs al Hasani wal Husaini.

89. *Al-Muhalla.* Al-Andalusī, Abū Muḥammad 'Alī ibn Aḥmad ibn Sa'īd ibn Ḥazm. Research by Ahmad Muḥammad Shakir. Beirut, n.d.

90.   *Al-Mu'jam al-Kabir.* At-Ṭabarāni, Abū 'l-Qāwsim Sulaymān Ibn Ahmad ibn Ayyub ibn Muṭawyyir al-Lakhmī al-Shāmī. Offset Publication, 1404 AH/ 1984 CE.

91.   *Mu'jam mā Ista'jam.* Al-Bakrī, Abū 'Ubayd 'Abdullāh ibn 'Abd al-'Azīz ibn Muhammad ibn Ayyūb ibn 'Amr. Cairo, 1945-1949 CE.

92.   *Mu'jam Rijāl al-Ḥadīth wa Tafṣīl Ṭabaqāt al-Ruwāt.* Al-Khoeī, Al-Sayyid Abū l-Qāsim al-Mūsawī. Lebanon: Dār az-Zahra Publication, 1413 AH/ 1993 CE.

93.   *Mu'jam al-Shu'arā'.* Marzubānī, Abū 'Ubayd Allah Muhammad ibn 'Imrān ibn Musa. Research by Abd as-Sattar Ahmad Faraj. Egypt, 1379 AH/ 1960 CE.

94.   *Al-Mukhtasar fi Akhbar al-Bashar.* Shāfi'ī, Imad ad-Din Abū al-Fidā' Ismā'īl ibn 'Alī.

95.   *Al-Murāja'āt.* Al-Mūsawī, 'Abd al-Ḥusayn Sharaf al-Dīn. Translated by Muhammad Ja'far Imami.

96.   *Murūj aḏ-Ḏahab wa-Ma'ādin al-Jawhar* (Meadows of Gold and Mines of Gems) In the margin of *Al-Kāmil fit-Tārīkh Ibn al-Athir.* Al-Mas'ūdī al-Shāfi'ī, Abū al-Ḥasan 'Alī ibn al-Ḥusayn ibn 'Alī. Research by Muhammad Muhyi ad-Din. Egypt, 1303 AH/ 1886 CE.

97.   *Al-Mustadrak 'ala al-Saḥiḥayn.* Al-Hakim al-Nīsābūrī Abū 'Abdullāh Muhammad ibn 'Abdullāh. Heydarabad, 1334 AH/ 1916 CE.

98.   *Musnad Ahmad ibn Ḥanbal.* Ḥanbal, Ahmad. Cairo: Sharh Ahmad Muhammad Shakir Publication, 1313 AH/ 1896 CE.

99.   *Musnad al-Tayalisi.* Al-Tayalisi, Sulayman ibn Dawud. Heydarabad, 1321 AH/ 1903 CE.

100.   Muntakhab Kanz al-Ummāl (A Selection of Kanz al-Ummāl)

101.   *Al-Muwahib al-Ladunniyya bi al-Minah al-Muhammadiyya.* Al-Qastallānī Shihāb al-Dīn Abu'l-'Abbās Ahmad ibn Muhammad ibn Abī Bakr al-Qastallānī al-Qutaybī al-Shāfi'ī. Beirut: Dār al-Kutub al-Ilmieh Publication.

102.   *Al-Muwaṭṭa'* (The Well-Trodden Path). Al-Aṣbahī al-Madanī, Mālik ibn Anas ibn Mālik ibn Abī 'Āmir ibn 'Amr ibn Al-Ḥārith ibn Ghaymān ibn Khuthayn ibn 'Amr ibn Al-Ḥārith. Cairo: Dār Ihya' al-Kutub al-Arabi Publication, 1343 AH/ 1925 CE.

103.   *Al-Muwafaqiat.* (Narrated by Ibn Abī l-Ḥadīd in *Sharh Nahj al-Balāgha*). Bakkar, Zubayr ibn Bakkar ibn 'Abdullāh ibn Mas'ab ibn Thabit ibn

'Abdullāh ibn Zubayr ibn al-Awwam. 1st Edition. Baghdād, 1392 AH/ 1972 CE.

104. *Nahj al-Balāghah*. Salih, Dr. Subhi. 1st Edition. Beirut, 1378 AH/ 1959 CE.

105. *Naqsh A'emeh Dar Ihya'e Din* (The Role of the Imams in Reviving the Religion). Allamah 'Askarī, Sayyid Murtaḍā Sharif. Tehran: Majma' Ilmi Islāmi.

106. *Naqsh Ā'ishah dar Trikh Islām* (Traslation of *Ahadith Umm al-Mu'minin Ā'ishah*). Allamah 'Askarī, Sayyid Murtaḍā Sharif. Tehran: Majma' Ilmi Islāmi.

107. *An-Nihāyato fi Qarīb al-Hadīth wa al-Āthār*. Ibn al-Athir al-Jazari, Abū al-Hasan 'Alī ibn Muḥammad ibn Muḥammad ash-Shaybani.

108. *An-Nizā' wa at-Takhāṣom*. Al-Maqrīzī, Taqī al-Dīn Abū al-'Abbās Aḥmad ibn 'Alī ibn 'Abd al-Qādir ibn Muḥammad.

109. Nūr al-Abṣār fī Manāqib Āl Bayt al-Nabī al-Mukhtār. Al-Shablanji al-Shāfi'ī Mu'min ibn al-Hasan.

110. *Al-Qāmus al-Muḥīṭ* (The Surrounding Ocean). Al-Fīrūzābādī, Muḥammad ibn Ya'qūb ibn Muḥammad ibn Ibrāhīm al-Shīrāzī al-Shāfi'ī.

111. *Qur'ān al-Karīm wa Riwāyāt al-Madrasatayn* (The Qur'ān in the Narrations and Monuments). Allamah 'Askarī, Sayyid Murtada Sharif. 1st Edition. Majma' Alam Islāmi, 1417 AH/ 1996 CE.

112. Ar-Rawḍ an-Naḍīr.

113. *Al-Riaz an-Nazra*. Ṭabarī Shāfi'ī, Abū Jafar Aḥmad ibn 'Abullāh Muḥibb al-Dīn. 2nd Edition. Cairo: Ad-Dār Publication, 1372 AH/ 1953 CE.

114. *Safwat u-Safwah*. Ibn al Jawzi, Abū al-Faraj 'Abd al-Raḥmān ibn 'Alī ibn Muḥammad Bakri Hanbali. Heydarabad, 1357 AH/ 1938 CE. (This same book has been also published as *Sifat as-Safwah*. Research by Mahmud Fakhuri. 1399 AH/ 1979 CE.)

115. *Ṣaḥīḥ al-Bukhārī*. Al-Bukhārī, Abū 'Abdullāh Muḥammad ibn Ismā'īl ibn Ibrahim ibn Mughīra. Egypt, 1327 AH/ 1909 CE.

116. *Ṣaḥīḥ Muslim*. Al-Qushayrī an-Naysābūrī, Abū al-Ḥusayn 'Asākir ad-Dīn Muslim ibn al-Ḥajjāj. Egypt, 1334 AH/ 1916 CE.

117. *Al-Saqīfa*. Muẓaffar, Muḥammad Riḍā.

118. *Al-Saqīfa*. Johari Basri, Abī Bakr Ahmad ibn 'Abdul Aziz.

119. *Al-Saqīfah wa al-Khilāfah*. 'Abd al-Maqṣūd, 'Abd al-Fattāḥ.

120. *As-Sawayiq al-Muhriqah ala Ahl al-Bidayi wa'd Dalali wa'z Zandaqah*. Ibn Hajar al-Haythami al-Shāfi'ī, Shibab al-Dīn Abū al-'Abbās Aḥmad ibn Muḥammad ibn 'Alī ibn Hajar. Egypt, 1324 AH/ 1906 CE.

121. *Shadarāt al-Dahab fī Akhbār man Dahab*. Ibn al-'Imād al-'Akarī al-Ḥanbalī, Abd al-Ḥayy ibn Aḥmad ibn Muḥammad.

122. *Sharaf As'hab al-Hadith*. Al-Khaṭīb al-Baghdādī, Abū Bakr Aḥmad ibn 'Alī ibn Thābit ibn Aḥmad ibn Māhdī al-Shafi'ī. Research by Dr. Muḥammad Sa'id Khatib Uqli. Dār Ihya as-Sunat an-Nabawiyah Publication, n.d.

123. *Sharḥ Nahj al-Balāgha* (Commentary of Nahj al-Balāgha). Ibn Abī al-Ḥadīd, 'Izz al-Dīn Abū Ḥāmid 'Abd al-Ḥamīd ibn Hibat Allāh. Research by Muḥammad Abū al-Fadl Ibrahim. 1st Edition. Egypt: Halabi Publication & Iranian Lithography.

124. *Sharḥ Nahj al-Balāgha*. 'Abduh, Muḥammad. Egypt.

125. *Shawāhid al-Tanzīl li Qawā'id al-Tafḍīl*. Al-Haskani al-Hanafi al-Nīsābūrī, Ubaydullah ibn Adullah ibn Ahmad. Research by Muḥammad Baqir Mahmudi. 1st Edition. Lebanon, 1393 Ah/ 1973 CE.

126. *As-Sirat al-Halabieh* (Insan al-'Uyun fi Sirat al-Amin al-Ma'mun). Halabi al-Shāfi'ī, 'Alī ibn Burhan al-Din. 1353 AH/ 1934 CE.

127. *Sirat Ibn Hisham* aka *Sirat an-Nabawi* (Biography of the Prophet). Al-Himyari al-Mu'afiri al-Baṣri, Abū Muḥammad 'Abd al-Malik ibn Hisham ibn Ayyub. Research by Muḥammad Muhyi al-Din; Research by Muṣṭafā as-Suqa, Ibrahim al-Abyari & abdul Hafiẓ al-Shibli. 2nd Edition. 1375 AH/ 1956 CE.

128. *Sireye Alawi: Fasli az Tarikh Sadr-e-Islām* (A Chapter on Early Islām). Behbudi, Muḥammad Baqir.

129. *Siyar A'lam al-Nubala*. Aḏ-Ḏahabī, Shams ad-Dīn Abū 'Abdullāh Muḥammad ibn Aḥmad ibn 'Uthmān ibn Qāymāẓ ibn 'Abdullāh at-Turkumānī Misri Shafi'ī. Cairo: Dār al-Ma'arif Publication, 1957 CE.

130. *Ṣubḥ al-A'shā fī Ṣinā'at al-Inshā'* (Daybreak for the Night-Blind Regarding the Composition of Chancery Documents). Al-Qalqashandī, Shihāb al-Dīn Abū al-'Abbās Aḥmad ibn 'Alī ibn Aḥmad 'Abdullāh al-Fazārī al-Shāfi'ī. Lebanon: Dār al-Fikr Publication.

131. *Sunan al-Bayhaqī* aka *as-Sunan al-Kabir* or *as-Sunan al-Kubra*. Bayhaqī Shāfi'ī, Abū Bakr Aḥmad ibn Ḥusayn ibn 'Alī ibn Mūsa al-Khosrojerdi. Heydarabad, 1344-1355 AH/ 1926-1936 CE.

132. *Sunan al-Dārimi*. Ad-Dārimi, Abū Muḥammad 'Abdullāh ibn 'Abdur Rahman. Damascus: Al_I'itidal & Muḥammad Ahman Dehman.

133. *Sunan Abī Dāwūd*. Abū Dāwūd al-Sijistānī, Sulaymān ibn al-Ash'ath ibn Isḥāq ibn Bashir ibn Shaddad ibn 'Amr ibn Umran al-Azdī al-Hanbali. Lucknow [India], 1321 AH/ 1903 CE.

134. *Sunan Ibn Mājah*. Ibn Mājah al-Rab'ī al-Qazwīnī, Abū 'Abdullāh Muḥammad ibn Yazīd. Research by Muḥammad Fo'ad Abdul Baqi. Cairo, 1373 AH/ 1954 CE.

135. *Sunan an-Nasā'ī* aka *Al-Sunan al-Sughra*. Sīnān al-Nasā'ī, Abū `Abd ar-Raḥmān Aḥmad ibn Shu`ayb ibn 'Alī. Cairo, 1312 AH/ 1895 CE.

136. *Sunan at-Tirmiḏī* aka *Jami' at-Tirmiḏī*. At-Tirmiḏī, Abū 'Īsā Muḥammad ibn 'Īsā as-Sulamī. 1st Edition. Būlāq [Cairo], 1292 AH/ 1875 CE; Egyptian Publication, 1350-1352 AH/ 1931-1933 CE.

137. *Tabsarat al-Awām fi Ma'arif Maqālāt al-Anam*. Ḥusayni Razi, Sayyid Murtaḍā Alam al-Hadi. Edited by Abbas Iqbal. Tehran: Majlis Publication.

138. *Taḏkirat al-Huffaz* (The Memorial of the Hadith Masters). Aḏ-Ḏahabī, Shams ad-Dīn Abū 'Abdullāh Muḥammad ibn Aḥmad ibn 'Uthmān ibn Qāymāẓ ibn 'Abdullāh at-Turkumānī Misri Shafī`ī. Heydarabad, 1357 AH/ 1956 CE.

139. *Taḏkirat al-Khawāṣ min al-Umma fi ḏikr Khaṣā'iṣ al-A'imma*. Sibṭ ibn al-Jawzi, Shams al-din Abū al- Muẓaffar Yusuf ibn Kizoghlu ibn 'Abdullāh Baghdādi Hanafi. Najaf, 1369 AH/ 1950 CE.

140. *Tafsīr al-Qur'ān al-Azim by Ibn Kathīr*. Ibn Kathīr al-Qurashī Al-Dimashqī, Abū al-Fiḏā 'Imād Ad-Din Ismā'īl ibn 'Umar.

141. Al-Tafsir al-Kabir aka Mafatih al-Ghayb. Al-Rāzī, Fakhr al-Dīn.

142. *Tafsīr al-Ṭabarī Jāmi' al-Bayān 'an ta'wīl āyāt al-Qur'ān* (Collection of Statements on the Interpretation of the Verses of the Qur'an). Al-Ṭabarī, Abū Ja'far Muḥammad ibn Jarīr ibn Yazīd.

143. *Tafsīr al-Qurṭubī* aka *Al-Jami' li Ahkam al-Qur'ān*. Al-Qurtubi, Abū 'Abdullāh Muḥammad ibn Ahmad ibn Abū Bakr al-Anṣārī. Tafsīr al-Qurtubi. 3rd Edition. Egypt, 1387 AH/ 1967 CE.

144. *Tafsīr al-Qummi*. Al-Qummi, Abū al-Hasan 'Alī ibn Ibrāhim.

145. *Tafsīr al-Nīsābūrī* aka *Gharā'ib al-Qur'ān wa-Raghā'ib al-Furqān*. Al-Nīsābūrī Niẓām al-Dīn Ḥasan ibn Muḥammad ibn Ḥusayn. Research by Ibrahim 'Itwah 'Awaḍ. 1st Edition. Egypt, 1381 AH/ 1962 CE.

146. *Tāj al-'Ārūs min Jawāhir al-Qāmūs*. Al-Zabīdī, Al-Murtaḍā al-Ḥusaynī Wasiti Hanafi. 1205 AH/ 1791 CE.

147. *Taqrīb al-Tahzīb*. Ibn Ḥajar al-'Asqalānī al-Kināni, Shihābud-Dīn Abul-Faḍl Aḥmad ibn Nūrud-Dīn 'Alī ibn Muḥammad. 1st Edition. Cairo, 1380 Ah/ 1961 CE.

148. *At-Tanbih wal-'Ishraf* (Book of Admonition and Revision). Al-Mas'ūdī, Abū al-Ḥasan 'Alī ibn al-Ḥusayn ibn 'Alī Shāfi'ī. Edited by as-Ṣāwi. Egypt; Beirut: Maktabat Khayyāṭ Publication.

149. *Tahzīb Ibn 'Asākir* (The Refinement of the History). Ibn 'Asākir, 'Abdul Qadir ibn Ahmad ibn Muṣṭafā ibn 'Abdul Rahim ibn Muḥammad Badran. 1st Edition. Damascus, 1329-1330 AH/ 1911-1912 CE.

150. *Tahḏīb al-Tahḏīb*. Ibn Ḥajar al-'Asqalānī, Shihābud-Dīn Abul-Faḍl Aḥmad ibn Nūrud-Dīn 'Alī ibn Muḥammad Shāfi'ī. Heydarabad, 1325-1327 AH/ 1907-1909 CE.

151. *Ta'rīkh Baghdād* (The History of Baghdād). Al-Khaṭīb al-Baghdādī, Abū Bakr Aḥmad ibn 'Alī ibn Thābit ibn Aḥmad ibn Māhdī al-Shafi'ī.

152. *Tārīkh Ibn al-Shihnah (Rowḍa al-Manāẓer Fi Akhbar al-Awa'el wa al-Awakher)* (Teaching Scenes in the Science of the Early and the Latter). In the margins of *Al-Kāmil fit-Tārīkh Ibn al-Athir*. Ibn Shiḥnah Ḥalabi. Cairo, 1348-1356 AH/ 1929-1937 CE; European Edition, 1290-1303 AH/ 1873-1886 CE.

153. *Tārīkh al-Islām al-Kabir aḏ-Ḏahabī* (Great History of Islām). Aḏ-Ḏahabī, Shams ad-Dīn Abū 'Abdullāh Muḥammad ibn Aḥmad ibn 'Uthmān ibn Qāymāẓ ibn 'Abdullāh at-Turkumānī Misri Shafi'ī. Cairo, 1367-1368 AH/ 1948-1949 CE.

154. *Tārīkh Madinat Dimashq* (History of Damascus). Ibn 'Asākir. 1st, 2nd & 10th volume, Damascus: Majma' Ilmi Arabi.

155. *Al-Bidaya wa an-Nihaya Ibn Kathīr*. Ibn Kathīr al-Qurashī Al-Dimashqī, Abū al-Fiḍā 'Imād Ad-Din Ismā'īl ibn 'Umar. Sa'adeh Publication, 1351-1358 AH/ 1932-1939 CE.

156. *Tārīkh al-Mukhtasar fi Akhbar al-Bashar* (An Abridgment of the History at the Human Race) aka *Tārīkh Abī al-Fada'*. Abī al-Fada', Ismā'īl ibn 'Alī ibn Maḥmūd ibn Muḥammad ibn 'Umar ibn Shāhanshāh ibn Ayyūb ibn Shādī ibn Marwān.

157. *Tārīkh al-Khulafā'* (History of the Caliphs). As-Suyūṭī, Jalāl al-Dīn 'Abd al-Raḥmān ibn Abī Bakr ibn Nasir ad-Din Muḥammad al-Shāfi'ī. Egypt, 1351 AH/ 1932 CE.

158. *Tārīkh al-Khamis fi Aḥwāl Anfās Nafis* aka *Tārīkh al-Khamis.* Diyar Bakri Maleki, Ḥusayn ibn Muḥammad ibn Ḥasan.

159. *Tārīkh al-Ṭabari (Tārīkh al-Rusul wa al-Mulūk)* (The History of the Prophets and Kings). Al-Ṭabari, Abū Ja'far Muḥammad ibn Jarīr ibn Yazīd. Reasearch by Muḥammad Abul-Faḍl Ibrahim. Europe (Leiden).

160. *Tārīkh al-Ya'qūbī* (The History of al-Ya'qūbī). Al-Ya'qūbī, 'Abū l-'Abbās 'Aḥmad ibn Abī Ya'qūb ibn Ġa'far ibn Wahb ibn Waḍīḥ. Najaf, 1358 AH; Beirut: Dār Ṣadir Publication.

161. *Tārīkh Ya'qūbī.* Al-Ya'qūbī, 'Abū l-'Abbās 'Aḥmad ibn Abī Ya'qūb ibn Ġa'far ibn Wahb ibn Waḍīḥ. Translated by Dr. Muḥammad Ibrahim Ayati.

162. *Tarjumeh va Sharheh Nahj al-Balāgha* (Translation of Nahj al-Balāgha). Feyz al-Islām.

163. *Taysīr al-Wusūl ila Jamei al-Usūl min Hadīth al-Rasūl* (Facilitating Access to the Collector of Assets from the Hadith of the Messenger). Ibn al-Diba' al-Shaibani az-Zubaidi al-Shāfi'ī. Egypt, 1346 AH/ 1928 CE.

164. *The Succession to Muḥammad: A Study of the Early Caliphate.* Madelung, Wilferd.

165. *'Umdat al-Qari* (Sharḥ Ṣaḥīḥ al-Bukhārī). Al-Badr al-'Ayni, Abī Muḥammad Muhamud ibn Ahmad ibn Musa. Lebanon: Muḥammad Amin Damaj Publication, n.d.

166. *Al-Usd al-Ġābah fi Ma'rifat al-Ṣaḥābah* (The Lions of the Forest in the Knowledge about the Aṣḥāb). Ibn al-Athir al-Jazari, Abū al-Ḥasan 'Alī ibn Muḥammad ibn Muḥammad al-Shaybani. Cairo, 1280 AH/ 1864 CE.

167. *Al-'Uthmāniyah.* Al-Jāḥiz, Abū 'Uthmān 'Amr ibn Baḥr al-Kinānī al-Baṣrī. Research by Abd as-Salam Muḥammad Harun. Egypt, 1374 AH/ 1955 CE.

168. *Uyūn al-Athar fi Funūn al-Maghāzī wa al-Shamā'il wa al-Sayr* (The Eyes of the Effect in al-Maghāzī wa al-Shamā'il wa al-Sayr Techniques). Al-Nas, Ibn Sayyid.

169. *Wafā' al-Wafā bi 'Akhbār Dār al-Muṣṭafā.* Al-Samhūdī, Nur ad-Din 'Alī ibn 'Abdullāh. Beirut: Dār al-Kutub al-Ilmieh Publication, 1374 AH/ 1955 CE.

170. Wafayat al-'Ayan. Ibn Khallikan.

171. *Waq'at Ṣiffīn*. Al-Minqari, Naṣr ibn Muzāḥim. Ressearch by Abd as-Sallam Muḥammad Harun. Qum, n.d.; 2nd Edition. Egypt, 1382 AH/ 1962 CE.

172. *Yanābī' al-Mawadda lī Ḏawī l-qūrbā*. Khajah Killan al-Balkhi al-Qunduzi, Sulaiman ibn Ibrahim. Beirut: Mu'asisah al-A'lami.

173. *Zahr al-Ādāb wa Thamar al-Albāb*. Abū Ishaq Ḥuṣrī, Ibrāhīm ibn 'Alī Ibn Tamim. Research & edit by Dr. Zaki Mubarak. 4th Edition. Lebanon: Dār al-Jayl Publication, n.d.

Index

Abū Sufyān, 42, 60, 61, 62, 87, 137, 151,
154, 158, 202

Abū Zubayd Naṣrānī, 147, 202

Adi ibn Ḥātim a'ṭ-Ṭā'iyy, 152, 202

Age of Ignorance, 24, 71

Al-Ahkam al-Sultania, 93, 94, 95, 96, 209

al-Dīnawarī, 11, 31, 77, 188, 211, 214

Al-Dīnawarī, 191, 193, 195

Alexandria, 114, 119, 126

al-Fath al-Kabir, 42

Alī ibn 'Abdullāh ibn 'Abbās, 194, 203

Alī ibn Abī Ṭālib, 28, 30, 31, 39, 41, 42, 49,
53, 80, 81, 132, 162, 185, 203, 204, 205,
211, 213

Alī ibn al-Ḥusayn (as), 194

Al-Imāma wal-Siyāsa, 11, 81, 83, 86, 87,
111, 157, 211

al-Jamal, 51, 52

al-Kulaynī, 111

al-Mas'ūdī, 11, 97, 188, 189

Al-Mufradat, 42, 215

Al-Muhajjal Samaratal Muhajja, 12, 215

al-Muttaqi al-Hindi, 12, 131

al-Qāḍī Abū Ya'lā, 93, 209

al-Qāḍī al-Māwardī, 93, 94, 95, 96, 209

Al-Suyūṭī, 193

Ammār ibn Yāsir, 78, 128, 147, 157, 202

Amr ibn Abd al-Wud, 104, 203

Amr ibn al-'Āṣ, 59, 150, 166, 203

Amr ibn Zurārah, 154, 203

Ansāb al-Ashrāf, 11, 73, 74, 79, 80, 111,
116, 117, 128, 129, 130, 131, 133, 134,
135, 138, 139, 141, 142, 143, 144, 145,
147, 148, 149, 150, 151, 154, 155, 156,
157, 158, 159, 160, 162, 165, 166, 167,
169, 170, 171, 172, 173, 174, 175, 177,
209

Asim ibn 'Adi, 46, 203

Attāb Thaqafi, 140, 203

Awāna ibn al-Ḥakam, 101, 203

Aws, 9, 30, 31, 62, 203

B

Baghdād, 88, 119, 209, 217, 220

Balāḏurī, 11, 73, 74, 79, 80, 97, 129, 130,
133, 135, 148, 165, 209, 213

Balāghāt al-nisā', 98

Banī 'Ajlan, 46

Banī Adi, 124

Banī al-Mustaliq, 138

Banī al-Qayn, 143

Banī Ghunm, 32

Banī Hāshim, 25, 52, 57, 61, 63, 76, 79, 83,
84, 91, 93, 116, 117, 124, 125, 126, 127,
173, 174, 197

Banī Kalb, 143

Banī Naḍīr, 92, 93

Banī Qaynuqa, 92

Banī Qurayza, 92, 95

Banī Tamīm, 67

Banī Taym, 124

Banī Umayya, 124, 130, 134, 137, 158, 173

Banū 'Adi ibn al-Najjar, 60

Banū al-Ḥārith, 192

Banū Aslam, 51, 52

Banū Umayya, 35, 39, 63

Baqī' Cemetery, 111, 147, 176

Bara' ibn 'Azib, 78, 203

Bashir ibn Sa'ad, 44, 48, 50, 65, 85, 203

Bashir ibn Sa'ad Khazraji, 48

Baṣrah, 38, 113, 119, 126, 155, 156, 160,
165, 170

Battle of Badr, 107, 138, 144, 145, 146,
196, 197

Battle of Ḥarrah, 110, 115, 183, 193, 195

Battle of Khandaq, 116

Battle of Uhud, 46, 107, 146, 196

Bayt al-mal, 60, 62